U.S. TRADE POLICY

U.S. TRADE POLICY

HISTORY, THEORY, AND THE WTO

SECOND EDITION

WILLIAM A. LOVETT, ALFRED E. ECKES JR., AND RICHARD L. BRINKMAN

M.E.Sharpe
Armonk, New York
London, England

Library of Congress Cataloging-in-Publication Data

Lovett, William Anthony.
    U.S. trade policy : history, theory, and the WTO / William A. Lovett, Alfred E. Eckes, Jr.
and Richard L. Brinkman.—2nd ed.
        p. cm.
    Includes bibliographical references and index.
    ISBN 0-7656-1307-7 (hardcover : alk. paper) ISBN 0-7656-1308-5 (pbk. : alk. paper)
        1. World Trade Organization. 2. United States—Commercial policy. I. Eckes, Alfred E.,
1942– II. Brinkman, Richard L. III. Title.

HF1455.L66 2004
382′.3′0973–dc22

2003055794

Printed in the United States of America

The paper used in this publication meets the minimum requirements of
American National Standard for Information Sciences
Permanence of Paper for Printed Library Materials,
ANSI Z 39.48-1984.

BM (c) 10 9 8 7 6 5 4 3 2 1
BM (p) 10 9 8 7 6 5 4 3 2 1

Contents

Tables and Figures

Tables

Figures

Preface

U.S. trade and industrial policies must engage the global economy more successfully. Millions of jobs have been lost by a failure to enforce overall balance and effective reciprocity. Between 1981 and 2003, U.S. trade deficits totaled –$4,000 billion; U.S. current account deficits total –$3,500 billion. The United States switched from the world's leading creditor to become its largest debtor. U.S. economic growth, resiliency, and industrial competitiveness suffered. Structural dislocations, greater inequality, and social stress followed. America's middle class feels squeezed and uneasy, worried about jobs, income security, and pensions. The U.S. economy has become unbalanced and increasingly vulnerable to economic shocks, speculative disruptions, devaluation pressures, and slowdowns. This neglect cannot continue.

This book represents a post–Cold War reassessment of U.S. trade policy. It reviews U.S. trade history, theory, and the evolution of General Agreement on Tariffs and Trade (GATT) 1947 into GATT 1994 and the World Trade Organization (WTO) Agreement. In Chapter 1, William Lovett provides an introductory overview. Chapter 2 by Alfred Eckes traces U.S. trade history, beginning with the new republic emerging from colonialism. The United States had trouble breaking into foreign markets in an era of mercantilism. The United States, like most countries, including Britain between 1650 and the 1840s, used tariffs and industrial development as a nation-building strategy. U.S. trade policy was very successful between 1791 and the 1920s in building up industrial strength, which created the world's most powerful economy.

In Franklin D. Roosevelt's New Deal era, the United States switched to a freer trade policy—supposedly emphasizing reciprocity. Then World War II and the Cold War led the United States to aid allies and accept trading relations that were not fully reciprocal. Because the United States was stronger in technology, industry, and finance after World War II, it could afford to tolerate asymmetries and unequal access, *at least for a while*. But by the 1970s, U.S. industry was beginning to suffer competitiveness problems. These difficulties and trade deficits grew worse in the 1980s and the 1990s.

A temporary boom-bubble "blessed" the United States between 1994 and

2000 (fueled in part by foreign capital inflows). A subsequent stock slump and global slowdown were not surprising. But the September 11, 2001 terrorist attacks on the United States, the Taliban war in Afghanistan, another war with Iraq, and continued crises in the Middle East, Korea, and the Caribbean basin (Venezuela and Colombia) were not anticipated. But all these security challenges, unresolved trade imbalances, and financial strains were hard to handle and unavoidably controversial.

Richard Brinkman traces the evolution of modern trade theory in Chapters 3 and 4. From the freer trade of Adam Smith, through Ricardian Comparative Advantage to Neo-Classical models (often labeled the "pure theory of international trade"), Brinkman clarifies assumptions and explains the shortcomings of the Heckscher-Ohlin model. In Chapter 4, Brinkman offers a revised, more realistic, and dynamic approach to trade and economic growth. It includes more emphasis on asymmetries, imbalances, and nonreciprocity problems. It argues that Adam Smith's productivity doctrine serves better than Ricardo's comparative statics as the basis for a theory of dynamic comparative advantage. This approach is more realistic for macroeconomic instability, external disruptions, and the need for more effective shock absorbers.

Finally, in Chapter 5, William Lovett comes back to problems for U.S. trade policy in the late 1990s and the early twenty-first century. Alternative solutions for U.S. trade imbalances are dollar devaluation, industrial renewal, and/or reciprocal trade policy. The 1992 election was a mandate, many believe, for a stronger U.S. policy. Yet no significant change occurred. Instead, a flawed GATT 1994 and WTO agreement were implemented without much debate in the United States. But Americans need to get serious about eliminating external deficits and rejuvenating their industrial network. More extensive trade supervision and industrial promotion efforts are essential. The advantages of greater realism, improved teamwork, and sustainable internationalism are explained. If the United States fails to take responsible, corrective action, Americans face weaker economic growth, continued imbalances, growing vulnerability to economic crises, and a blend of stagnation and decline. And U.S. influence in the world will erode along with a weakening economy.

All three coauthors endorse freer trade and the global marketplace. They argue that U.S. policy must now reemphasize greater trade balance and reciprocity. The United States still has an important role as the world's leading democracy. But European unification, increased prosperity elsewhere, and the spread of modern industry and technology to most of the world mean that the United States cannot dominate the global economy. This is a blessing for Americans, though, because we should now focus more realistically on improving the terms of U.S. engagement with the world economy. Americans are only 4 percent of the world's people. We cannot afford to subsidize or support the whole world. We can, with the collaboration of other friendly nations, improve and stabilize a global economic regime that helps all nations. In the end, most nations must learn to help themselves. The United States, like other countries, must fix our own social and industrial problems. Only the United States can rejuvenate its own industry, eliminate excessive trade deficits, and restore healthy external account discipline and trade reciprocity. This is a top priority for America as we enter the twenty-first century.

Recent financial crises and trade imbalances from Mexico (1994–1995), Asia and Russia (1997–1998), and parts of Latin America (1998–2001) highlight the dangers of neglect. Badly informed capital flows, excessive currency speculation, and unsustainable trading and lending relationships are risky. Surging market forces can make serious mistakes. The Great Depression (1929–1938) taught this lesson through two generations of economists. Global market euphoria of the mid- to late 1990s brought back a naive faith in laissez-faire. But the recent crises and disruptions remind us of the need for effective shock absorbers, safeguarding, and stabilization measures.

More realistic trading is needed for the twenty-first century. A global marketplace, with better reciprocity and reliable property-contracts rights, promotes wide prosperity. Key international institutions, including the International Monetary Fund, Bank for International Settlements, and the World Bank, can facilitate responsible markets. But there are limits to any multilateral governance. There is no substitute for responsible national governments as providers of sound incentives, healthy education, industrial vitality, infrastructure, and policies to promote full employment and social harmony. This requires self-discipline by each country for its engagement with the global marketplace. Excessive trade imbalances, heavy debt burdens, and speculative capital flows are problems for many countries, and they erode the good order and prosperity of the world economy, too. Thus, a healthier global economy requires reasonable efforts by individual nations to live within their means, avoid excessive budget and external deficits, and correct serious imbalance problems. This can often be done by collaboration with other nations. But ultimately every nation bears the main responsibility for making the best of its own resources, trading opportunities, and industrial development.

U.S. TRADE POLICY

1

Introduction

WILLIAM A. LOVETT

Britain's Free Trade Experiment

During the nineteenth century, Great Britain moved away from mercantilist practices in a freer trade experiment.[1] This had great impact on subsequent controversies about trading policy. Although many nations (including the United States, Germany, France, Russia, Japan, Austria, and Italy) used more protectionist policies to catch up with "free trade" Britain, economic thought was focused upon these issues and the extent to which tariffs and other encouragements to industries were desirable. But throughout the British free trade experiment, Britain's colonies were kept largely secure for British investments, companies, and trading activity. Also, Britain could afford to eliminate tariffs in the 1830s and 1840s because it enjoyed a substantial lead in technology, industrial scale economies, maritime predominance, and stronger banking-investment resources. Yet by 1900, when the United States, Germany, and others had caught up with British industries, British manufacturers began to seek imperial preference tariffs as a means to greater reciprocity. In the 1920s, as Britain suffered adjustment and competitiveness problems, British trade policy became increasingly controversial. The Safeguarding of Industries Act of 1921 was implemented timidly, but finally in 1932 Britain rejoined the great majority of industrial nations by establishing Imperial Preference tariffs.

Despite unequal trade openness, with tariffs and industrial development policies, economic progress flourished in much of Europe, the United States, and other areas. International investments and loans expanded greatly, opening up new markets. Technological progress was dramatic in most fields, including, in particular, armaments, warships, and even aircraft.

Then World War I (1914–1918) disrupted things. Casualties and war costs were heavy. A harsh peace was imposed upon Germany, with unsustainable reparations burdens. The Austro-Hungarian Empire disintegrated, and Russia came under Bolshevik rule. Confidence, trade, and capital flows weakened. Britain's exports, steel, and coal slumped. Although the 1920s brought unbalanced economic recovery, a boom in the United States proved fragile.

The stock market crash of 1929 brought a worldwide depression. Many defaults occurred on international loans. Hard times brought militaristic governments to Germany, Japan, Italy, and some smaller countries. World War II (1939–1945) followed, with heavy casualties and further dislocations.

Bretton Woods, GATT 1947, and Trade Asymmetries

But now the Allied democracies realized that better postwar arrangements were needed. At the 1944 Bretton Woods Conference, Britain, the United States, and other Allies agreed upon more collaboration after the war. This led to the International Monetary Fund (IMF), the World Bank, and the General Agreement on Tariffs and Trade (GATT 1947).[2] The United States moved away from its long history of protectionist tariff policies (1791–1934); it began to sponsor more open markets, rather like Britain's efforts toward freer trade between the 1840s and 1931. (Like Britain in most of the nineteenth century, the United States now enjoyed a substantial lead in technology, industrial scale economies, maritime leadership, and stronger banking-investment resources. Like Britain, the United States could now afford freer trade.) Accordingly, in eight GATT rounds between 1947 and 1994, the United States led the way toward reductions in tariff levels among the industrial nations (more recently labeled the OECD countries). U.S. multinational corporations (MNCs) felt an increasing stake in world trade, and they provided support for the multilateral trade process.

Unfortunately, Stalin's USSR chose not to collaborate with Western-style economic recovery. Instead, Communist governments were imposed in most of Eastern Europe. A rival COMECON was established for the USSR and satellite countries. A Communist government was set up in North Korea, and the Kuomingtang government of China fell to the Red Chinese under Mao Zedong. Communist parties and subversion efforts were encouraged elsewhere. In this way, a Cold War threat of aggression and/or subversion developed against the Western democracies and their allies.

Ironically, in response to this Cold War threat, U.S. policies allowed more generous aid (through the Marshall Plan, military assistance, and help to developing countries) than would have been possible otherwise. Under the slogan "trade, not aid," the U.S. political establishment was kind to its allies and trading partners. Less than fully reciprocal trade deals were accepted by the United States, especially with developing nations. For less developed countries (LDCs), it was understood that substantial tariffs and other restrictions would promote industrialization and broader prosperity.

However, GATT 1947 allowed safeguard relief under Article XIX, balance of payments relief under Article XII, and antidumping and countervailing duty for subsidy relief under Article VI.[3] In addition, imports could be limited to maintain national security or to protect agriculture, product standards, consumer safety, and environmental interests. While GATT signatories accepted an obligation to apply these and other regulatory policies in a nondiscriminatory manner and to give national treatment to foreign companies, implementation was left up to each importing country. Trade disputes among nations were to be negotiated among them, largely by mutual conciliation. GATT dispute resolution panels could be constituted, but their function was essentially advisory and for mediation purposes.

Most nations learned from the Great Depression that Keynesian budget deficit policies would be needed to maintain full employment, at least in slumps or recessions.[4] Unemployment compensation, education, and social security measures were popular after World War II in the countries with moderate social democratic governments. Farm price support/subsidy measures were well established, too. Industrial growth and export expansion were desired, but few wanted much import disruption or job losses. Trade unions were powerful in most industrial countries, so that GATT safeguard, offset, subsidy, or voluntary import restraint measures were used to limit disruptive imports.

Another lesson from the Great Depression and early post–World War II years was the need for balance of payments discipline in order to avoid large and chronic external deficits.[5] Most countries were forced, sooner or later, to live within their means and maintain current account discipline. Countries that failed to discipline themselves suffered recurrent devaluations or became dependent upon foreign aid or loans. Accordingly, GATT safeguard and offset measures, exchange controls (for most NICs [new industrial countries] and LDCs), and/or other industrial and trade policies that allowed countries to "live within their means" became important instruments of macroeconomic policy for the majority of nations.

Dollar Hegemony, Indiscipline, and Euro Challenges

One big exception to this macroeconomic self-discipline, at least since the early 1980s, was the United States.[6] Large U.S. budget deficits became entrenched in the 1980s, caused by political gridlock and a lack of consensus over tax loads and spending. Tighter U.S. monetary policy was used to offset bigger U.S. budget deficits, which meant higher U.S. interest rates. This attracted heavy borrowing from abroad, and for a while the U.S. dollar became substantially overvalued. By the mid-1980s, the United States had become a net debtor country (for the first time since World War I). By the end of 1997, net U.S. external debt reached at least –$1,250 billion (the biggest debt in the world).[7] Between 1998 and 2003, U.S. current account deficits and external debts grew substantially, with net debt reaching at least –$3,000 billion by the end of 2003. Nevertheless, sustained, heavy foreign capital inflows allowed U.S. imports to expand, while U.S. exports slowed (Tables 1.1 and 1.2). Between 1981 and 2003 U.S. merchandise trade deficits totaled –$4,000 billion or more, while U.S. current account deficits totaled at least –$3,500 billion. In the period from 1981 to 2003, the U.S. gross federal debt ballooned from –$1,000 billion to –$7,300 billion, with greatly increased federal debt service burdens (Table 1.3). By 2000, the annual federal debt service for the United States approached its defense spending. Sadly, in the 1980s, the United States lost both its fiscal discipline and balance of payments or external accounts discipline. Large U.S. budget, trade, and current account deficits became entrenched. Increasingly, economists saw this predicament as the "twin deficits problem."

Why was the United States allowed more slack in recent years for excessive budget, trade, and current account deficits? Basically, because the U.S. dollar continued to serve as the primary reserve currency. U.S. capital markets were bigger, wider, more stable and reliable. No other currency (the Japanese yen, the Swiss franc, the British pound, or the German mark) could offer comparable opportunities as a medium-term, large-scale "parking place," or store of value, than the U.S. dollar, U.S. government securities, and/or U.S. corporate stocks or bonds. Japanese, Swiss, British, and German capital markets simply were not big enough or sufficiently reliable to accommodate large inflows (*and outflows*) of foreign capital. Nor were emerging markets big enough or sufficiently reliable to place large amounts of foreign capital for liquidity or longer-term secure investments.

Only the new European Monetary System (EMS) and the euro offered a possible challenge to the U.S. dollar and its capital markets as a reserve currency and as a major store of value.[8] In the fall of 1997, prospects for the euro and EMS remained uncertain, because of difficulties faced by many countries in Europe in reducing budget deficits, social insurance, and chronic unemployment. Also, European growth was slower between 1994 and 2000, while the U.S. boom sucked in a lot of foreign investment from Europe, Asia, and many emerging markets. This kept the U.S. dollar overvalued despite increasing trade and current account deficits for the United States. In the meantime, the United States and the dollar continued to enjoy the mixed blessings and "privileges" of primary reserve currency, the "profits" of seigneurage for U.S. investment bankers and financial markets, and a generous "tolerance" for excessive, large-scale U.S. budget, trade, and current account deficits, at least a while longer.

But from 2002 to 2003 the tide of foreign exchange flows turned against the dollar and in favor of the euro. When the U.S. stock market bubble sagged in the spring and summer of 2001, it was not that clear at first how long a retreat was involved. Investors everywhere took a while to decide that a larger correction and slump were needed. But as the Federal Reserve forced U.S. interest rates to low levels (below the European Central Bank's short-term rates), the September 11, 2001, terrorism attack occurred. Then prospects of war in the Middle East and/or Korea developed for 2003 and beyond; Europeans and others began moving capital out of the United States into the euro and a few other currencies (e.g., Australian and New Zealand dollars). China, Japan, and most of Asia, however, continued to peg their currencies relatively low against the U.S. dollar to sustain their very large export surpluses in trade with the United States.

MNCs, Integration Economies, and Sharing Benefits

Another big development, although gradual, over the past twenty to twenty-five years has been the ascendancy of multinational corporations (MNCs) and financial institutions in the global marketplace. U.S. companies led the way in this trend. Marketing outlets, assembly plants, processing centers, basic manufacturing, research and development, financial accounting, and other operations were located for optimal convenience in various countries. Of course, national economic development, industrial, and export promotion policies tried to foster (at least for many OECD and most developing countries) the relocation of plants, operations, and headquarters in their own territories. In this way, countries sought to promote their own employment, economic growth, and national interests.

Interestingly, the U.S. government's policies (especially since the 1980s) have been more generous to MNCs (regardless of national origin) than the policies of most other countries. Why this asymmetry? The explanation is partly ideological. U.S. free market thinking (in both the Republican and Democratic parties) was more inclined to see global markets as "good for us," or at least as favorable to U.S. MNC interests. Political processes, lobbying influence, and financial capitalism in the United States (at least for the last twenty to twenty-five years) were more MNC dominated and less constrained by national policies, labor union pressures, or other concerns than in many other nations. Accordingly, U.S. policy favored MNC interests (regardless of national origin) and did not really try to maintain a "fair share" for U.S. MNCs as opposed to companies from foreign nations.

An important consequence of this one-sided, "friendly" treatment for MNCs by U.S. policy is that the American share of economic growth has been less substantial since the mid-1970s (Table 1.5), except for its brief boom (1996–2000). By contrast, if U.S. trade policy had been tougher and reciprocity-oriented, U.S. MNCs and national growth could have retained a steadier share of global markets.

Because of trade asymmetries and this lack of concern for reciprocity for U.S. companies, industries, and workers, U.S. per capita income grew less rapidly than the per capita income in some other countries (Table 1.5). Real wages (adjusted for inflation) stagnated in the United States after 1973, with families able to keep up only by putting their women more fully to work (Table 1.6). Single-earner families lost ground, and the poor and the low-middle class were squeezed. By the mid-1990s, a number of countries had forged ahead of the United States in per capita income. Many Western European countries caught up to U.S. living standards. Singapore, Taiwan, South Korea, and Southeast Asian countries were moving up fast, while China and India have enjoyed rapid growth since the late 1970s.

Strictly speaking, it is good for more countries to enjoy prosperity. But U.S. industrial-trade policies need not concede more than Asian, European, or other NIC trade policies. A growing majority of Americans came to believe in the late 1990s that U.S. policy could have enforced more effective reciprocity in its trading relationships. U.S. tolerance of entrenched trade deficits and asymmetries (Table 1.2) was simply weak policy. This does not mean, of course, that growing world trade was wrong. No—fairly shared, mutual growth in the benefits of global economic integration, expanding trade, and increased productivity is desirable for most countries.

GATT 1994 and the World Trade Organization

In the early 1980s, the United States suggested a broader GATT round to include services and agriculture, and to open more NIC and LDC markets. But few other countries supported another trade negotiation at that stage. Yet when the LDC debt overload–debt rescheduling crisis threatened insolvency for leading international banks (from 1982 to 1985) and when protectionist interests gained ground in many countries, a "consensus" developed for a broad Uruguay GATT round trade negotiation effort. Initial U.S. goals were ambitious; they included greatly reduced subsidies, more open markets in agriculture, access to developing countries, stronger intellectual property and investment protection, and stronger remedies for unfair trade practices. Many Americans felt that a more level playing field was essential. From the standpoint of MNC interests, however, the goals of the Uruguay Round negotiation were defensive—that is, to "save" the global trading system from breakdown. The Great Depression's financial collapse and reductions in trade in the early to mid-1930s were recalled as warnings. Meanwhile, Mikhail Gorbachev's reform efforts for the USSR—perestroika (restructuring) and glasnost (openness)—could revitalize economic competition from the Russians. But most developing countries resisted any large market opening, while the European Union (EU) resisted any great liberalization for agriculture. Soon it became apparent that "progress" for the Uruguay Round would be slow and difficult and that U.S. hopes for major changes in the world trading system were probably unrealistic.

The mid to late 1980s were controversial for U.S. trade policy.[9] Democrats and some Republicans in Congress pushed for greater use of U.S. trade law remedies (e.g., countervailing duties for subsidies, antidumping remedies, and stronger Section 301 unfair trade practice enforcement) to level the playing field. An omnibus trade act was proposed between 1984 and 1988 for these purposes, but was greatly weakened and finally enacted in 1988 with a "Super 301" provision that mainly amounted to a reporting requirement for foreign trade barriers. Unfortunately, the United States Trade Representative (USTR) made a crucial concession at the outset of the Uruguay Round in pledging the United States to "stand still" in use of trade restrictions. From the MNCs' viewpoint, this pledge was important for their interests in allowing MNCs to rely on existing openness to major U.S. and, to a lesser extent, European markets, so that more plants could be relocated to lower-wage countries. But from the standpoint of trade asymmetries and efforts to level the playing field, this was a blunder. U.S. negotiating leverage to open markets, equalize tariffs downward, and eliminate foreign restrictions would have been substantially greater without the "standstill" concession.

In the late 1980s, Mexico made a historic shift toward greater trade openness, having realized that excessive subsidies, restrictions, and protectionism had become counterproductive. Thus, Mexico proposed to expand the recent U.S.–Canada Free Trade Agreement (negotiated from 1985 to 1988) into a North American Free Trade Agreement (NAFTA). The Bush administration welcomed NAFTA, mainly seeking to protect U.S. investment and MNC interests. U.S. labor and environmental interests opposed NAFTA, fearing more relocation of manufacturing jobs and lowered levels of environmental protection. Meanwhile, the Gorbachev reform efforts in the USSR worked out badly for the Communists. Pressures for a free press and for democracy boiled up quickly, but Russian restructuring efforts were timid and inadequate and only made the economy weaker. Between 1989 and 1991, Communism collapsed as a political system in the USSR and Eastern Europe. But China's economic-oriented liberalization gained momentum, unleashing expanded production and attracting foreign investment that accelerated China's success. Finally, the European Community moved to deepen integration with its Single Europe Act, Maastricht Treaty, and efforts toward a European Monetary System (EMS) and common currency (later named the "euro"). All these developments increased world confidence in freer markets for a while in many developing countries. By the early 1990s, an investment boom (from the United States, Europe, Japan, and elsewhere) began to shift more capital into "emerging markets"—broadly speaking, many NICs and LDCs.

Between 1991 and 1993, final negotiations for the Uruguay Round GATT were completed. Results were controversial.[10] Tariffs were already low among most OECD nations, but NICs and LDCs only lowered tariffs modestly (from levels previously averaging 30 to 50 percent down to 20 to 35 percent). Thus, manufacturing markets in developing countries remained substantially protected. Meanwhile, safeguard, antisubsidy, and anti-dumping remedies for the U.S. were made more difficult to use. Agreements on services (GATS) and intellectual property (TRIPs) were reached, but remained largely aspirational. Reservations were used by most developing countries to limit market opening in services. MNC lobbies, however, were pleased overall, because U.S. and European markets became more securely open, and a trend toward greater investment opportunities in many NICs and LDCs seemed to be under way. But labor and environmental interests, especially in the United States, were greatly disappointed. More jobs would move now to low-wage countries, and the playing field had not been leveled. Structural asymmetries, leading to chronic U.S. trade and current account deficits, were, in fact, entrenched by the 1994 GATT (the Uruguay Round).

An important element of the final Uruguay Round GATT deal was the new World Trade Organization (WTO) Agreement.[11] This expanded the GATT's secretariat into a continuing multilateral agency. The most controversial features, from the U.S. viewpoint, were voting arrangements and the dispute resolution process. Voting for most purposes in the WTO is by majority—that is, one country/one vote (as in the United Nations General Assembly). Accession of new members (for example, China, Cuba, or Russia) or Amendments require merely a two-thirds majority, while Interpretations require a three-fourths majority. But the EU got fifteen votes directly, with another ten to fifteen candidates for EU membership and sixty Lomé Convention states (mostly former European colonies) likely to vote with Europe for many purposes. From another perspective, developing countries have about three-fourths of the votes in the WTO. In dramatic contrast, the International Monetary Fund (IMF) has weighted voting—according to financial quotas and economic strength. Supermajority requirements are higher (85 percent) for key issues, with the United States having 17 percent of the quotas—that is, a blocking vote power.

In addition, WTO dispute resolution panels come close to mandatory arbitration. Thus, if the United States invokes Section 301 unfair trade practice proceedings (the strongest weapon in U.S. trade law), countries that feel disfavored can challenge this process and convene a WTO dispute settlement panel. Panel decisions upheld by the WTO's Appellate Body (a seven-member court) cannot be overturned except by consensus (a unanimous vote by all WTO members). Ordinarily, any country or group of countries that wins a decision adverse to the United States would not support its overturn. Thus, negative consensus makes it almost impossible to overturn adverse WTO panel decisions.

Experience since 1994 with the new WTO and its dispute resolution process shows that broad, sustained prosperity and growth did not come to all countries. Even though MNCs largely benefited, many domestic industries, workers, farmers, and communities suffered disruption—often after excessive booms, panics, banking crises, and capital flight. Widening market freedoms without adequate supervision, stabilizers, and shock absorbers brought greater instability. The IMF found difficulty in assisting some countries with stabilization policies from 1998 to 2003. And many nations lacked the healthy governance that could take proper advantage of expanding trade, capital flows, and international investments. This led to greater defensiveness, and most countries wanted more safeguard relief, limits on disruptions, and constraints upon excessive capital flows. Meanwhile, hopes for rapid and mutually satisfying dispute resolution by WTO panels have been disappointed. Many trade conflicts remain unresolved. Environmental, labor, and farming interests feel shortchanged. Pressures for antidumping relief and voluntary important restraints have increased. Some experts now believe, in fact, that the mediation-oriented dispute resolution process under GATT 1947 was more politically sensitive and more successful in the longer run than the last eight years of WTO panel experience.

Meanwhile, efforts toward another WTO round collapsed in Seattle in 1999. Disorderly demonstrations against "globalization" erupted and have become a public nuisance in many international gatherings since then. Although another WTO round of tariff and trade restriction negotiations was launched at Doha, Qatar, in 2001, a logjam of conflicting goals and interests makes progress doubtful. Developing countries want major cutbacks on drug patent protection, opposed by leading OECD nations. Developing and "Cairns group" agricultural exporting nations want substantial cuts in agricultural tariffs and subsidies, strongly resisted by the EU and Japan. Most developing countries want more immediate benefits and more "sacrifices" by wealthy nations. But the United States, EU, and Japan have been suffering slumps in the last several years, so they cannot be very generous now.

Goals for U.S. Trade Policy

U.S. trade policy for the twenty-first century should promote the overall interests of Americans in the global economy. Fortunately, the United States no longer needs to "subsidize" economic development abroad with one-sided trade concessions. The Communist challenge ended in collapse and transformation to market-oriented economies, with more mutual tolerance and respect among most nations. Now most countries accept the logic of market-oriented, decentralized enterprise, and self-sustaining development. The United States, along with other OECD nations, should be reasonably kind to a larger number of poor, unstable countries that have not yet established strong, fully secure governments and institutions. Some multilateral aid, IMF support, foreign investment, and export opportunities need to be extended to these troubled countries. But the post–World War II experience demonstrates, with many economic success stories in Europe, Asia, and Latin America, that self-sustaining, healthy development and progress require sound and responsible governments in each country. Foreign aid, investment, and export opportunities can build upon and reinforce domestic progress, but they cannot substitute for a basic lack of security and respect for property or for inadequate incentives provided by local governments.

Accordingly, U.S. trade and external policies must engage the global economy more successfully. By not enforcing sufficient balance and reciprocity in trade relations, the United States "gave up" some of its industrial strength, technology, and growth potential. We estimate that 10 million to 12 million U.S. jobs were lost by a failure to enforce trade reciprocity.[12] By not enforcing reciprocity, the United States lost economic growth. With stronger U.S. trade policies, especially since the 1980s, the country would have enjoyed fuller employment, less social stress, and more cohesion. While some interests did all right (especially the MNCs), overall prosperity in the United States would have been greater if its industrial and trade interests had not been neglected.

Now the time has come to correct this accumulated neglect of U.S. industrial-trade interests. Between 1981 and 2003, U.S. trade deficits totaled –$4,000 billion; U.S. current account (or net balance of payments) deficits totaled –$3,500 billion. The United States switched from the world's leading creditor to become its largest debtor. The U.S. gave up a strong lead in many areas of manufacturing. U.S. industrial competitiveness declined. This neglect cannot continue.

Consequently, U.S. policy should focus upon restoring its own good health, broad prosperity, and full employment.[13] Gradually Americans have come to understand that their excessive budget deficits had to be disciplined, and both political parties moved in that direction. But U.S. trade, current account, and external deficits must be eliminated also. This requires four changes: (1) U.S. trade and investment flows need more careful supervision; (2) the United States must enforce more balance and reciprocity in trading

Figure 1.1 **Conflicting "Freer Trade" Outlooks**

- **Adam Smith's Freer Trade**
  (Reciprocity-oriented)

- **National Development Freer Trade** (with development tariffs, e.g., Hamilton and Friedrich List)

- **British Empire Freer Trade** (with restricted foreign access to British colonies)

- **Neoclassical Freer Trade**
  (One world model: everyone supposedly gains)

- **Socialist Internationalism**
  (Liberated from class oppression, with fraternal socialist cooperation)

- **Cobdenite, Wilsonian Freer Trade** (Free trade, democracy, and world peace)

- **UNCTAD – Group of 77 Plus Freer Trade** (with strong NIC and LDC preferences)

- **U.S. Cold War Freer Trade**
  (Led by United States and OECD; preferences for the developing nations accepted by United States)

- **WTO Model Freer Trade**
  (Strong LDC preferences, with aspirations for gradually more opening)

- **Reciprocity Freer Trade**
  (Led by United States; more equal openness, with preference only for poorer countries treating foreign capital fairly)

- **MNC-Oriented Freer Trade**
  (Freedom for MNCs to operate everywhere, subject to restrictions by developing nations to promote their industrialization)

- **Neo-Mercantilist Freer Trade**
  (Exploit openness of others, but insist upon limits to protect key interests, industries, or trades)

relationships; (3) unconditional most favored nation (MFN) status needs to be replaced by conditional MFN for those countries that do not allow comparable trade openness or that are well out of reasonable balance in longer-term trade flows; (4) U.S. industries need considerable renewal, with more efforts devoted to offsetting foreign trade restrictions, subsidies, and marginal cost discounting activity. How to achieve these objectives raises many important and interesting technical issues.

Table 1.1A

U.S. GNP, Debt, and External Accounts 1961–2002 (in billions of US$)

Year	GNP	Gross federal debt	Merchandise imports[a]	Merchandise exports[b]	Merchandise trade balance	Current account balance[c]	Customs merchandise trade balance[d]	Customs current account balance[e]
1961	520.1	292.6	14.8	20.2	5.5	3.8	5.5	3.8
1962	560.3	302.9	16.5	21.0	4.5	3.4	4.5	3.4
1963	590.5	310.3	17.2	22.5	5.3	4.4	5.3	4.4
1964	632.4	316.1	18.7	25.8	7.1	6.8	7.1	6.8
1965	684.9	322.3	21.4	26.7	5.3	5.4	5.3	5.4
1966	749.9	328.5	25.6	29.5	3.9	3.0	3.9	3.0
1967	793.9	340.4	28.7	30.0	1.3	-0.3	4.1	2.6
1968	865.0	368.7	35.3	34.1	-1.3	-1.5	0.8	0.6
1969	930.3	365.8	38.2	37.3	-0.9	-1.8	1.3	0.4
1970	977.1	380.9	42.4	42.7	0.2	-0.1	2.7	2.3
1971	1,054.9	408.2	48.3	43.5	-4.8	-4.2	-2.0	-1.4
1972	1,158.0	435.9	58.9	49.2	-9.7	-9.8	-5.7	-5.8
1973	1,294.9	466.3	73.6	71.9	-1.7	3.1	2.4	7.1
1974	1,397.4	483.9	110.9	99.4	-11.5	-5.6	-3.9	2.0
1975	1,528.8	541.9	105.9	108.9	3.0	11.5	9.6	18.1
1976	1,700.1	629.0	132.5	116.8	-15.7	-3.6	-7.8	4.3
1977	1,887.2	706.4	160.4	123.2	-37.2	-23.1	-28.4	-14.3
1978	2,156.1	776.6	186.0	145.8	-40.2	-25.1	-30.2	-15.1
1979	2,413.9	829.5	222.2	186.4	-35.8	-12.2	-23.9	-0.3
1980	2,626.1	909.1	257.0	225.7	-31.3	-9.2	-19.7	2.3
1981	2,957.8	994.8	273.4	238.7	-34.7	-7.3	-22.3	5.0
1982	3,069.3	1,137.3	254.9	216.4	-38.4	-22.4	-27.5	-11.4
1983	3,304.8	1,371.7	269.9	205.6	-64.2	-54.0	-54.2	-44.0
1984	3,772.2	1,564.7	346.4	224.0	-122.4	-114.6	-106.7	-99.0

1985	4,010.3	1,817.5	352.5	218.8	−133.6	−139.9	−117.7	−124.0
1986	4,235.0	2,120.6	382.3	227.2	−155.1	−170.0	−138.3	−153.2
1987	4,545.6	2,346.1	424.4	254.1	−170.3	−186.3	−152.1	−168.1
1988	5,062.6	2,601.3	460.2	321.8	−138.4	−148.1	−118.5	−128.2
1989	5,452.8	2,868.0	487.6	363.8	−123.7	−118.6	−109.4	−104.2
1990	5,764.9	3,026.6	512.5	393.6	−119.0	−109.1	−101.7	−91.9
1991	5,932.4	3,598.5	504.4	421.7	−82.6	−14.2	−74.1	−5.7
1992	6,255.5	4,002.1	546.0	448.2	−97.9	−58.1	−96.1	−56.4
1993	6,576.8	4,351.4	597.4	465.1	−132.3	−90.5	−132.6	−90.8
1994	6,955.2	4,643.7	689.2	512.6	−176.6	−143.9	−166.2	−133.5
1995	7,270.6	4,920.9	770.9	582.1	−188.8	−144.4	−173.6	−129.1
1996	7,637.7	5,181.9	817.8	622.8	−195.0	−152.0	−191.2	−148.2
1997	8,060.1	5,369.7	898.3	687.6	−210.7	−178.1	−199.0	−166.4
1998	8,778.1	5,478.2	942.6	682.1	−260.5	—	−229.8	−220.6
1999	9,297.1	5,605.5	1,059.9	695.0	−364.9	—	−330.0	−331.5
2000	9,848.0	5,628.7	1,259.3	781.9	−415.9	—	−380.5	447.7
2001	10,104.1	5,769.9	1,179.2	729.1	−450.1	—	−411.9	−393.4
2002	10,600.0	6,198.4	1,202.5	693.5	−509.0	—	−470.1	−500(e)

Sources: U.S. Dept. of Commerce, Economic and Statistics Administration, Bureau of Economic Analysis, National Accounts Data (Dec. 9, 1997), www.fedstats.gov/index20.html.; Bureau of Economic Analysis. *Survey of Current Business*, July 1997; Bureau of Economic Analysis, U.S. Council of Economic Advisors, Economic Indicators, various issues 1965–1998; *Economic Report of the President*, 1982, 1984, 1986, 1993, 1996, 1997, 1998, and 2003.

[a] Merchandise imports are based on CIF (cost-insurance-freight) values. However, CIF figures are not available for 1961–1966: those imports are based on Customs values. CIF figures for 1967 to 1998 are based on estimates.

[b] Exports are based on FAS (free along shipside) value.

[c] Current account balance reflects the net balance on merchandise trade, services, trade, investment income, and other unilateral transfers. However, the years 1961 to 1964 show only the results of merchandise imports, exports, services, and income from investments.

[d] The U.S. government publishes its merchandise trade figures using Customs values for imports and FAS values for exports.

[e] The discrepancy between the estimated and U.S. government published current account balances is due to the difference in the merchandise trade balance arising from valuing imports using CIF values versus valuing imports using Customs values.

Table 1.1B

Composition of U.S. Current Accounts, 1980–2002 (in billions of US$)

	1980	1981	1982	1983
Merchandise trade balance[a]	−31.3	−34.7	−38.4	−64.2
Services trade balance				
~Imports	−41.5	−45.5	−51.7	−55.0
~Exports	47.6	57.4	64.1	64.3
Net services trade balance	6.1	11.9	12.3	9.3
Investment income balance				
~Income receipts on U.S. assets abroad				
*Direct investment receipts	37.1	32.5	23.9	27.0
*Other private receipts	32.9	50.3	58.2	53.4
*U.S. government receipts	2.6	3.7	4.1	4.8
~Income payments on foreign assets in U.S.				
*Direct investment payments	−8.6	−6.9	−1.9	−4.2
*Other private payments	−21.2	−29.4	−35.2	−30.5
*U.S. government payments	−12.7	−17.3	−19.3	−19.0
Net investment income balance	30.1	32.9	29.8	31.5
Net unilateral transfers	−8.3	−11.7	−17.1	−17.7
Current account balance	−3.4	−1.6	−13.4	−41.1

	1992	1993	1994	1995
Merchandise trade balance[a]	−97.9	−132.2	−176.6	−188.8
Services trade balance				
~Imports	−120.3	−126.4	−135.5	−147.0
~Exports	177.2	186.7	197.2	218.7
Net services trade balance	56.9	60.3	61.8	71.7
Investment income balance				
~Income receipts on U.S. assets abroad				
*Direct investment receipts	51.9	61.2	70.9	90.3
*Other private receipts	66.8	63.5	79.5	101.8
*U.S. government receipts	7.1	−5.1	4.1	4.7
~Income payments on foreign assets in U.S.				
*Direct investment payments	−0.3	−5.6	−20.2	−30.3
*Other private payments	−67.1	−63.0	−77.6	−98.4
*U.S. government payments	−40.5	−41.6	−47.0	−61.3
Net investment income balance	18.0	−19.7	9.7	6.8
Net unilateral transfers	−35.2	−38.1	−38.8	−34.0
Current account balance	−58.1	−90.5	−143.9	−144.4

Sources: Table 1, U.S. International Transactions, *Survey of Current Business*, July 1997, March 1998, July 1998, March 2003. Table 2, U.S. International Transactions, *Survey of Current Business*, June 1999, March 2003.

[a]Imports based on CIF value; exports based on FAS value. See Table 1.2 for detailed presentation.

1984	1985	1986	1987	1988	1989	1990	1991
−122.4	−133.6	−155.1	−170.3	−138.4	−123.7	−119.0	−82.6
−67.7	−72.9	−81.8	−92.3	−100.0	−104.2	−120.0	−121.2
71.2	73.2	86.3	98.6	111.0	127.1	147.8	164.2
3.4	0.3	4.5	6.2	11.1	23.0	27.8	43.0
31.3	30.5	32.0	39.6	52.1	55.4	58.7	52.2
68.3	57.6	52.8	55.6	70.6	92.6	94.1	81.2
5.2	5.5	6.4	5.3	6.7	5.7	10.5	8.0
−8.7	−7.2	−7.1	−7.4	−11.7	−6.5	−2.9	3.4
−44.2	−42.7	−47.4	−57.7	−72.3	−93.8	−95.5	−83.1
−21.2	−23.1	−24.6	−26.2	−31.7	−38.4	−41.0	−41.5
30.7	20.6	12.1	9.2	13.6	15.0	23.9	20.2
−20.6	−22.7	−24.7	−23.9	−26.0	−27.0	−34.6	5.1
−108.8	−135.5	−163.2	−178.8	−139.7	−112.7	−101.8	−14.2

1996	1997	1998	1999	2000	2001	2002
−195.0	−210.7	−260.5	−364.9	−415.9	−450.1	−509.0
−156.6	−167.9	−181.5	−189.4	−218.5	−210.4	−240.5
236.8	253.2	260.3	273.2	292.2	279.3	289.3
80.1	85.3	78.8	83.8	73.7	68.9	48.8
98.9	109.2	100.4	128.5	149.7	126.0	128.1
102.9	123.3	138.6	156.7	197.1	151.8	110.8
4.6	3.5	3.6	3.2	3.8	3.6	3.3
−32.1	−41.5	−45.8	−53.4	−60.8	−23.4	−50.1
−100.1	−117.7	−128.6	−136.5	−179.2	−156.8	−124.5
−71.3	−91.1	−90.7	−75.5	−83.0	−80.7	−72.9
2.8	−14.3	−22.5	18.1	21.8	14.4	−11.9
−40.0	−38.5	−41.9	−48.8	53.4	−49.5	−56.0
−152.0	−178.1	−246.1	−292.9	−410.3	−393.4	−504.4

Table 1.2

U.S. Merchandise Trade Balances, 1998–2002 (in billions of US$)

Country	1998				1999			
	Imports	Exports	Balance	Ratio	Imports	Exports	Balance	Ratio
World	944.586	682.977	−261.6	1.38	1059.435	695.797	−363.64	1.52
North America								
~Canada	178.048	156.308	−21.74	1.14	201.988	166.600	−35.39	1.21
~Mexico	96.078	79.010	−17.07	1.21	111.103	86.909	−24.10	1.28
Europe								
~Western Europe: Non-EU	15.283	13.149	−2.13	1.10	17.415	13.712	−3.70	1.27
Norway	3.037	1.709	−1.33	1.94	4.231	1.439	−2.79	2.94
Switzerland	8.897	7.251	−1.65	1.23	9.727	8.371	−1.36	1.16
Turkey	2.677	3.513	+8.36	0.76	2.764	3.217	+0.453	0.86
~Western Europe: EU	182.063	149.470	−32.60	1.22	201.021	151.814	−49.21	1.32
Austria	2.653	2.506	−0.15	1.06	3.007	2.588	−0.420	1.16
Denmark	2.482	1.874	−64.0	1.32	2.926	1.726	−1.20	1.70
Finland	2.747	1.915	−0.832	1.43	3.041	1.669	−1.37	1.82
France	24.712	17.728	−6.98	1.39	26.349	18.887	−7.47	1.40
Germany	51.283	26.642	−24.64	1.92	56.740	26.800	−29.94	2.12
Greece	0.515	1.355	+0.840	0.38	0.613	0.996	+3.83	0.62
Ireland	8.479	5.653	−283.0	1.50	11.084	6.384	−4.70	1.74
Italy	21.910	9.027	−12.88	2.43	23.260	10.091	−13.17	2.31
Netherlands	8.009	19.004	+11.0	0.42	8.882	19.437	+10.56	0.46
Portugal	1.327	0.888	−0.440	1.49	1.415	1.092	−0.323	1.20
Spain	5.112	5.465	+0.353	0.94	5.410	6.133	+0.723	0.88
Sweden	8.076	3.819	−4.26	2.11	8.336	4.251	−4.09	1.97
United Kingdom	35.721	39.070	+3.35	0.91	40.216	38.407	−1.81	1.05
~Eastern Europe	11.451	7.474	−3.98	1.53	12.366	5.882	−6.48	2.10
Czech Republic	0.699	0.568	−0.131	1.23	0.784	0.610	−1.74	1.29

Table 1.2 (continued)

USSR (former)	7.466	4.962	-2.50	1.50	7.902	3.511	-4.39	2.25
Russia	6.009	3.585	2.42	1.68	6.133	2.060	4.07	2.98
Central America	9.752	8.415	-1.34	1.16	11.551	8.455	-3.10	1.37
Costa Rica	2.927	2.229	-0.630	1.27	4.177	2.381	-1.80	1.75
El Salvador	1.479	1.515	+0.036	0.98	1.648	1.519	-0.130	1.08
Guatemala	2.2112	1.941	-0.271	1.14	2.406	1.812	-0.594	1.33
Honduras	2.662	2.322	-0.340	1.15	2.806	2.370	-0.436	1.18
Nicaragua	0.472	0.336	-0.136	1.40	0.514	0.374	-0.140	1.37
Panama	0.330	1.753	+1.42	0.19	0.396	1.742	+1.35	0.23
South America								
Argentina	2.441	5.885	+3.44	0.41	2.794	4.950	+2.16	0.56
Bolivia	0.234	0.103	+0.170	0.58	0.232	0.298	+0.07	0.78
Brazil	10.642	15.157	+4.52	0.70	11.897	13.203	+1.31	0.90
Chile	2.811	3.985	+1.17	0.71	3.306	3.078	-0.23	1.07
Colombia	4.940	4.817	+0.123	1.03	6.593	3.560	-3.03	1.85
Ecuador	1.989	1.687	-0.302	1.18	2.053	0.910	-1.14	2.26
Paraguay	0.36	0.786	+4.30	0.46	0.52	0.515	-0.01	1.01
Venezuela	10.073	6.520	-3.55	1.54	12.017	5.354	-6.66	2.24
~Caribbean basin								
Bahamas	0.154	0.815	+0.661	0.19	0.207	0.842	+0.635	0.25
Dominican Republic	4.551	3.977	-0.574	1.14	4.382	4.100	-2.82	1.07
Jamaica	0.798	1.304	+0.510	0.61	0.723	1.293	+0.570	0.56
Netherland Antilles	0.327	0.742	0.435	+0.420	0.409	0.597	+0.19	0.64
Trinidad & Tobago	1.071	0.983	0.12	-0.09	1.417	0.785	-0.632	1.81
Asia								
China	75.109	13.258	-60.85	5.27	87.790	13.111	-74.68	6.70
Japan	125.091	57.888	-67.20	2.16	134.322	57.466	-76.9	2.34
~East Asia NICs	88.738	63.292	-25.45	1.40	98.702	70.989	-27.71	1.39
Hong Kong	10.935	12.934	+2.0	0.85	10.996	12.652	+1.66	0.87
Singapore	18.654	15.674	-8.27	1.50	18.547	16.247	-2.30	1.14
South Korea	24.805	16.538	-8.27	1.50	32.391	22.958	-9.43	1.41

Sources and notes located at end of table.

Table 1.2 (continued)

Country	1998				1999			
	Imports	Exports	Balance	Ratio	Imports	Exports	Balance	Ratio
Taiwan	34.343	18.157	-16.19	1.89	36.769	19.131	-17.64	1.92
~Other Asia								
Burma	0.175	0.32	+1.50	0.54	0.251	0.09	-0.16	2.79
Cambodia	0.388	0.11	-0.280	3.53	0.635	0.20	-0.44	3.18
India	8.659	3.545	-5.11	2.44	9.578	3.688	-5.89	2.60
Indonesia	9.973	2.291	-7.68	4.35	10.284	2.038	-8.25	5.05
Malaysia	19.519	8.953	-10.57	2.18	22.085	9.060	-13.03	2.44
Pakistan	1.788	0.726	-1.06	2.46	1.872	0.497	-1.38	3.77
Philippines	12.335	6.736	-5.60	1.88	12.809	7.222	-5.59	1.77
Sri Lanka	1.856	0.190	-1.67	9.77	1.858	0.167	-1.69	11.13
Thailand	13.971	5.233	-8.74	2.67	15.163	4.985	-10.18	3.04
Vietnam	0.596	0.274	-0.322	2.18	0.654	0.292	-0.362	2.24
Middle East								
Israel	8.785	6.978	-1.81	1.26	10.028	7.691	-2.34	1.30
Kuwait	1.471	1.479	+0.01	0.99	1.571	0.864	-0.710	1.82
Saudi Arabia	7.169	10.525	+3.36	0.68	8.919	7.912	-1.01	1.13
United Arab Emirates	0.709	2.370	+1.66	0.30	0.760	2.708	+1.95	0.28
Africa								
Algeria	1.799	0.650	-1.15	2.77	1.944	0.459	-1.49	4.24
Angola	2.451	0.354	-2.10	6.92	2.568	0.252	-2.32	10.19
Egypt	0.699	3.060	+2.36	0.23	0.651	3.001	+2.35	0.22
Gabon	1.382	0.062	-1.32	2.23	1.644	0.45	-1.19	3.65
Ivory Coast	0.448	0.152	-3.00	2.95	0.377	0.104	-0.273	3.63
Morocco	0.367	0.552	+0.19	0.66	0.416	0.566	+0.150	0.73
Nigeria	4.548	0.820	-3.73	5.55	4.656	0.630	-4.03	7.39
South Africa	3.190	3.626	+4.40	0.88	3.331	2.586	-.750	1.29
Oceania								
Australia	5.179	11.929	+6.21	0.48	5.596	11.818	+0.622	0.47
New Zealand	1.803	1.885	+0.082	0.96	1.916	1.923	+0.01	1.0

Table 1.2 (continued)

Country	2000				2001			
	Imports	Exports	Balance	Ratio	Imports	Exports	Balance	Ratio
World	1,258.027	782.429	−475.60	1.61	1,179.177	729.100	−450.1	1.62
~North America								
Canada	232.700	178.786	−53.91	1.30	219.438	163.424	−56.01	1.34
Mexico	137.452	111.721	−25.73	1.23	132.678	101.297	−31.38	1.31
Europe								
~Western Europe: Non-EU	20.376	16.015	−4.36	1.27	19.220	15.499	−3.72	1.24
Norway	5.960	1.544	−4.42	3.86	5.466	1.835	−3.63	2.98
Switzerland	10.387	9.943	−0.444	1.04	9.841	9.807	−0.03	1.00
Turkey	3.238	3.731	+0.493	0.87	3.255	3.095	−0.16	1.05
~Western Europe: EU	248.129	181.240	−66.86	1.37	226.128	158.768	−67.36	1.42
Austria	3.353	2.554	−0.800	1.31	4.091	2.605	−1.49	1.57
Denmark	3.093	1.513	−1.58	2.04	3.531	1.609	−1.92	2.19
Finland	3.384	1.571	−1.81	2.15	3.529	1.554	−1.98	2.27
France	30.447	20.253	−10.19	1.50	31.072	19.865	−11.21	1.56
Germany	60.163	29.244	−30.92	2.06	60.413	29.995	−30.42	2.01
Greece	0.644	1.218	+0.574	0.53	0.554	1.294	+0.74	0.43
Ireland	16.517	7.727	−8.79	2.14	18.586	7.144	−11.44	2.60
Italy	26.200	11.000	−15.20	2.38	24.915	9.916	−15.0	2.51
Netherlands	10.164	21.974	+11.81	0.46	9.969	19.485	+9.52	0.51
Portugal	1.649	0.957	−0.692	1.72	1.620	1.240	−0.38	1.31
Spain	6.150	6.323	+0.173	0.97	5.587	5.756	+0.17	0.97
Sweden	9.904	4.557	−5.35	2.17	9.186	3.541	−5.65	2.59
United Kingdom	44.542	41.579	−2.96	1.07	42.338	40.714	−1.62	1.04
~Eastern Europe	16.936	6.144	−10.79	2.76	15.058	6.832	−8.23	2.20
Czech Republic	1.117	0.734	−0.383	1.52	1.169	0.706	−0.463	1.66
USSR (former)	10.919	3.608	−7.34	3.03	8.672	4.085	−4.59	2.12
Russia	8.039	2.318	−5.72	3.76	6.535	2.716	−3.82	2.41

Sources and notes located at end of table.

Table 1.2 (continued)

Country	2000				2001			
	Imports	Exports	Balance	Ratio	Imports	Exports	Balance	Ratio
Central America								
Costa Rica	12.334	9.069	-3.27	1.36	11.648	8.990	-2.66	1.30
El Salvador	3.764	2.445	-1.32	1.54	3.090	2.502	-0.59	1.24
Guatemala	1.989	1.775	-2.14	1.12	1.933	1.760	-0.173	1.10
Honduras	2.766	1.895	-0.871	1.46	2.746	1.870	-0.88	1.47
Nicaragua	3.203	2.575	-0.63	1.24	3.249	2.416	-0.83	1.34
Panama	0.613	0.379	-0.234	1.62	0.630	0.443	-0.19	1.42
	0.328	1.609	+1.28	0.20	0.310	1.331	+1.02	0.23
South America								
Argentina	3.314	4.700	+1.39	0.71	3.254	3.920	+0.67	0.83
Bolivia	0.198	0.251	+0.65	0.79	0.173	0.216	+0.04	0.80
Brazil	14.641	15.360	+0.75	0.95	15.263	15.880	+0.62	0.96
Chile	3.667	3.455	-0.212	1.06	4.020	3.118	-0.902	1.29
Colombia	7.355	3.689	-3.67	1.99	6.082	3.583	-2.50	1.70
Ecuador	2.464	1.037	1.43	2.38	2.281	1.412	-0.87	1.62
Paraguay	0.46	0.444	-0.02	1.04	0.36	0.389	+0.03	0.93
Venezuela	19.602	5.552	-14.05	3.43	16.153	5.642	-10.51	2.86
~Caribbean basin								
Bahamas	0.290	1.065	+0.780	0.27	0.329	1.026	+0.70	0.32
Dominican Republic	4.486	4.443	-0.43	1.01	4.287	4.398	+0.11	0.97
Jamaica	0.681	1.378	+0.700	0.49	0.496	1.406	+0.91	0.35
Netherland Antilles	0.751	0.674	0.49	1.14	0.515	0.816	+0.30	0.63
Trinidad & Tobago	2.405	1.097	-1.31	2.19	2.589	1.087	-1.50	2.38
Asia								
China	107.621	16.253	-91.37	6.62	109.388	19.182	90.206	5.70
Japan	150.632	65.254	-85.38	2.31	129.576	57.452	-72.124	2.26
~East Asia NICs	115.517	84.724	-30.791	1.36	96.604	71.902	-24.662	1.34
Hong Kong	11.974	14.625	+2.65	0.82	10.071	14.028	+3.96	0.72
South Korea	41.724	27.902	-13.82	1.50	36.488	22.181	-14.31	1.65

Table 1.2 *(continued)*

Singapore	19.558	17.816	-1.74	1.10	15.284	17.652	+2.37	0.87
Taiwan	42.261	24.380	-17.38	1.73	34.762	18.122	-16.64	1.92
~Other Asia								
Burma	0.507	0.17	-3.40	2.98	0.502	0.11	-0.392	4.56
Cambodia	0.880	0.32	-5.60	2.75	1.017	0.30	-0.72	3.39
India	11.312	3.663	-7.65	3.09	10.290	3.757	-6.53	2.74
Indonesia	11.215	2.547	-8.67	4.40	10.906	2.521	-8.39	4.33
Malaysia	26.394	10.996	-15.40	2.40	23.076	9.358	-13.72	2.47
Pakistan	2.341	0.462	-1.88	5.07	2.420	0.541	-1.88	4.47
Philippines	14.454	8.790	-5.66	1.64	11.769	7.660	4.11	1.54
Sri Lanka	2.145	0.204	-1.94	10.51	2.100	0.183	-0.192	11.48
Thailand	17.375	6.643	-10.73	2.62	15.565	5.989	-9.58	2.60
Vietnam	0.885	0.368	-5.20	2.40	1.139	0.460	-0.68	2.48
Middle East								
Israel	13.213	7.750	-5.46	1.70	12.146	7.475	-4.67	1.62
Kuwait	3.001	0.791	-2.21	3.79	2.209	0.902	-1.31	2.45
Saudi Arabia	15.078	6.230	-8.85	2.42	14.342	5.958	-8.38	2.41
United Arab Emirates	1.037	2.291	+1.25	0.45	1.284	2.638	+1.35	0.49
Africa								
Algeria	2.879	0.867	-2.01	3.32	2.914	1.038	-1.88	2.81
Angola	3.759	0.226	-0.353	16.63	3.273	0.276	-3.0	11.86
Egypt	0.941	3.329	+2.39	0.28	0.943	3.564	+2.62	0.26
Gabon	2.333	0.63	-1.70	3.70	1.740	0.73	-1.01	2.38
Ivory Coast	0.422	0.95	+0.53	0.44	0.358	0.97	+0.61	0.37
Morocco	0.471	0.525	+0.05	0.90	0.467	0.282	-1.85	1.66
Nigeria	11.052	0.719	-10.33	15.37	9.167	0.955	-8.21	9.60
South Africa	4.362	3.085	-1.28	1.41	4.593	2.960	-1.63	1.55
Oceania								
Australia	6.803	12.466	+5.66	0.55	6.810	10.931	+4.12	0.62

Sources and notes located at end of table.

Table 1.2 (continued)

Country	2002							
	Imports	Exports	Balance	Ratio				
New Zealand	2.258	1.974	-2.84	1.14				
World	1,202.499	693.516	-509.0	1.73	2.384	2.111	-0.27	1.13
~North America								
Canada	213.954	160.829	-53.1	1.33				
Mexico	137.144	97.531	-39.9	1.41				
Europe								
~Western Europe: Non-EU	20.031	12.944	-7.09	1.55				
Norway	6.075	1.407	-4.67	4.32				
Switzerland	9.543	7.782	-1.76	1.23				
Turkey	3.760	3.106	-0.654	1.21				
Western Europe: EU	232.142	143.748	-88.39	1.61				
Austria	3.939	2.424	-1.52	1.63				
Denmark	3.346	1.496	-1.85	2.24				
Finland	3.607	1.537	-2.07	2.35				
France	28.944	19.019	-9.98	1.52				
Germany	63.884	26.628	-37.26	2.40				
Greece	0.602	1.153	0.551	0.52				
Ireland	22.485	6.749	-15.736	3.33				
Italy	25.415	10.089	-15.326	2.52				
Netherlands	10.308	18.335	8.03	0.56				
Portugal	1.740	0.863	-0.877	2.02				
Spain	6.063	5.226	-0.837	1.16				
Sweden	9.552	3.154	-6.40	3.03				
United Kingdom	41.825	33.253	-8.57	1.26				
~Eastern Europe	15.617	6.599	-9.02	2.37				
Czech Republic	1.293	0.654	-0.639	1.98				
USSR (former)	9.072	4.113	-4.96	2.21				
Russia	7.146	2.399	-4.75	2.98				

Table 1.2 (continued)

Central America	12.457	9.841	-2.62	1.27
Costa Rica	3.339	3.132	-0.21	1.07
El Salvador	2.039	1.665	-0.374	1.22
Guatemala	2.976	2.042	-0.934	1.46
Honduras	3.396	2.565	-0.831	1.32
Nicaragua	0.707	0.438	-0.270	1.61
Panama	0.321	1.408	1.09	0.23
South America				
Argentina	3.432	1.591	-1.84	2.16
Bolivia	0.167	0.192	0.03	0.87
Brazil	16.722	12.409	-4.31	1.35
Chile	4.350	2.612	-1.74	1.67
Colombia	5.936	3.589	-2.35	1.65
Ecuador	2.391	1.607	-0.784	1.49
Paraguay	0.48	0.433	0.05	1.11
Venezuela	15.828	4.447	-11.381	3.56
~Caribbean basin				
Bahamas	0.478	0.975	0.50	0.49
Dominican Republic	4.271	4.261	-0.01	1.00
Jamaica	0.421	1.420	1.0	0.30
Netherland Antilles	0.382	0.742	0.36	0.51
Trinidad & Tobago	2.664	1.018	-1.65	2.62
Asia				
China	133.490	22.053	-111.437	6.05

Sources and notes located at end of table.

Table 1.2 (continued)

Country	2002			
	Imports	Exports	Balance	Ratio
Japan	124.633	51.440	−73.2	2.42
~East Asia NICs	95.297	69.823	−25.5	1.36
Hong Kong	9.774	12.612	2.84	0.77
South Korea	36.910	22.596	−14.31	1.63
Singapore	15.093	16.221	1.13	0.93
Taiwan	33.520	18.394	−15.13	1.82
~Other Asia				
Burma	0.380	0.10	−0.28	3.80
Cambodia	1.146	0.29	−0.86	3.95
India	12.450	4.098	−8.35	3.04
Indonesia	10.385	2.581	−7.80	4.02
Malaysia	24.734	10.348	−14.39	2.39
Pakistan	2.482	0.694	−1.79	3.58
Philippines	11.431	7.270	−4.16	1.57
Sri Lanka	1.924	0.172	−1.75	11.19
Thailand	15.683	4.860	−108.23	0.23
Vietnam	2.585	0.580	−2.01	4.46
Middle East				
Israel	12.644	7.039	−5.61	1.80
Kuwait	2.052	1.015	−1.04	2.02
Saudi Arabia	3.892	4.779	−9.11	2.91
United Arab Emirates	0.998	3.599	2.60	0.28
Africa				

Table 1.2 (continued)

Algeria	2.560	0.984	-1.58	2.60
Angola	3.275	0.373	-2.90	8.78
Egypt	1.417	2.866	1.45	0.49
Gabon	1.666	0.66	-1.01	2.52
Ivory Coast	0.399	0.76	0.36	0.53
Morocco	0.425	0.566	0.141	0.75
Nigeria	6.219	1.057	-5.16	5.89
South Africa				
Oceania	4.183	2.525	-1.66	1.66
Australia	6.824	13.084	6.26	0.52
Newe Zealand	2.471	1.814	-0.66	1.36

Sources: U.S. Department of Commerce, International Trade Administration, *U.S. Foreign Trade Highlights*, and www.ita.doc.gov/industry/otea/usfth/aggregate/H198+06.txt

Notes: Imports based on CIF value; exports based on FAS value.

Table 1.3

U.S. GNP and Federal Government Expenditures, Selected Years, 1980–2002 (in billions of US$)

Year	1980	1984	1988	1990	1991	1992	1993	1994
GNP[a]	2,819.5	3,933.5	5,062.6	5,764.9	5,932.4	6,255.5	6,563.5	6,931.9
Gross federal debt[b]	908.5	1,564.1	2,600.8	3,206.3	3,599.0	4,002.1	4,351.4	4,643.7
Total federal expenditures[c]	613.1	892.7	1,109.0	1,273.6	1,332.7	1,479.4	1,530.9	1,567.3
Federal receipts	553.0	725.8	972.3	1,107.4	1,122.2	1,198.5	1,275.3	1,377.0
Federal deficits (or surplus)	−60.1	−166.9	−136.7	−166.2	−210.5	−280.9	−255.6	−190.3
Interest paid on federal debt[d]	64.5	137.7	175.5	209.2	220.9	217.9	214.4	224.1
National defense outlays (total)[e]	134.0	227.4	290.4	299.3	273.3	298.4	291.1	281.6
Military retirement and disability[f]	11.9	16.5	19.0	21.5	23.1	24.5	25.7	26.7
Veterans' benefits[g]	11.0	12.8	14.8	13.4	14.4	15.7	18.0	18.0
Social security[h]	118.5	178.2	219.3	248.6	269.0	287.6	304.6	319.6
Medicare[i]	34.0	61.0	85.7	107.4	114.2	129.4	143.2	159.6
Income security[j]	80.6	113.4	130.4	130.4	148.7	172.4	199.5	209.9

Year	1995	1996	1997	1998	1999	2000	2001	2002
GNP[k]	7,246.7	7,567.1	8,060	8,778	9,288	9,861	10,104	10,600
Gross federal debt[l]	4,921.0	5,181.9	5,369	5,478	5,606	5,629	5,670	6,198
Total federal expenditures[m]	1,637.6	1,698.1	1,601	1,653	1,750	1,828	1,936	2,125
Federal receipts	1,463.2	1,587.6	1,579	1,722	1,875	2,047	2,008	1,875
Federal deficits (or surplus)	−174.4	−110.5	−22	+69	+125	+236	+127	−158
Interest paid on federal debt[n]	250.0	253.1	244	241	230	223	206	171
National defense outlays (total)[o]	272.1	265.7	271	269	275	295	306	355
Military retirement and disability[p]	27.8	28.8	30	31	32	33	34	35
Veterans' benefits[q]	20.8	21.6	19	21	22	22	23	24
Social security[r]	335.8	349.7	365	375	390	409	433	456
Medicare[s]	177.1	174.2	190	193	190	197	217	236
Income security[t]	217.0	223.7	235	238	242	254	270	312

[a] Table 1, Gross Domestic Product (1929–1996), *Survey of Current Business* (May 1997), U.S. Department of Commerce, Economics and Statistics Administration, Bureau of Economic Analysis. 1997 data from Table 1.9, Relation of Gross Domestic Product, Gross National Product, Net National Product, Net National Product and Personal Income, *Survey of Current Business* (March 2003).

[b] Table 1-15, Federal Finances and the Federal Debt (1955–1996), *Green Book*, U.S. House of Representatives Ways and Means Committee.

[c] Data for: 1980–1988 taken from Table 3.2, Federal Government Receipts and Expenditures, *National Income and Product Accounts of the United States, Volume 2, 1959–1988,* U.S. Department of Commerce, Economics and Statistics Administration, Bureau of Economic Analysis; 1989–1990 from Table 3.2, Federal Government Receipts and Expenditures, *Survey of Current Business* (Dec. 1991); 1991 from Table 3.2, Federal Government Receipts and Current Expenditures, *Survey of Current Business* (Aug. 1996); 1995–1997 from Table 3.2, Federal Government Receipts and Current Expenditures, *Survey of Current Business* (March 2003).

[d] Ibid.

[e] Table B-78, Federal Receipts and Outlays, by Major Category, and Surplus or Deficit (Fiscal Years 1940–2003) *Economic Report of the President.*

[f] Table 1-5, Historical Outlays for Entitlements and Other Mandatory Spending, Selected Fiscal Years 1975–03, *2003 Green Book.*

[g] (Including Veterans' compensation, readjustment benefits, life insurance, and housing programs.) 1980–1994 from Table 1.5, Historical Outlays for Entitlements and Other Mandatory Spending, Selected Years, 1975–95; *1996 Green Book.* 1995–1997 from Table 2.1, Personal Incomes and Disposition, *Survey of Current Business* (March 2003).

[h] Table B-78, Federal Receipts and Outlays, by Major Category, and Surplus or Deficit (Fiscal Years 1940–1998), *Economic Report of the President* (March 2003).

[i] Table 1-5, Historical Outlays for Entitlements and Other Mandatory Spending, Selected Fiscal Year, *Green Book.*

[j] Table B-80, *Economic Report of the President* (2003).

[k] *Survey of Current Business,* U.S. Dept. of Commerce, Economics and Statistics Administration, Bureau of Economic Analysis, various years; *Economic Report of the President,* various years (including 2003).

(continued)

Table 1.3 (continued)

[l] Federal Finances and the Federal Debt, *Green Book*, U.S. House of Representatives Ways and Means Committee.

[m] Federal Government Receipts and Expenditures, *National Income and Product Accounts of the United States, Volume 2, 1959–1988*, U.S. Department of Commerce, Economics and Statistics Administration, Bureau of Economic Analysis; 1989–1990 from Table 3.2, Federal Government Receipts and Expenditures, *Survey of Current Business* (various years).

[n] Ibid.

[o] Table B-78, Federal Receipts and Outlays, by Major Category, and Surplus or Deficit, *Economic Report of the President* (various years).

[p] Table 1-5, Historical Outlays for Entitlements and Other Mandatory Spending, Selected Fiscal Years 1975–2003, *2003 Green Book*.

[q] (Includes Veterans' compensation, readjustment benefits, life insurance, and housing programs.) 1980–1994 from Table 1.5, Historical Outlays for Entitlements and Other Mandatory Spending, Selected Years, 1975–95 *1996 Green Book*. 1995–1997 from Table 2.1, Personal Incomes and Disposition, *Survey of Current Business* (March 2003).

[r] Table B-78, Federal Receipts and Outlays, by Major Category, and Surplus or Deficit (Fiscal Years 1940–1998), *Economic Report of the President* (1997, 2003).

[s] Table 1-5, Federal Receipts and Outlays, by Major Category, and Surplus or Deficit (Fiscal Years 1940–1998), *Economic Report of the President* (1997, 2003).

[t] Table B-80, *Economic Report of the President* (2003).

Table 1.4

Foreign Exchange Rates, Selected Years, 1971–2003 (in currency units per US$)

Country/currency:	Jan. 1971	Sept. 1973	Dec. 1976	Dec. 1980	Jan. 1985	Dec. 1987	Dec. 1994	May 1995
United States/dollar[a]	120.4000	95.1100	105.3300	90.9900	152.8300	88.7000	89.6400	82.7300
Japan/yen	358.0100	265.4800	294.7000	209.4400	254.1800	128.2400	100.1800	85.1100
Germany/deutsche mark	3.6369	2.4245	2.3829	1.9697	3.1706	1.6335	1.5716	1.4096
Switzerland/franc	4.3053	3.1070	2.4496	1.7850	2.6590	1.3304	1.3289	1.1693
Taiwan/dollar	n/a	n/a	n/a	n/a	39.2090	29.0040	26.2860	25.5370
South Korea/won	n/a	n/a	n/a	n/a	832.1600	798.3400	793.8100	764.4300
United Kingdom/pound[b]	240.5800	241.8300	167.8400	234.5900	112.7100	182.8800	155.8700	158.7400

Country/currency:	May 1996	Jan 1997	Jan 1998[e]	Jan 1999[f]	Jun 1999[g]	Aug 2001[h]	Dec 2002[i]	Jun 2003[j]
United States/dollar[a]	88.2800	91.0100	101.0800	93.6200	96.2800	103.03	97.95	88.96
Japan/yen	106.3400	117.9100	133.9900	116.3600	119.4700	118.75	119.92	118.39
Germany/deutsche mark[b]	1.5324	1.6047	1.8223	2.2287	2.0202	—	—	—
Switzerland/franc	1.2539	1.3913	1.4803	1.4165	1.5455	1.6698	1.3954	1.3290
Taiwan/dollar	27.3520	27.4770	33.6000	323.8000	32.3600	34.580	34.830	34.590
South Korea/won	780.8600	854.0700	1,790.0000	1,176.5000	1,167.0000	1284.00	1198.00	1190.60
United Kingdom/pound[c]	151.5200	165.8500	163.3000	164.7000	159.2500	1.4510	160.22	166.44
European Union/Euro[d]				113.9500	103.2900	90.90	104.11	1.1616

Sources: (unless otherwise noted) *Federal Reserve Bulletin*, Board of Governors of the Federal Reserve System (various issues).
a Index of weighted-average exchange value of U.S. dollar against the currencies of ten industrial countries. The weight for each of the ten countries is the 1972–76 average world trade of that country divided by the average world trade of all ten countries combined. Series revised as of August 1978.

(continued)

Table 1.4 *(continued)*

[b] German mark exchange rate derived from euro rate as of January 11, 1999: euro = 1.95583 German marks; Foreign Exchange Rates (weekly), Board of Governors of the Federal Reserve System (rel. date February 1, 1999).

[c] Value in U.S. cents per pound.

[d] Euro reported as of January 11, 1999 release, in place of EMU member currencies (Belgian francs, German marks, Spanish pesetas, French francs, Irish pounds, Italian lire, Luxembourg francs, Dutch guilders, Austrian schillings, Portuguese escudos, and Finnish markkas); Foreign Exchange Rates (weekly), Board of Governors of the Federal Reserve System (rel. date January 11, 1999) www.bog.frb.fed.us/releasesH10/19990111/>; value is in U.S. cents per euro.

[e] Rates as of April 1, 1998; Foreign Exchange Rates (weekly), Board of Governors of the Federal Reserve System (rel. date April 27, 1998).

[f] Rates as of Jan. 28, 1999; Foreign Exchange Rates (weekly), Board of Governors of the Federal Reserve System (rel. date Feb. 1, 1999).

[g] Rates as of June 17, 1999; Foreign Exchange Rates (weekly), Board of Governors of the Federal Reserve System (rel. date Mar. 17, 2003).

[h] Rates as of Aug. 31, 2001; Foreign Exchange Rates (weekly), Board of Governors of the Federal Reserve System (rel. date Sept. 4, 2002).

[i] Rates as of Dec. 27, 2002; Foreign Exchange Rates (weekly), Board of Governors of the Federal Reserve System (rel. date Dec. 30, 2002).

[j] Rates as of June 20, 2003; Foreign Exchange Rates (weekly), Board of Governors of the Federal Reserve System (rel. date June 23, 2003).

Table 1.5

Per Capita Gross National Product by Nation, Selected Years, 1953–2000

Year	1953	1960	1965	1970	1975	1980	1985	1991	1994	1995	2000
United States	2,310	2,830	3,580	4,826	7,141	11,446	16,693	22,240	25,860	26,980	34,100
USSR (Russia)	—	1,600	1,900	2,300	2,700	5,730	5,749	3,220	2,650	2,240	1,660
Japan	230	460	900	1,964	4,481	9,069	11,024	26,930	34,630	39,640	35,620
West Germany	740	1,310	1,950	3,042	6,751	13,216	10,123	23,650	25,580	27,510	25,120
France	1,010	1,350	2,050	2,775	6,430	12,163	9,270	20,380	23,470	24,990	24,090
United Kingdom	940	1,380	1,640	2,213	4,162	9,470	8,039	16,550	18,410	18,700	24,430
Belgium	940	1,250	1,610	2,616	6,304	11,927	8,068	18,950	22,920	24,710	24,540
Italy	430	700	1,120	1,875	3,464	7,011	6,278	18,520	19,270	19,020	20,160
Sweden	1,120	1,740	2,660	4,139	8,843	14,938	11,975	25,110	23,630	23,750	27,140
Switzerland	1,150	1,600	2,330	3,308	8,477	15,920	14,194	33,610	37,180	40,630	38,160
Spain	—	340	680	1,086	2,952	5,665	4,340	12,490	13,280	13,580	15,080
Netherlands	610	990	1,570	2,567	6,364	11,970	8,525	18,780	21,970	24,000	24,970
Norway	870	1,240	1,890	2,883	7,100	14,121	13,953	24,220	26,480	31,250	34,530
Hungary	—	1,500	1,800	2,000	2,400	4,180	1,956	2,720	3,840	4,120	4,710
Yugoslavia	—	590	520	714	1,557	2,470	1,878	—	—	—	—
Poland	—	1,500	1,800	2,100	2,800	—	2,241	1,790	2,470	2,790	4,190
China	93	117	134	167	209	240	333	370	530	620	840
South Korea	—	152	115	266	583	1,620	1,986	6,350	8,220	9,700	8,910
Taiwan	100	150	199	227	910	2,260	3,140	7,190	11,597	12,439	—
India	62	74	103	100	147	210	255	330	310	340	450
Canada	1,710	2,090	2,460	3,870	7,213	10,800	13,096	20,440	19,570	19,380	21,130
Mexico	232	334	455	701	1,463	1,950	2,260	3,030	4,010	3,320	5,070
Brazil	—	208	236	505	1,219	2,060	1,623	2,940	3,370	3,640	3,580

(continued)

34

Table 1.5 (continued)

Sources: National Accounts of OECD Countries, 1950–1968, p. 10; National Accounts of OECD Countries, 1960–1984, Comparative Table 21, OECD, Department of Economics and Statistics. Yearbook of National Account Statistics, 1969, Vol. 11, Table 1C and 1972, Vol. III, Table 1A, United Nations, Department of Economics and Social Affairs, Statistics Office. Geographical Distribution of Financial Flows, 1981–84, Section C, pp. 274–75. OECD (Paris 1986). Worldmark Encyclopedia of the Nations, Vol. V, Hungary, Poland, and USSR, Worldmark Press Ltd. Paul S. Shoup, The East European and Society Data Handbook: Political and Development Indicators, 1965–75, Table 11.4, Columbia University Press (New York 1991). Willy Kraus, Economic Development and Social Change in the People's Republic of China, Table A1, Springer-Verlag (New York 1979). Morgan International Data, Table A-1, Morgan Guaranty Trust International, Economic Department (June 1986). World Financial Markets, Morgan Guaranty Trust (Oct./Nov. 1986). OECD Economic Outlook (Dec. 1986). "Korea Business Brief," Asia Wall Street Journal (June 5, 1987), p. 4. World Bank Atlas, 1990; World Development Report, 1992–94, World Bank, 1990; World Bank Atlas 1996, World Bank Atlas, 1997, World Bank Atlas, 2002. World Information Country Outlooks, Bank of America, Taiwan (Nov. 1990). Taiwan Statistical Data Book, 1996. Council for Economic Planning and Development, Republic of China.

Note: The fluctuations in relative GNPs in 1980, 1985, 1991, 1994, 1995, and 2000 reflect a "low" dollar in 1980, a "high" dollar in 1985, a "declining dollar" in 1991, a somewhat "lower" dollar in 1994, a "low" dollar in 1995, and a "higher" dollar in 2000.

Table 1.6

Average Weekly Earnings of U.S. Production or Nonsupervisory Workers on Nonagricultural Payrolls, Selected Years, 1940–2002 (in US$)

Year	Total private		Manufacturing	
	Current dollars	Constant dollars[a]	Current dollars	Constant dollars[a]
1940	n.a.	n.a.	24.96	n.a.
1947	45.58	196.47	49.13	211.77
1955	67.72	243.60	75.30	270.87
1965	95.45	291.90	107.53	328.84
1972	136.90	315.44	154.71	356.48
1978	203.70	300.89	249.27	368.20
1980	235.10	274.65	288.62	337.17
1981	255.20	270.63	318.00	337.23
1982	267.26	267.26	330.26	330.26
1983	280.70	272.52	354.08	343.76
1984	292.86	274.73	374.03	350.88
1985	299.09	271.16	386.37	350.29
1986	304.85	271.94	396.01	353.26
1987	312.50	269.16	406.31	349.96
1988	322.02	266.79	418.81	346.98
1989	334.24	264.22	429.68	339.67
1990	345.35	259.47	441.86	331.98
1991	353.98	255.40	455.03	328.31
1992	363.61	254.99	469.86	329.50
1993	373.64	254.87	486.04	331.54
1994	385.86	256.73	506.94	337.29
1995	394.34	255.07	514.59	332.85
1996	406.61	255.73	531.65	334.37
1997	424.89	261.31	553.14	337.99[b]
2002	505.13	276.02[c]	625.77	342.73[c]

Source: National Employment, Hours and Earnings, U.S. Department of Labor, Bureau of Labor Statistics.
Note: n.a. = not available.
[a] Constant dollars in 1982 base year.
[b] Average from February 1997 to February 1998.
[c] January 2002.

2

U.S. Trade History

ALFRED E. ECKES JR.

Products and Partners

To survive and prosper in the New World, the courageous settlers of British North America relied on trade. Beginning in the seventeenth century, the colonists shipped large quantities of foodstuffs and raw materials across the Atlantic to England—particularly furs, tobacco, rice, indigo, rum, grain, potash, coal, fish, timber, and naval stores. This external trade contributed 20 percent of total income during colonial times and established a pattern that would endure for many years. Until the 1960s, the majority of U.S. exports (by value) consisted of food products and industrial materials, although paradoxically the United States became the world's leading manufacturing power before World War I. Early American settlers also built ships, and U.S. shipping soon played a big role in the Atlantic carrying trade. But it was in primary and semiprocessed products, not finished goods and services, that colonial America prospered and penetrated world markets.[1]

Europe soon developed an insatiable appetite for American commodities—especially tobacco, cotton, wheat, and petroleum. Tobacco brought prosperity to the Chesapeake region and it quickly emerged as the leading export crop, amounting to one-third to one-half of total exports. Despite the health hazards of smoking, American tobacco remains an important export. In 2002, this country sold abroad $2.8 billion in tobacco and tobacco products. But early in the nineteenth century cotton displaced tobacco as the leading export. American-grown long-staple cotton quickly became an essential raw material for the spindles of Lancashire. In the generation before the American Civil War, cotton was considered king. It constituted more than half of total U.S. exports, and during the war the South hoped that English dependence on American cotton would bring favorable intervention. As late as the 1920s, raw cotton still accounted for more than 20 percent of U.S. exports, and in 2001 it earned a respectable $2.2 billion from foreign sales.[2]

By the middle of the nineteenth century, an industrializing Europe developed an appetite for other American raw materials and farm products, such as wheat, lard, pork, and petroleum. Wheat and flour exports soared as improved railroad transportation integrated the American Midwest into the international economy. Wheat would remain a sizable export, amounting to $3.4 billion in 2001. Petroleum never became America's leading export, but late in the nineteenth century the United States emerged for a while as the world's leading oil exporter. American oil proved critical to Allied victory in World War I, supplying 80 percent of petroleum needs. Lord Curzon observed how "the Allied cause had floated to victory upon a wave of [American] oil." As late as 1929, the United States produced 68 percent of the world's oil.[3]

American imports exhibited a more complex pattern. From colonial times until the Civil War, finished manufactures and consumer goods composed the majority of imports. These included clothing, tools, equipment, and home furnishings. A different pattern emerged after the Civil War and continued for more than a century—until the 1980s. During this period a majority of American imports were food (particularly coffee and sugar) and industrial supplies (rubber and petroleum). This shift reflected the requirements of the American protective system, which imposed high duties on manufactures and encouraged the importation of tropical foods and raw materials. As tariff levels declined to minimal levels and as a global economy took shape in the 1980s, the composition of American imports changed again. With large quantities of foreign-made cars, machine tools, apparel, footwear, and other consumer goods entering the open American market, it is not surprising that finished goods again came to dominate the import trade (see Table 2.1).

This second shift in import composition coincided with the emergence of major new trading partners in Asia (see Table 2.2). At the beginning of the twentieth century, Europe accounted for most of total U.S. trade. Indeed, until the 1890s, Britain had purchased more than half of exports—a statistic that reflected the importance of American cotton for the English textile industry—and the United Kingdom would remain the largest export market until World War I, when Canada took the lead. In 1900, 75 percent of U.S. exports crossed the Atlantic to Europe. As a market for U.S. products, Germany ranked second to Britain; France held fourth place behind Canada. In the early twentieth century, the Asian market was small but rising. Asia bought about 5 percent of exports, while Latin America purchased another 10 percent. In 1900 Great Britain remained the leading supplier of U.S. imports—and would remain so until the 1920s, when Canada moved to the front.

A century later Europe no longer dominates U.S. trade. During the last thirty years, Asian suppliers and markets rose rapidly in significance. In 1974 imports from that region surpassed imports from Europe, and in 1986 exports to Asia exceeded those to Europe (including Eastern Europe). By 2002, only 23.6 percent of U.S. merchandise exports crossed the Atlantic Ocean to Europe, while 27.1 percent went to Asian markets. This figure included Japan,

Table 2.1

Percentage of Exports and Imports by Broad End-Use Class, 1925–2002

Year	Food, feed, and beverages		Industrial supplies		Capital goods (excluding auto)		Automotive (including parts)		Consumer goods	
	Imports	Exports	Imports	Exports	Imports	Exports	Imports	Exports	Imports	Exports
1925	21.7	18.1	67.5	58.1	0.3	08.5	—	6.6	9.3	5.8
1929	21.7	14.4	64.5	54.0	0.8	12.5	—	10.4	11.7	6.5
1930	22.3	14.1	63.5	54.9	0.9	14.2	—	7.4	11.3	6.6
1935	31.0	9.5	57.8	60.0	0.7	11.6	—	10.2	8.9	6.4
1939	25.9	10.1	61.8	52.6	0.6	18.4	—	8.2	8.5	6.9
1946	26.5	22.6	61.3	39.5	0.6	17.0	0.26	5.7	9.8	11.1
1950	29.5	14.4	61.3	42.4	1.2	20.8	0.7	7.3	6.0	8.3
1955	26.9	13.6	59.2	39.0	2.2	19.7	4.2	8.2	8.6	7.3
1960	21.8	15.4	52.3	38.5	3.7	26.7	4.4	6.1	12.6	6.7
1965	18.3	17.9	51.2	32.4	6.8	29.2	14.9	7.0	15.4	6.5
1970	15.4	13.5	37.8	31.9	9.5	33.2	11.9	8.4	18.9	6.3
1975	9.8	18.5	52.0	27.9	10.4	34.2	11.3	9.9	13.5	6.2
1980	7.4	16.2	53.0	32.1	12.6	34.0	19.2	7.8	13.7	7.9
1985	6.5	11.4	33.7	28.3	18.1	36.7	17.8	11.6	19.6	6.8
1990	5.3	9.0	29.1	27.1	23.3	39.2	17.5	9.4	21.1	11.2
2002	4.3	7.1	23.1	22.6	25.6	41.9		11.3	26.4	12.2

Source: Survey of Current Business (June 1993, January 2003), U.S. Department of Commerce, Economics and Statistics Administration, Bureau of Economic Analysis; *Historical Statistics of the United States*, Bicentennial Edition, 2:895, U.S. Bureau of the Census (1975).

Table 2.2

Geography of American Trade as a Percentage of U.S. Exports and Imports by Country or Region, 1850–2002

Country/region	1850 Imports	1850 Exports	1900 Imports	1900 Exports	1929 Imports	1929 Exports	1960 Imports	1960 Exports	2002 Imports	2002 Exports
Canada	2.90	6.9	4.6	6.8	11.4	18.1	19.8	18.5	18.1	23.2
Mexico	0.5	1.4	3.4	2.5	2.7	2.6	3.0	4.0	11.6	14.1
Latin America	19.0	13.9	21.8	9.5	25.4	18.9	27.0	18.8	17.6	20.5
Great Britain	43.1	49.3	18.8	38.3	7.5	16.2	6.8	7.2	3.5	4.8
Germany	5.2	3.4	11.4	13.4	5.8	7.8	6.1	6.2	5.4	3.8
Europe	71.3	75.7	51.9	74.6	30.3	44.7	29.1	40.0	23.1	23.6
Japan	—	—	3.9	2.1	9.8	4.9	7.8	7.0	10.4	7.4
China	—	—	3.2	1.1	3.8	2.4	—	—	10.8	3.2
Asia	6.3	2.1	17.2	4.9	29.1	12.3	18.6	20.3	39.3	27.1

Source: Historical Statistics of the United States, Bicentennial Edition, 2: 895, U.S. Bureau of the Census (1975); Statistical Abstract of the United States (various issues); and Survey of Current Business (April 2002), U.S. Department of Commerce, Economics and Statistics Administration, Bureau of Economic Analysis.

7.4 percent, and China, 3.2 percent. By comparison, Canada took 23.2 percent of U.S. exports and Latin America took 20.5 percent. On the import side, the rise of Asia was even more pronounced. In 2002 Asia supplied 39.3 percent of all imports (China, 10.8 percent, and Japan, 10.4 percent), compared to 23.1 percent for all of Europe. Canada held another 18.1 percent of the U.S. import market, and Latin America 17.6 percent (Mexico, 11.6 percent).[4]

Colonial Antecedents

Colonial experiences and the lessons of the Revolutionary War both left an imprint on American trade policy after independence. On the one hand, many colonists prospered from participating in the eighteenth-century Atlantic economy, trading raw materials for import manufactures; they had a stake in trade expansion. But if commercial interdependence produced prosperity, it also brought vulnerability. When the great colonial powers of Europe fought, as Britain and France did for much of the period from 1689 to 1815, their wars disrupted commerce in the North Atlantic and dislocated colonial life. Britain's effort to finance the costs of empire led to higher taxes and commercial regulations intended to sustain the mercantile system. These aggravations (taxation without representation) radicalized colonial merchants and encouraged colonial leaders, like Benjamin Franklin, to think of establishing a new nation that would protect American commerce, develop American industry, promote American agriculture, and encourage settlement of the frontier. Noting how America's population grew more rapidly than England's, Franklin conceived a time when America would lead the Atlantic economy.[5]

From these experiences, America's founders drew several conclusions that shaped public policy for 150 years. To maintain its political independence in an unstable international environment, America needed to focus on balanced internal development—to include industry as well as agriculture and commerce. This meant a national government prepared to focus on developing the nation's resources and on securing respect for American rights. Leaders like Benjamin Franklin and Thomas Jefferson did not contemplate self-sufficiency. They thought an expanding but agricultural America could pay its way in the Atlantic economy if it had access to foreign markets for its agricultural products and raw materials. This strategy hinged on developing a navy and a merchant marine and on using diplomacy to obtain respect for neutral rights, particularly for the principle, "Free ships make free goods."

In commercial treaties, intended to provide access to major European markets, Americans desired reciprocity and nondiscrimination. They construed the latter as national treatment, meaning equality of treatment with foreign nations, not simply equality with the treatment accorded lesser third countries. Ideally, they wanted the benefits of unconditional most-favored-nation treatment, that is, trade conditions equal to those accorded most-favored parties.

Some merchants like Benjamin Franklin, planters like Thomas Jefferson, and New England lawyers like John Adams shaped early commercial policy with an initial predisposition toward free trade. Franklin knew the famous Scottish economist Adam Smith, author of *Wealth of Nations* (1776), a book that later generations have interpreted as a manifesto for free markets and freer trade. Jefferson, a young cosmopolitan, instinctively sympathized with such arguments. Indeed, in 1774 he boldly asserted that "free trade with all parts of the world" was a "natural right" that no law could abridge. Yet both Jefferson and his friend John Adams, who spoke publicly about removing the "shackles upon trade" and letting market forces dictate, worried about the conflict between economic prosperity and political independence. Said Adams in 1786:

> [I]f the United States would adopt the principle of the French economists, and allow the ships and merchants of all nations equal privileges with their own citizens, they need not give themselves any further trouble about treaties or ambassadors. The consequence nevertheless would be the sudden annihilation of all their manufactures and navigation. We should have the most luxurious set of farmers that ever existed, and should not be able to defend our sea coast against the insults of a pirate.[6]

These concerns about a lack of reciprocity were evident during the American Revolution when the Continental Congress sent Benjamin Franklin and several colleagues to Europe in pursuit of diplomatic recognition, assistance, and commercial agreements. With Britain's archenemy France, they succeeded in negotiating America's first trade treaty, the Franco-American Treaty of Amity and Commerce of February 1778. But that agreement represented only a modest beginning. It failed to secure either *equality* (national treatment) or *unconditional* most-favored-nation treatment. Indeed, the commercial treaty contained only a *conditional* form of the most-favored-nation clause that gave each party the right to purchase concessions either provided to third countries. Probably the negotiators adopted this approach in order to keep Britain from gaining reciprocal access to either the French or the American states. The king of France, Louis XVI, was wary of a reconciliation between England and its former colonies. The Americans later wanted a commercial agreement with England that provided reciprocal access to Britain's market. Resorting to the unconditional most-favored-nation clause might have jeopardized those objectives. Despite its imperfections and departure from principles, the 1778 agreement proved an important trade policy document. The preamble committed America to the pursuit of "the most perfect equality and reciprocity." Secretary of State John Quincy Adams would later claim that the preamble was "the foundation of our commercial intercourse with the rest of mankind." He asserted it "should be the political manual for every negotiator of the United States, in every quarter of the globe." It placed "the true principles of all fair commercial negotiation between independent states" on the "diplomatic record of nations" for the first time.[7]

As it turned out, this first generation of American trade negotiators had little other success in promoting commercial reciprocity and equality. Although the Netherlands and Sweden signed similar agreements before independence, and Prussia did later, the Americans could not pry open access to European colonies in the Western Hemisphere or obtain a commercial agreement with Great Britain. London excluded American ships from the British Isles and the West Indies and sought to dominate the Atlantic trade. Most monarchs of continental Europe regarded the American revolutionaries with suspicion. Even the agreement with France proved difficult to implement, despite the efforts of officials in Paris. French merchants refused credit, and ports openly discriminated against the Americans.[8]

Frustrated in Europe, the American traders had better luck accessing Asian markets. In February 1784, a group of New York merchants dispatched a 360-ton merchant ship, the *Empress of China*, to Canton with a cargo of ginseng. Exchanging it for tea, the ship returned in May 1785 having opened commercial relations with "the Eastern Extreme of the Globe." The merchants' return on capital was 25 percent, a strong inducement to further trade expansion.[9]

Confederation to Constitution

During the first years of American independence, Europeans also had commercial grievances, as American debtors sought to escape their obligations and as individual states indulged in various forms of trade discrimination. Under the Articles of Confederation, the thirteen states ceded only limited powers to the confederation government and retained power to levy taxes and regulate commerce. The thirteen pursued separate and discriminatory policies intended to raise revenues and protect local manufactures. Given the weakness of the central government in collecting taxes and regulating commerce, it is perhaps understandable that European powers adopted a wait-and-see attitude and discriminated against American shipping. Frustrated in his efforts to negotiate a commercial treaty with true reciprocity, John Adams could only lobby for a stronger central government, one having the power to regulate commerce and conduct foreign affairs. "[N]othing but retaliation, reciprocal prohibitions, and imposts, and putting ourselves in a posture of defense will have any effect," he wrote.[10]

It is important to remember that the commercial chaos of the Confederation period produced a consensus in favor of a strong central government. Chief Justice John Marshall observed later that "the deep and general conviction that commerce ought to be regulated by Congress" contributed significantly to the governmental revolution brought about by the Constitution.[11] That text, adopted by delegates to the Constitutional Convention and approved by individual states, established what economists now call a customs union with internal free trade and a common external tariff. Previously, under the Articles of Confederation, individual states had imposed both import tariffs and export tariffs on trade with sister states. Moreover, the weak national government had no authority to raise revenue, and it lacked the resources to promote internal development and to support a merchant marine and a navy.

The Constitution of 1787 specified a separation of powers between the legislative and executive branches. The former acquired specific authority to regulate commerce and levy taxes (Article I: Section 8); the latter gained the responsibility to conduct diplomatic negotiations and to negotiate treaties subject to the approval of Congress (Article II: Section 2). In effect, this arrangement provided the legal basis for a bifurcated trade policy. Only Congress could fix tariffs and regulate commerce; only the executive could negotiate with foreign powers.

The first act of Congress in 1789 indicated the overriding importance that the new government attached to commercial policy. On July 4, 1789, the anniversary of independence, Congress enacted a revenue tariff—averaging about 8.5 percent ad valorem—to raise revenue for President George Washington's new national government. Although some in Congress favored higher protective duties, Secretary of the Treasury Alexander Hamilton urged moderation. To fund the national debt he wanted a dependable source of revenue, and a moderate tariff would meet the new government's needs by taxing commerce, but not prohibiting it. In enacting the tariff, Congress opted for a single schedule, one that applied the same duties to imports from all countries. While this was consistent with the American desire for equal treatment and nondiscrimination, it left the executive branch without leverage to bargain down or retaliate against foreign trade barriers. In effect, the United States had chosen to treat its old friend France the same as its old adversary, Great Britain.[12]

America First

President George Washington's administration pursued a nationalistic course, one that reflected the general's own experiences and desire to promote development. He sought to strengthen the nation's economic base and reduce dependence on Europe, to develop internal transportation and communications, and to protect military security. Determined to promote domestic manufactures, the first president ordered an American-made suit for his inauguration in 1789 and pledged to give preference to domestic fabrics and produce.

Perhaps the most significant initiative to promote domestic industry was Treasury Secretary Hamilton's famous "Report on Manufactures." In it Hamilton made the case for active government. If laissez-faire were the prevailing practice of nations, he argued, the United States and other developing countries might forgo the production of manufactures. But he noted that manufacturing nations, like Great Britain, sought to preserve "a monopoly of the domestic market to its own manufacturers." In such circumstances, the United States needed to pursue a "similar policy" to secure for its citizens a "reciprocity of advantages." Hamilton was not worried about the short-run impact of trade barriers on domestic consumers. He argued that in a developing country the establishment of new manufactures would expand competition and that with new suppliers prices would inevitably fall.[13]

Congress, diverted by more immediate problems such as Indian unrest on the frontier, took no immediate action on the report, but Hamilton's basic recommendations reverberated for generations. Describing Hamilton as "the greatest American," Arthur H. Vandenberg, later a U.S. senator from Michigan, concluded: "His whole 'Report on Manufactures' remains . . . the most lucid and convincing and complete defense of a protective tariff system which has ever been given to the American people." Even the Jeffersonians, who feared a strong central government, came to espouse industrial policy when the French Revolution destabilized Europe and brought Napoleon Bonaparte to power. In 1810, President James Madison's treasury secretary, Albert Gallatin, an enthusiastic supporter of free trade, issued his own statement on manufactures. It recommended import duties, export subsidies, and government loans to promote manufactures.[14]

The relatively low-revenue tariff approved in the act of 1789 continued until conflict between Britain and France during the Napoleonic Wars led to widespread disregard for American neutral rights, to the impressments of American sailors, and to property losses. To cope with this challenge, Jefferson espoused unilateral retaliation. Indeed, the use of trade sanctions to obtain respect for American commercial rights had its origin in Secretary of State Jefferson's policy statements during the French Revolution. Later, as president, Jefferson experimented with sanctions—including nonintercourse and the embargo. Under pressure from war hawks in Congress to stand up for American rights and commerce, Jefferson's successor, President James Madison, made the fateful decision to seek a war declaration in

1812. This second conflict with Britain exposed America's vulnerabilities when British troops burned the White House and the Capitol. Afterward, British merchants indulged in discount pricing to move accumulated inventories. This dumping was intended, as a member of Parliament said, to "stifle in the cradle, those rising manufactures in the United States, which the war had forced into existence."[15]

American System

After the War of 1812, a more nationalistic Congress responded to the public desire for economic security and to industry requests for protection by enacting substantially higher duties on imports. This nationalistic trade policy, associated with House Speaker Henry Clay from Kentucky, became known as the American System, and it endured for more than a century. From the War of 1812 to World War II, American import duties averaged over 25 percent ad valorem on all dutiable goods in all but six years. In sixty of those years, the average rate was 40 percent or higher.[16]

Today many economists and pundits associate free trade with rapid economic growth. This assertion, frankly, is incompatible with American economic history. The most rapid growth occurred during periods of high protectionism, not free trade. From 1889 to 1929, a forty-year period ending in the Great Depression, U.S. growth averaged 3.6 percent, significantly above the 3 percentage point average real growth for the twentieth century. And for all but two of those years the United States enjoyed a merchandise trade surplus. Can protectionism spur economic growth? Paul Bairoch, a prominent Swiss economic historian, concluded that in the late nineteenth century countries pursuing protective policies (Germany and America) experienced higher growth rates than Great Britain, a country that unilaterally adopted free trade. Of course, it is arguable that developing countries typically have higher growth rates than mature economies. Nonetheless, the history of economic development suggests that protectionism is frequently one aspect of a successful development strategy. None of the world's present industrial nations achieved economic success without experiencing a sustained protectionist phase.[17] Of course, not every nation that practiced protectionism pursued successful development policies. And in the case of the United States and Germany, the establishment of large national markets (internal free trade areas) clearly gave stimulus to economic growth as business expanded to serve larger markets.

In the nineteenth century, many leaders, and most Republicans, considered protectionism indispensable to American development. Indeed, from the Civil War to World War II, Republicans regularly celebrated the success of their protectionist policies. Said the GOP platform in 1896: "We renew and emphasize our allegiance to the policy of protection, as the bulwark of American industrial independence, and the foundation of American development and prosperity. This true American policy taxes foreign products and encourages home industry." Four years later, Republicans renewed their faith in protectionism: "In that policy our industries have been established, diversified and maintained. By protecting the home market competition has been stimulated and production cheapened." As a result, American working people enjoyed "better conditions of life from those of any competing country."[18] In nineteenth-century America, substantial tariffs were not simply trade barriers imposed to advance the narrow interests of favored manufacturers. They served a larger national purpose, intended to secure American independence from foreign interference and to promote national prosperity. Economic data show that the United States achieved high levels of economic growth after the American Civil War, and declining prices for many protected goods suggest that in the context of a large continental market protectionism was not inconsistent with rapid economic development.

If America's industrial policy—the protective tariff—promoted national economic development, it complicated the efforts of export-oriented businesses and emerging industries to gain improved access to foreign markets. Because Congress legislated tariffs and subjected all imports to a uniform schedule, the executive branch had no leverage to effect preferential bilateral agreements with foreign powers. The State Department, which handled trade negotiations from 1789 to 1962, when Congress established the White House position of special trade representative, found several opportunities to test congressional resolve on this issue, but was unable to effect a modification.

One such episode occurred in the early 1840s after tobacco growers pressured the State Department to promote tobacco exports. The U.S. minister to Prussia, Henry Wheaton, a fervent free trader, opened negotiations with the Zollverein. He signed a treaty that opened the German market for agricultural exports while lowering American duties on manufactures. This had broad significance because the Convention of 1815 with Britain appeared to contain an unconditional most-favored-nation clause. London thus argued that approval of the Zollverein Treaty entitled British exporters to identical low-tariff treatment in the American market. The matter became moot after the Senate tabled the proposed treaty in June 1844. The Senate construed the agreement as an effort to undercut the authority of Congress to regulate commerce. Like many trade-policy disputes, this one had partisan elements, but fundamentally it involved a test of wills between Congress and the executive over which branch was to control trade policy. Eager to satisfy the tobacco industry and its many congressional supporters, a U.S. diplomatic representative tried to trade off domestic manufacturing interests to benefit agricultural exporters and promote foreign policy objectives. In the 1840s Congress had no disposition to accept a one-sided agreement that opened the American market without obtaining significant export opportunities.[19]

Cobden's Challenge

The Senate had good reason to worry about the efforts of doctrinaire free traders to subvert the American system. Across the Atlantic in Great Britain, doctrinaire free traders had effected a major change in British commercial policy when Parliament repealed the corn laws. Cotton manufacturer Richard Cobden and other reformers touted free trade as the "grand panacea" for promoting peace and prosperity. In 1843 they started a magazine called *The Economist* "solely for the purpose of advocating these principles." Said the magazine's founders: "we seriously believe that *free trade*, free intercourse, will do more than any other visible agent to extend civilization and morality throughout the world." Later, Cobden and his corn-law reformers persuaded Sir Robert Peel and Parliament to repeal Britain's tariff structure and adopt unilateral free trade, generally.[20]

They were less successful in exporting the free trade doctrine to America. Robert J. Walker, President James K. Polk's secretary of the treasury, who fancied himself a Democratic free trader, proposed major tariff reforms in the United States. As adopted, the Walker Tariff, the Tariff Act of 1846, lowered average duties on all imports from about 29 percent in 1845 to 23 percent. It also converted many duties from a specific to an ad valorem basis. Until the Civil War, Democrats flirted with tariff liberalization, including an 1854 reciprocity treaty with Canada lowering duties on raw materials. The Pierce administration wanted to move faster toward free trade, but Congress and the domestic business community remained skeptical and resisted fundamental change. Even so, "tariff-for-revenue-only" Democrats succeeded in whittling down the average ad valorem equivalent tariff on dutiable imports from 61.7 percent in 1830 to under 20 percent by 1860. Even these moderate tariffs had very substantial effects in fostering domestic manufacturing industries.[21]

Protectionists in Charge

From the Civil War to the Great Depression of 1930, protection was predominant. No Southern Democrat chaired the Senate Finance Committee from the outbreak of the Civil War to the election of Woodrow Wilson. Instead, strong committee leaders defended the American System against tariff liberalizers and do-gooders in the executive branch. The three most influential chairs were Republicans Justin Morrill of Vermont, Nelson Aldrich of Rhode Island, and Reed Smoot of Utah, three senators who dominated the Senate Finance Committee for some sixty-five years. They had strong allies in the House Ways and Means Committee, particularly chairs William "Pig Iron" Kelley and William McKinley, supporters of the protective system. Morrill, who had moved to the Senate in 1867 after chairing the House Ways and Means Committee as a Whig, served on the Senate Finance Committee for thirty-one years (1867–1898) and chaired it for twenty-two. He consistently opposed the "humbug" of reciprocity treaties, thinking them unconstitutional in law and one-sided in effect. He regularly lambasted free trade theorists: "There is a transcendental philosophy of free trade, with devotees as ardent as any of those who preach the millennium. . . . Free trade abjures patriotism and boasts of cosmopolitism. It regards the labor of our own people with no more favor than that of the barbarian on the Danube or the cooly on the Ganges." Concerned about balancing the federal budget, Morrill considered tariff reductions a threat to the nation's fiscal health. Aldrich apprenticed under Chairman Morrill, and Smoot learned from Aldrich. All three battled to protect congressional prerogatives and the American protective system.[22]

From 1860 to World War II, every Republican presidential candidate ran on platforms supporting the protective tariff. They preached class harmony and warned that removal of the protective tariff would "bring widespread discontent." As McKinley put it, "Free trade results in giving our money, our manufactures, and our markets to other nations." Protection, the policy of the Republican Party, "has made the lives of the masses of our countrymen sweeter and brighter, and has entered the homes of America carrying comfort and cheer and courage." Republicans during the Gilded Age embraced protection as the key component of industrial policy, which they favored. Said McKinley: "In the mind of every American workingman is the thought that this great American doctrine of protection is associated with wages and work, and linked with home, family, country, and prosperity. . . . [T]he people of this country want an industrial policy that is for America and Americans."[23]

In American political history, the tariff issue has usually ignited partisan debate. Until the Great Depression, Republicans generally favored the protective tariff, while Democrats backed a tariff for revenue only. With a strong base of support in the rural and nonindustrial South, Democrats, not surprisingly eagerly promoted export expansion and favored tariffs for revenue. In 1850, cotton and tobacco, the two most important southern export crops, accounted for 61 percent of all U.S. exports. Sixty-two years later, in 1912, when the Democrats elected Woodrow Wilson president, those two products still accounted for 28 percent of U.S. exports.[24] Eager to cut tariffs, Democrats proposed the income tax as an alternative revenue source.

As the Democratic Party revived in the generation after the Civil War, it offered a different interpretation of the tariff than Republican economic nationalists who backed import-sensitive industries. Democrats argued that the tariff exploited consumers for the benefit of rich monopolists. In Ida Minerva Tarbell, the muckraking journalist, they found a popular communicator to champion these antimonopoly, antitariff ideas. Tarbell's assault on the tariff so impressed Woodrow Wilson that he lobbied hard to place her on the Tariff Commission in 1917.[25]

In 1884, Democrat Grover Cleveland, the governor of New York, won the presidential election and attempted to pursue a low-tariff Democratic agenda. Complaining that existing tariffs generated far more revenue than the government could spend prudently, Cleveland urged downward revision. Republican critics lampooned Cleveland as a dupe of John Bull, the symbol of Great Britain, and suggested that unilateral tariff reductions, such as Cleveland proposed, benefited English monopolists eager to exploit the American market. But the absence of a Democratic majority in Congress and the 1893 depression defeated Cleveland's plans to reduce the tariff and substitute an income tax. The Supreme Court also held the income tax unconstitutional.[26]

During the McKinley, Roosevelt, and Taft administrations, some public pressure for downward tariff revision continued. Whereas American industry long defended high tariffs, export-competing industries increasingly sought access to foreign markets. The National Association of Manufacturers (NAM), founded in 1895, declared that one of its main purposes was "the discussion of ways and means whereby trade relations between the United States and foreign countries may be developed and extended." While favoring the principle of protection, the NAM favored making duties "as low as possible consistent with the fair protection of our industries and the labor they employ." Concerned about discrimination against America's export industries, the NAM urged adoption of a dual schedule tariff, with maximum and minimum rates. Such a provision would give the executive branch discretion to negotiate reciprocal access to foreign markets. But early in the twentieth century most U.S. business opposed free trade. Said the NAM in 1907: "The National Association of Manufacturers is unalterably opposed to free trade in any particular. It stands first, last and always for the protection of American industries and American manufacturers, and . . . protection in liberal measure, not in scant measure."[27]

But some big business also endorsed reforms to take the tariff out of politics. The congressional tariff-writing process had proven costly and cumbersome. Campaign contributions from special interests and legislative logrolling compounded business uncertainty. In 1907 the NAM urged establishment of a nonpartisan tariff commission "with semi-judicial powers . . . to investigate thoroughly and scientifically the various schedules." Elements of the business community embraced progressive tariff reforms before the major political parties. Not until 1912 would one of the major political parties, the Progressives, endorse a "non-partisan scientific tariff commission."

While Presidents William McKinley and Theodore Roosevelt later embraced reciprocity, they were reluctant to undertake sweeping tariff revision, knowing that it would divide the Republican Party. For them reciprocity must be treated as the handmaiden of protection. It must come without injury to domestic workers and to producers of import-competing products. They did make exceptions, however, for territory acquired in the Spanish-American War. In order to assist Cuba, President Roosevelt persuaded Congress to adopt a Cuban reciprocity agreement in 1903. It provided a 20 percent uniform reduction in tariffs on dutiable imports from Cuba. In effect, by giving Cuban sugar producers a price premium, it represented backdoor aid to the Cuban economy. Security concerns also led the Republicans to provide duty-free access for Philippine sugar.

In 1909, however, President William Howard Taft yielded to the public mood and summoned a special session of Congress to revise the tariff. The new Payne-Aldrich Tariff embodied for the first time the concept of a maximum and minimum tariff. In writing the bill, Republicans in Congress bowed to business desires for a more flexible tariff mechanism, one that the executive could use to improve market access abroad. As it turned out, Taft and the State Department, fearful of foreign reactions, chose not to apply the maximum schedule, claiming that it was not flexible enough to permit the selective imposition of penalty duties.

But Payne-Aldrich did facilitate reciprocal negotiations with Canada. Taft, who spent his summers at a home along the St. Lawrence River, wanted to make improved Canadian relations a hallmark of his administration. After brief secret negotiations, the Taft administration signed a bilateral agreement placing more than 40 percent of U.S. imports from Canada on the free list and about 10 percent of Canadian imports from the United States. Canadians would gain access to the U.S. market for agricultural produce, fish, and raw materials but retain duties on manufactured imports. Despite the asymmetries benefiting Canada, Congress approved the agreement; the Canadian Parliament did not. In a general election, Canadian voters soundly rejected the Liberal Party and reciprocity.[28]

Wilson's Low-Tariff Revolution

An important turning point in U.S. trade policy came after the election of 1912. In that presidential election, Democrat Woodrow Wilson, a former Princeton University professor of history and government, triumphed over a divided Republican Party. Gaining control of the presidency and both houses of Congress for the first time since 1892, the Democrats moved promptly to reduce protective rates. The Underwood-Simmons Act of 1913 sharply lowered American tariffs from an average of 19.3 percent on dutiable and free imports under the Payne-Aldrich Tariff of 1895 to 9.1 percent in 1916. Unfortunately, the Democrats ignored the opportunity to bargain down foreign trade barriers. Instead, eager to redeem domestic campaign pledges to cut duties and aid consumers, Wilson and the Democratic Congress unilaterally lowered the U.S. tariff.

The outbreak of World War I in Europe in 1914, and the consequent disruption of ocean shipping, provided a new form of temporary protection to U.S. industries during wartime. But as the conflict came to an end, American business began to worry about cheap foreign competition—particularly from the German chemicals industry—and about how to negotiate access to closed European markets for U.S. exporters. The Wilson administration, preoccupied with the League of Nations and plans for global free trade, apparently hoped that international economic government would promote market access and reduce foreign trade barriers to American exports. It remained faithful to the traditional Democratic panacea of a tariff for revenue only, while endorsing the use of a nonpartisan tariff commission to suggest tariff revisions.

Protection Restored

Skeptical of Wilson's motives, the Republicans skillfully campaigned in 1920 on public fears that "a flood of imports will cheapen our cost of living . . . [and] destroy our capacity to buy." Soon after his inauguration in 1921, President Warren Harding asked Congress for emergency tariff legislation. "I believe in the protection of American industry, and it is our purpose to prosper America first," Harding said. In May 1921, Congress enacted an emergency tariff measure raising duties on agricultural products and amending the anti-dumping laws.[29]

Dumping occurs when a firm sells goods more cheaply in the export market than in the home market, frequently at less than the cost of production. For the United States, dumping first became a disruptive factor before the American Revolution. After each war with France, British merchants unloaded inventories of unsold goods at bargain basement prices. Late in the nineteenth century, large American steel and German chemical companies engaged in differential pricing to penetrate foreign markets. Canada enacted the first antidumping statute in 1904, authorizing the government to impose offsetting duties. In proposing the measure, the Canadian finance minister, W.S. Fielding, rebutted the argument of laissez-faire economists that cheap imports benefit consumers.

> If we could be guaranteed for ever or for a long period that we would obtain cheap goods . . . it would probably be wise for us to close up some of our industries and turn the energies of our people to other branches. But surely none of us imagine that when these high tariff trusts and combines send goods into Canada at sacrifice prices they do it for any benevolent purpose. . . . They send the goods here with the hope and the expectation that they will crush out the native Canadian industries.[30]

Fearful that German manufacturers might dump products such as chemicals, steel, and newsprint in the U.S. market after the war, Congress passed two laws. The first, the Revenue Act of 1916, provided criminal and civil penalties for predatory dumping. But this law proved difficult to enforce because it was necessary to show that importers had "intent" and "conspired" to destroy or injure an industry in the United States. As an alternative to criminal laws, Congress passed the 1921 Antidumping Act providing administrative remedies. This law gave the treasury secretary broad discretionary power to conduct investigations and to impose duties offsetting the injurious effects of dumping. Avoiding the issue of intent, it focused on import pricing. In effect, it authorized the secretary of the treasury to conduct an inquiry to determine whether, as a matter of policy, merchandise was being sold in the United States at less than its "fair" value and whether such sales were injuring or threatening the injury of a U.S. industry. The 1921 law gave broad discretionary powers to the secretary of the treasury. It provided no standards for determining injury, imposed no deadlines, and authorized no outside review of injury findings. In effect, Congress made administration of the antidumping law an executive function and subordinated legal considerations to policy concerns. Nothing barred the Treasury Department from considering other relevant factors, such as how enforcement might impact bilateral political and military relations.

In 1922 the Republican Congress completed a comprehensive tariff revision—the Fordney-McCumber Act. It raised the average duty on all imports from 9.1 percent under Underwood to 14 percent. The final bill contained both a flexible tariff provision, which permitted the independent Tariff Commission to recommend tariff changes to the president, and a retaliation provision, which authorized the president to retaliate unilaterally against foreign tariff discrimination.

In deciding how to administer the new tariff, the Harding administration made a fateful decision. In August 1923, Secretary of State Hughes announced that the United States would adopt the unconditional most-favored-nation policy. Eager to advance the principle of equality and to address the problem of growing discrimination against U.S. exports, the Republican officials effectively abandoned the long-established approach of extending concessions to third countries only after equivalent compensation. This process was tedious and time-consuming, and the State Department hoped to encourage other nations to voluntarily provide equal treatment to all trading partners. It did not apparently foresee the situation in which emerging competitors might become free riders, using the unconditional policy to gain access to the U.S. market while declining to provide reciprocal access to home markets. Eager to avoid commercial antagonisms, the Harding State Department also declined to invoke the retaliation provision. Reluctant to risk political relations for commercial advantage, the State Department was unsuccessful in the 1920s in opening the most important foreign markets to American exports—namely Canada, Great Britain, and France.

During the 1920s, higher U.S. tariffs do not appear to have harmed the international economy. They had little impact on U.S. imports and economic growth. During the 1920 to 1923 recession, for instance, imports of dutiable goods fell less than duty-free imports (measured by value). Despite the price declines, the quantity of imports continued to rise. During the immediate postwar period, American private lending, direct investments in postwar Europe, and an outflow of tourists helped finance large merchandise trade surpluses: 2.6 million Americans traveled to Europe and the Mediterranean during the 1920s; only 350,000 Europeans came to the United States. Paris was a popular tourist destination, and American tourists reportedly spent $180 million annually in France—more than offsetting the merchandise trade deficit. In 1929, for example, the United States experienced a travel expenditures deficit of $659 million, nearly offsetting a $734 million commodity trade surplus.[31]

Smoot-Hawley

One of the enduring myths concerns the Tariff Act of 1930, popularly known as the Smoot-Hawley Tariff. A widespread misconception, recycled in many newspaper columns and political speeches, holds that this tariff act represented the high-water mark of American protectionism, disrupting trade, exacerbating international relations, and contributing to the outbreak of World

War II. Many of these claims rest on a misunderstanding of the 1930 tariff, which was enacted after nearly eighteen months of hearings and debate in Congress from January 1929 to June 1930. Without a doubt, this last effort to effect a general tariff revision produced tense partisan debate—and a deadlock in Congress. In the Senate, majority Republicans lost control of the bill to a coalition of Midwestern Progressives and low-tariff Democrats. In effect, the bitter and protracted congressional debate, not the fear of higher tariffs, exacerbated the stock market collapse. Unable to forecast prices for inputs and end products, business might have postponed key investments and offered uncertain earnings forecasts to financial analysts.[32]

The seventy-first Congress did not enact the highest tariff in American history, as some texts and pundits assert. The highest was the "Tariff of Abominations" in 1828 at 61.7 percent. The average duty on dutiable goods enacted in 1930 was 44.9 percent, using 1930 trade data. It marked a return to Payne-Aldrich levels (40.8 percent) and did not exceed levels reached under the McKinley (48.4 percent) and Dingley tariffs (46.5 percent) in the 1890s. During the Great Depression, falling prices did ratchet up ad valorem equivalents for goods with specific duties (to a 59.1 percent average in 1932), but this would have occurred no matter what the tariff schedule was. A twenty cent specific duty on an item priced at one dollar effectively becomes a 40 percent duty if the good's price falls to fifty cents per unit. While Smoot-Hawley represents a return to the high Republican tariffs of post–Civil War America, there is one important difference. In the late nineteenth century, roughly one-half of imports entered duty-free; under Smoot-Hawley, two-thirds did. Thus, the ratio of duties calculated to total free and dutiable imports is considerably lower under Smoot-Hawley (13.7 percent in 1930) than under the Tariff of Abominations (57.3 percent), McKinley (23.0 percent), and Dingley (25.5 percent).[33]

Some writers have alleged that the 1929 to 1930 general tariff revision spooked the stock market and caused the Great Depression. Of course, the stock market collapsed in October 1929, about eight months before Smoot-Hawley cleared Congress and was signed into law. There is no evidence that the final act influenced the October equities sell-off and the resulting financial collapse. But there is testimony that the extended deadlock in Congress may have heightened business uncertainty, slowed investment, and complicated efforts to stabilize financial markets. It was not really fear of tariffs that spooked the market, but continued uncertainties. In 1929 to 1930 business overwhelmingly favored a substantial protective tariff, but deplored political logrolling and capricious decision making.

How did Smoot-Hawley affect American commerce? Many economists and commentators continue to assert that the 1930 tariff disrupted world trade. But official data show that higher U.S. tariffs had little impact on American imports. From 1929 to 1932 imports of dutiable and duty-free goods fell almost the same percentage, suggesting that higher tariffs had little impact on most trading partners. Nor did foreign governments protest and retaliate against U.S. exports, as many pundits seem to think. While newspapers did warn of foreign protests and retaliation, as they do whenever Congress considers a trade bill, U.S. diplomatic records show that only two or three countries actually lodged formal diplomatic protests. Others may have sought to influence the policy process through leaks to newspapers, but exports to the countries most concerned about higher tariffs—Austria, Canada, France, Italy, Spain, Switzerland, and the United Kingdom—fell less than average. The sharpest drop in exports involved commodity-exporting countries, including some like Brazil, largely unaffected by higher U.S. tariffs.[34]

Finally, the political lesson of Smoot-Hawley. For years critics have alleged that the public was so dissatisfied with Smoot-Hawley protectionism that the authors of the act, Senator Reed Smoot of Utah and Congressman Willis Hawley of Oregon, lost their seats in the 1932 election. A review of local press, however, suggests that the tariff had little effect. Hawley, the chair of the House Ways and Means Committee, lost a primary battle to a much younger opponent. He did not return to Oregon to campaign. According to Oregon newspapers, a dispute over the location of a veterans' home and the battle over Prohibition cost Hawley his elected position. Smoot, one of the leaders in the Mormon church, also went down to defeat in the 1932 general election. He was a victim of the Roosevelt landslide, although popular enough to outpoll President Hoover and the Republican candidate for governor. His opponent also endorsed protectionism for Utah products like lead, copper, and sugar.

Secretary Hull's Trade Policy Revolution

The presidential election of 1932 produced a revolution in American trade policy. But that was not evident in the campaign. As might be expected, President Hoover defended Smoot-Hawley and warned that Democratic proposals for a revenue tariff would "place our farmers and workers in competition with peasant and sweated labor." The Democratic nominee, New York governor Franklin D. Roosevelt, followed his own pragmatic instincts, attempting to satisfy both protectionists and free traders. He endorsed barter trade and interpreted his party's platform as calling for a tariff that "equalizes the differences in the cost of production." During the campaign, it was apparent that Roosevelt wanted modified protectionism to safeguard his domestic policies intended to boost wages and prices.[35]

In selecting Tennessee senator Cordell Hull as secretary of state, Roosevelt made a fateful decision. He turned trade policy over to the most determined tariff cutter and free trade idealist in the Democratic Party. During his service on congressional oversight committees, Hull had gained a reputation as a tariff expert. His views reflected the agricultural export orientation of his middle Tennessee district and his experiences as chairman of the Democratic National Executive Committee (during the Harding administration). At a time when high-tariff industrial interests funded the Republican Party, he saw an opportunity to create a new export-oriented coalition with its base in southern agriculture and emerging mass production industries, like automobiles.

In 1934 Hull persuaded Congress to enact his "reciprocal" trade program. The bill (HR 8687) contained no direct reference to tariff reduction as a goal. Instead, it authorized "expanding foreign markets for the products of the United States . . . by regulating the admission of foreign goods into the United States in accordance with the characteristics and needs of various branches of American production." To achieve this goal, Congress granted the executive branch temporary authority, for three years, to *raise or lower* tariffs as much as 50 percent from 1930 levels. Hull explained the plan as "an emergency measure to deal with emergency panic conditions." He emphasized that the "entire policy of this bill would rest under trade relationships which would be *mutually and equally profitable* both to our own and other countries." In his transmittal message, President Roosevelt emphasized the "no-injury concept": "The successful building up of trade *without injury to American producers* depends upon a cautious and gradual evolution of plans . . . *no sound and important American interest will be injuriously disturbed*" (emphasis added).[36]

In effect, the 1934 act transferred tariff making from Congress, where the process was relatively transparent and the decisions made by elected officials, to the executive branch. Hull established two interdepartmental committees, composed of representatives of several cabinet-level agencies and chaired by the State Department. In contrast to the congressional process, the powerful interagency committees operated anonymously. For twenty years Congress could not learn the identities of the middle-level officials who made life-or-death decisions about protection for American industries.

We now know that many members of the all-powerful Committee on Trade Agreements were recently hired academic economists without significant private sector experience. Given their academic backgrounds and Hull's disposition to lower tariffs as quickly as possible, it is not surprising that members of the Trade Agreements Committee held that the "primary object" of the Reciprocal Trade Agreements Program (RTAP) "is to reduce trade barriers rather than to drive a sharp bargain." Their policy envisioned "permitting a greater increase in imports than in exports with a view to correcting the trade balance problem of the United States."[37]

In a series of so-called reciprocal trade agreements during the 1930s and during World War II, U.S. trade policy makers proceeded to roll back the American tariff system. From 1934 to 1947, the United States concluded thirty-two reciprocal trade agreements, all, except for the agreement with Iran, being with countries in the Americas or Western Europe. A substantial number of the agreements, such as those with Central American countries, Ecuador, Paraguay, and Uruguay, as well as those with Turkey, Iran, and Finland, were shadow agreements without real substance. They contained duplicative or inconsequential concessions and lacked immediate commercial significance. For instance, the United States padded its list of concessions by binding coffee duty-free (par. 1654) in separate agreements with eleven countries. Such agreements constituted window-dressing for the reciprocal trade program, allowing the State Department to claim momentum for the program.

In reciprocal trade negotiations U.S. officials offered and sought maximum 50 percent reductions; in negotiations with principal suppliers, this was on an item-by-item basis. U.S. officials did not seek to drive hard bargains. Instead, they often accepted commitments to bind existing duties as consideration for real U.S. cuts! When reciprocal trade partners depreciated their currencies or imposed quantitative controls, as the Belgians and Swiss did, the State Department did not insist on reopening negotiations. It turned a blind eye.

After the February 1935 agreement with Belgium, the first with an industrial country, the State Department made a key interpretation about which countries could benefit from the lower rates. Although the United States had adopted an unconditional most-favored-nation policy in 1923, the United States might have denied concessions to many countries because they discriminated against U.S. trade. Industrialist George Peek, who sought to fashion New Deal trade policy, and President Franklin Roosevelt himself favored the conditional approach, in which concessions were extended only to countries making equivalent concessions. Peek wanted the United States to get its money's worth for reductions. But Hull's State Department insisted on continuing the unconditional approach and on withholding benefits only to countries flagrantly discriminating against the United States. This avoided the need for multiple follow-on negotiations with other trading partners and for weighing each individual concession carefully. Had Peek and Roosevelt prevailed, the United States might have limited concessions made in bilateral agreements to many third countries like Canada, Great Britain, Germany, and France—all of which discriminated substantially against U.S. trade. Instead, the State Department took a "conciliatory" approach, concluding that only Nazi Germany discriminated substantially against American trade and should be denied benefits. Even the Soviet Union, Italy, and Japan, among many nations, qualified for the lowest tariff rates.[38]

By 1937, when the program faced congressional reauthorization, the emergency trade program had become an instrument of foreign policy. During congressional oversight hearings, the State Department described reciprocal trade as both an "essential requirement of a full and balanced economic recovery" and as "a powerful instrument of *economic appeasement* and stability . . . to strengthen the foundations of world peace." The "successful" trade negotiations with Great Britain in 1938 reflected the influence of foreign policy considerations. In the months after Munich, when Germany presented a threat to European stability, diplomats from the British Foreign Office and the U.S. State Department insisted that the agreement could not fail. Although the United States achieved a major reduction in U.S. tariffs extending across hundreds of items (621 concessions on trade valued at $457.8 million in 1937, or 37 percent of U.S. dutiable imports), Washington was not prepared to press Britain for major modifications in the system of imperial agricultural preferences, nor for significant concessions on manufactured exports in the British market.[39]

Building the Bretton Woods World

Hull's vision of a peaceful, prosperous world without trade barriers guided America's postwar planners. From 1942 to 1945 they devised plans for three postwar international economic institutions—the International Monetary Fund, the International Bank for Reconstruction and Development (World Bank), and the International Trade Organization (ITO). Each would operate under the auspices of the United Nations and have universal membership for its function. At Bretton Woods, New Hampshire, in July 1944, planners led by economists Harry Dexter White, representing the U.S. Treasury, and John Maynard Keynes, an adviser to the British Treasury, completed work on the postwar financial institutions. Preparations for the postwar trade organization, supervised by Hull's reciprocal trade policy team, lagged. But Hull's aides deemed it the centerpiece of the postwar economic order. It would establish the intergovernmental structure and rules for regulating world trade.

At a preparatory meeting in 1946, economist Clair Wilcox, leader of the U.S. delegation, asserted: "If political and economic order is to be rebuilt, we must provide, in our world trade charter, the solid foundation upon which the superstructure of international cooperation is to stand." A final proposal would not emerge until the winter of 1948, when trade policy officials met in Havana, Cuba, to complete this section of the postwar structure.[40]

American business favored trade expansion, sharing generally the Truman administration's enthusiasm for equal and nondiscriminatory access to world markets. But big business disliked the charter for the ITO. In particular, business groups like the NAM and the Chamber of Commerce of the United States worried that the ITO would prove too bureaucratic, too tolerant of exchange and trade restrictions, and too much a forum for developing and debtor countries. Big business worried that the investment provisions would complicate prompt and just compensation for expropriations. Said the NAM, the Havana charter promised to make the world "safe for socialistic planning" but a "very precarious place" for private enterprise.

Appreciating that the United States might need to increase imports to facilitate postwar reconstruction, big American business worried that an ITO in which the United States had one vote, like developing and war-damaged nations, would produce asymmetrical and unbalanced results. The charter established a structure and rules in which the United States would likely not receive "an adequate *quid pro quo* for any liberalization that it might adopt in its commercial policy." In essence, the ITO would accelerate America's market opening, but tolerate restrictions against American exports and investments.[41]

Like the League of Nations a generation earlier, the ITO seemed a grandiose abstraction. Business groups balked, disturbed over investment provisions and the proposed international bureaucracy. In the United States, Philip Cortney, a business leader, launched a successful campaign against the Havana charter, claiming that it condoned socialistic planning and had a bias toward full employment and inflation. He complained that the charter authorized the use of quotas and exchange controls for balance of payments reasons. In ratifying the charter, Cortney alleged, the United States would "surrender our main weapon against nationalistic economic wickedness, namely the power to retaliate."[42] The American Bar Association (ABA) also issued a critical assessment: "The ITO commits its members to action to conform their national policies and laws to the policies and decisions or findings or rules or regulations of the ITO, in the fields of trade, employment, and general economic development." Some ABA members commented that "the charter has more the appearance of a world-government constitution than that of an agency of the United Nations." Unable to persuade Congress, the Truman administration finally withdrew the ITO proposal in 1950.[43]

Five years later—during the Eisenhower administration—State Department planners revived the concept. After minor changes to the ITO proposal, they renamed it the Organization for Trade Cooperation (OTC).[44] Once again the sovereignty issue enraged Congress. In 1956 House Ways and Means Committee Republicans, including Howard Baker of Tennessee, complained that "authorization of United States membership in OTC will result in an almost complete transfer by the Congress to an international organization of its constitutional authority over United States foreign commerce policy."[45] Some Democrats had similar concerns.

To accelerate trade liberalization after World War II, the United States invited nineteen foreign countries, including the Soviet Union, to participate in the negotiation of a multilateral agreement at Geneva in 1947. Although the Soviets opted to pursue an autarkic course, twenty-three countries engaged in negotiations, conducted bilaterally on a product-by-product basis with principal suppliers. The various bilateral agreements became the multilateral General Agreement on Tariffs and Trade (GATT). Every country signing the agreement was eligible to enjoy the concessions of every other signatory and thus gained unconditional most-favored-nation status. Nine countries, accounting at that time for 80 percent of world trade, put the GATT agreement into effect on January 1, 1948. They were Australia, Belgium, Canada, Cuba, France, Luxembourg, the Netherlands, the United Kingdom, and the United States.

As a temporary forum for trade negotiations, pending creation of the ITO, the GATT endured for nearly a half-century until establishment of the World Trade Organization on January 1, 1995. Under GATT auspices, a series of multilateral trade negotiating rounds took place beginning with the 1947 session in Geneva. The next four rounds, held in Annecy, France (1949), Torquay, England (1950–1951), Geneva (1956 and 1960–1962), employed the same bilateral product-by-product negotiating approach. Beginning with the Kennedy Round (1962–1967), negotiators adopted, with some exceptions, a linear formula for across-the-board percentage cuts, an approach that avoided some cumbersome bilateral negotiations with principal suppliers. In successive rounds more countries acceded, notably Italy (1949), West Germany (1951), Japan (1955), and Israel, Switzerland, and Spain (1962). By the end of the Kennedy Round in 1967, GATT had 75 members. By December 31, 1994, GATT's final day, membership had expanded to 128 countries, and the most significant nonmembers—Russia, China, and Taiwan—wanted to join. In terms of duty reductions, the most important multilateral rounds were the ones ending in 1947 and 1967. The first Geneva Round and the Kennedy Round were the only ones in which the U.S. Congress authorized major duty reductions (up to 50 percent of existing rates), and in both the depth of tariff reductions averaged 35 percent. But these figures, which suggest reciprocal concessions, mask conspicuous asymmetries. In the first rounds after World War II, the United States, of course, promptly implemented its concessions, but trading partners in Western Europe, who were recovering from the devastation of World War II, delayed the impact of their concessions, using exchange controls and quantitative restrictions. Obviously, given the enormous disruption caused by the war and the problems of rebuilding economies, some controls were justified. But in some instances the perpetuation of controls into the late 1950s reflected the strength of local protectionist forces or government enthusiasm for using national industrial policy to achieve competitive advantages. In Great Britain, for instance, agricultural interests used political pressure to discriminate against American apples, pears, grapefruit, and other products. Conceded trade official Reginald Maudling to Prime Minister Harold Macmillan in 1959: "The Americans have put more into G.A.T.T., and got less out of it, than any of the other big trading countries . . . by and large the Americans have kept their doors wide open to our trade (and at a time when they might have urged that we were shutting out their goods by quotas long after we were genuinely short of dollars to pay for them)." In the Kennedy Round, similar asymmetries occurred as Japan and most developing countries avoided meaningful reciprocal concessions.[46]

Marshall Plan Mentality

As noted, the ambitious plans for trade liberalization conceived in Hull's State Department soon took a back seat to recovery from World War II and to Cold War circumstances. During this period—unlike the period immediately after World War I—American political and business leaders chose to provide assistance to devastated allies and defeated adversaries to recover and become full participants in the global economy. But there was another key aspect—the emerging Cold War struggle with Soviet Russia. By late 1946 it was evident to leaders in Washington that the wartime alliance binding America, Britain, and Soviet Russia had disintegrated. In place of global peacekeeping solutions, the United States had to seek regional and bloc cooperation to offset and contain the threat of Communist expansionism.

The economic crisis of 1946–1947 precipitated action. With wartime allies in Western Europe exhausted—their industries outmoded, their finances weakened—and with Axis nations enduring a bleak recovery from wartime devastation, the United States faced a tough challenge. It could disengage from events, as it did after World War I, or use its vast power and influence to help rebuild Western Europe and Japan and reconstruct the international economy. Adopting a "Marshall Plan mentality," American leaders chose the latter course. They pursued foreign economic policies designed to make U.S. allies self-sustaining participants in a thriving, open, international economy, even at the expense of domestic American economic interests.

American presidents in the post–World War II period from Harry Truman to George W. Bush felt that America had a responsibility to lead the world economy, placing the interests of the system ahead of U.S. national interests. In the Cold War competition with the Soviet Union, foreign policy took priority. Reflecting pride in what publisher Henry Luce called the "American Century," Truman boasted, "Our industry dominates world markets . . . American labor can now produce so much more than low-priced foreign labor in a given day's work that our workingmen need no longer fear, as they were justified in fearing in the past, the competition of foreign workers."[47]

It is not surprising that Truman's successor, President Dwight Eisenhower, a former military leader, also gave priority to strategic considerations. Indeed, he criticized protectionist U.S. businesses for "shortsightedness bordering upon tragic stupidity." In the face of aggressive Communism, he considered freer trade essential to help other nations "make a living": "We are not talking about trying to put American people out of work or undersell an American manufacturer and drive him to the wall or anything else. We are striving to make a better world for ourselves and for our children."[48]

Trade was important, Eisenhower thought, to sound political relationships. To secure allied support for strategic export controls against the Soviet Union, the United States had to provide alternative markets in the West.

This emphasis on opening the huge American market to aid foreign allies and promote international economic reconstruction surfaced during World War II and, publicly, during the 1947 Geneva trade negotiations. Eager to construct a liberal economic order without high tariffs and exchange controls, State Department planners contemplated drastic, and disproportionate, cuts in U.S. tariffs to stimulate imports and assist foreign reconstruction and participation in an open trading community. To them, the statute requiring mutually balanced tariff concessions seemed overly restrictive and inappropriate to postwar circumstances.

Others in Congress and the private sector were less sensitive to the dollar shortage and problems of international economic adjustment, less enthusiastic about textbook solutions, and more cautious about the implications of opening the U.S. market for the sake of humankind. To the Republican Congress elected in 1946, further tariff reductions immediately after the war seemed imprudent and overly idealistic. The war had disrupted economies and created distortions. It was not clear whether previous cuts, especially the steep reductions effected in the 1938 reciprocal trade agreement with Britain, could be accommodated without injury to domestic industries and workers. Nonetheless, the congressional critics hesitated to vote down RTAP and to undercut Truman's effort to provide leadership. Instead, Senator Arthur Vandenberg, chair of the Senate Foreign Relations Committee, and Senator

Eugene D. Millikin, chair of the Senate Finance Committee, negotiated with the administration. The Republicans would renew reciprocal trade tariff cutting if President Truman reiterated the no-injury-to-domestic-industry pledge of preceding presidents. Truman promised that "domestic interests will be safeguarded in this process of expanding trade."[49]

GATT and Unreciprocal Trade

Notwithstanding President Truman's commitment, foreign policy considerations drove U.S. trade policy for the next forty years—until the Uruguay Round. In a series of multilateral negotiations held under auspices of the GATT, U.S. negotiators yielded unbalanced concessions and tolerated free riders. The Geneva negotiations of 1947 were a distinct example. During these negotiations with fifteen countries, the primary U.S. goal was to bargain away what remained of the Smoot-Hawley protective system in exchange for the elimination of British preferences and discriminations against American exports. During the protracted talks, the Labor government of Clement Attlee battled to protect "at all costs the empire preference system," while U.S. officials took the view that this was an opportune time to break the preferential system. The United States, claiming that the master lend-lease agreement obligated London to dismantle the preferential system, thought that Britain's precarious financial situation and dependence on Washington for financial support and Marshall Plan assistance would tip the scales. When the Labor government refused, Washington chose in October 1947 to paper over differences with a thin agreement—one that provided major U.S. concessions on textiles and manufactures. The State Department acquiesced to a deal that failed to break down the preferential system. Four years later, during the Torquay negotiations, the British again attempted to win an agreement unbalanced in their favor, but this time the reciprocal trade program faced reauthorization scrutiny in Congress. The Truman administration pragmatically broke off negotiations, seeking to demonstrate toughness at the bargaining table.

For presidents Truman and Eisenhower, trade concessions represented an alternative to foreign aid, which never appealed to Congress or the voting public. Concerned about Soviet motives and the problems of recovery in Western Europe, the State Department promoted imports and acquiesced to discrimination against U.S. exports.

Perhaps the classic example of asymmetrical trade agreements involved the 1955 bilateral agreement with Japan. Although Britain and some European countries attempted to block Japanese membership in GATT and to deny Japanese textiles access to international markets, the Eisenhower administration considered a trade agreement a high priority. As Eisenhower told congressional leaders, "all problems of local industry pale into insignificance in relation to the world crisis." He said that "Japan cannot live, and Japan cannot remain in the free world unless something is done to allow her to make a living."[50]

In light of later developments, the minutes of the negotiating sessions make fascinating reading. C. Thayer White, the chief of the U.S. delegation, reminded the Japanese that "some of the most powerful support for the trade agreements program comes from American agriculture and the automobile industry." The minutes also cited international economic justifications for Japanese concessions. Arguing for a Japanese duty reduction on automobiles, White stated:

> (1) [T]he United States industry is the largest and most efficient in the world; (2) the industry is strongly in favor of expanding the opportunities for world trade; (3) its access to foreign markets in recent years has been limited by import controls. . . . (4) although the United States Government appreciates that it is necessary for some countries to impose import restrictions for balance of payments reasons . . . it would be in Japan's interest to import automobiles from the United States and export items in which Japan could excel.

On another occasion, White, referring to a statement that Japan desired only to establish industries that could compete in world markets, said that "it would be inconsistent for Japan to attempt to establish an automobile industry because its prospects were not very promising for the future." He also urged a concession on machine-tool imports, doubting "that Japan could compete with the United States in world markets because of the difference in the relative efficiency of the industries in both countries." Establishment of "high cost industries behind a tariff wall does not contribute to the sound growth of national economy," White said.[51] He encouraged the Japanese not to use tariffs, but to increase productivity, favor foreign private direct investment, utilize technical assistance, facilitate domestic capital investment through tax incentives, and pursue a sound domestic fiscal policy.[52]

The Japanese had a different vision of their economy and their future in the international economy. Said K. Otabe, a Japanese delegate:

> (1) if the theory of international trade were pursued to its ultimate conclusion, the United States would specialize in the production of automobiles and Japan in the production of tuna; (2) such a division of labor does not take place . . . because each government encourages and protects those industries which it believes important for reasons of *national policy*.

Urged to reduce import duties on synthetic textiles, Otabe declined, saying that "the Japanese Government believes that a synthetic industry is necessary to diversify and promote the development of the Japanese economy." Asked to lower tariffs on hand tools, Otabe refused: "the domestic industry was having difficulty competing and it was concerned over the competitive effects of increased imports." A lower duty on raisins would "interfere with the consumption of domestically produced sugar confectionery." Reductions on boots and shoes might "destroy" an industry composed of small firms. Asked to reduce the Japanese duty on movie cameras, Otabe said his government "wished to advance the development of the Japanese optical industry." Asked about reductions on radios and television sets, Otabe demurred: the Japanese industry was at a "competitive disadvantage"; the government feared "political repercussions." On electronic equipment the story was similar: "The Japanese Government believes that an electronics industry is essential to the development of the Japanese economy, the communications industry and national defense." Similar explanations applied to petrochemicals, tractors, and heavy machinery. Heavy machinery and machine tools were essential to the development and diversification of the Japanese economy and to a skilled labor force. Indeed, Otabe reminded the Americans "that a protective tariff had contributed to the development of new industries in the early history of the United States and that similarly a protective tariff could promote the development of the petrochemical, heavy machinery and other promising industries in Japan."[53]

What was the outcome? The Japanese press trumpeted its government's negotiating success. Privately, some American officials conceded that the Japanese had negotiated successfully and skillfully taken advantage of American determination to make Japan a prosperous partner and ally supporting U.S. containment policy.

How did the 1955 bilateral agreement with Japan affect U.S. imports? Japan more than doubled its share of America's manufactured imports from 7.6 percent in 1955 to 15.4 percent in 1960. In essence, the 1955 trade negotiations with Japan, far more than the negotiations with Great Britain in 1938 and 1947, opened U.S. borders to imports of labor-intensive products and other manufactures. They also sparked a political reaction when reciprocal trade came up for renewal again in 1958. On this occasion, the Senate Finance Committee refused the Eisenhower administration's request for a five-year extension and authority to reduce tariffs an additional 25 percent. The White House agreed to shift trade-coordinating responsibilities from the State Department to the Commerce Department. In 1962, when President Kennedy requested a broad mandate permitting 50 percent reductions across the board, Congress insisted on establishing the office of Special Trade Representative with authority to negotiate and coordinate the interagency committees.

Kennedy Round Asymmetries

The most significant multilateral round of GATT tariff negotiations in the Cold War period took place from 1964 to 1967. President Lyndon Johnson called the Kennedy Round the "most successful multilateral agreement on tariff reduction ever negotiated." The agreement, announced in May 1967, produced cuts of 36 to 39 percent in tariffs among participating industrial countries. But, on agriculture, a crucial long-term goal of U.S. trade negotiators, the United States failed to make any significant progress in persuading the European Community to liberalize restrictions. Nor did the Kennedy Round negotiators persuade Japan, the beneficiary of many concessions, to prove real reciprocity and open its protected home market to foreign competition. Forty-one developing countries, members of GATT, refused to participate. These included Singapore and Malaysia, future trade powerhouses in the 1980s and 1990s. Another seventeen countries negotiated under special arrangements that did not require reciprocity. This second group included many big emerging markets such as Argentina, Brazil, India, Indonesia, Korea, and Pakistan.[54]

Despite evidence of unbalanced trade concessions, President Lyndon Johnson and the State Department wanted an agreement. The latter saw the negotiations as critical in promoting the U.S. foreign policy goal of a unified and prosperous Europe able to withstand Soviet pressure. The president, his leadership under assault at home, wanted a victory. In the Middle East, Israel and Egypt were on the brink of war. France's president, Charles DeGaulle, and some other governments wanted to impose discipline on the dollar's unique role in the world monetary system and thus restrict a flood of American direct investments and influence.

Evidence of asymmetrical results can be found in the record of U.S. negotiations with Japan and nine important developing countries. Japan kept a low profile in the Kennedy Round, letting the Americans and Europeans slug out differences. Because of the unconditional most-favored-nation principle, the Japanese could anticipate benefiting from others' tariff cuts. Their negotiating tactic was to delay, knowing that the Americans faced a congressional deadline for concluding negotiations. Special Trade Representative (STR) Carl Gilbert told President Richard Nixon later that "the Japanese took advantage of this situation along toward the close of the Kennedy Round." Congress weighed in with its own complaints. In the Trade Act of 1974, Congress inserted a provision requiring the president to determine after the conclusion of future negotiations whether any major industrial country (defined as Canada, the European Economic Community, or Japan) had failed to make concessions "substantially equivalent" to U.S. concessions.[55]

Other evidence that the Kennedy Round left asymmetries in the U.S.–Japan relationship appears in bilateral trade data. In the three years before the Kennedy Round cuts took effect (1965–1967), imports from Japan exceeded exports by 17 percent. A decade later (1975–1977), imports from Japan exceeded U.S. exports by 50 percent. Much of this represented a surge in Japanese automobile exports as the energy crisis encouraged Americans to shift to fuel-efficient cars. But a decline in the U.S. automobile tariff from 6.5 to 3 percent during the Kennedy Round, while Europe maintained 11 percent duties and quantitative restraints on Japanese cars, encouraged Japanese auto exports to the American market.[56]

With the developing countries the United States made concessions on $700 million in imports (almost all of these being duty reductions of 50 percent or more). What did the nine developing countries provide in return? They made concessions on $200 million in trade, but only $20 million of that amount involved actual tariff reductions. The rest consisted of commitments to bind existing tariffs. In the Kennedy Round, as in early tariff negotiations, the United States did not insist on parallel reductions. In 1967 American negotiators did not anticipate that one day Argentina, Brazil, and India might be big emerging markets for American exports. In effect, the Kennedy Round opened the American market to cheap imports from the world but did virtually nothing to open the markets of emerging countries. Instead, the United States reduced its tariffs, bound rates, and effectively gave away leverage that might over time have promoted free and balanced international trade.[57]

Under such circumstances, it is not surprising that White House aides worked overtime to put the best face on results. According to journalist Steve Dryden, author of *Trade Warriors*, a history of the U.S. Trade Representative's office, Francis Bator, a National Security Council aide who briefed Johnson on the subject, instructed a young Oxford-trained economist on the staff to "use some creative thinking and make some new tables" showing a positive outcome. Imaginative staff work may have fashioned a paper victory, but the episode infuriated trade specialists in the Commerce, Labor, and Agriculture Departments who had negotiated for more reciprocal outcomes.[58]

More than any other single round of tariff negotiations, the Kennedy Round opened the American market to global competition and contributed to a growing merchandise trade imbalance. Said Secretary of Commerce Alexander Trowbridge, the "American domestic market—the greatest and most lucrative market in the world is no longer the private preserve of the American businessman." As the concessions were phased in over a five-year period, border barriers no longer shielded high-wage American manufacturing workers from global competition. The average ad valorem equivalent on dutiable U.S. imports fell from 12.2 percent in 1967 to 8.6 percent in 1972.[59]

Leaders of large multinational corporations understood the Kennedy Round's policy significance. The agreements indicated that the U.S. government still wished to promote imports, and foreign prosperity, using a "trade, not aid," strategy. To support this policy, Washington would invoke only in extraordinary circumstances protectionist import-remedy laws, intended to shelter domestic industries from low-cost and unfair foreign competition. Business also appreciated how parallel technological innovations in transportation and communications were transforming the international business environment and enhancing overseas opportunities. The arrival of containerization and wide-bodied aircraft, such as the Boeing 747, in the late 1960s, helped erase barriers of time and distance, while communications satellites accelerated exchanges of information among widely dispersed units of multinational operations. Previously, Fortune 500 firms tended to focus on the domestic U.S. market for growth and profits, leaving overseas sales and production to somewhat autonomous operations. But the Kennedy Round tariff reductions opened the American market, and many foreign markets, to increased competition. Meanwhile, technological innovations enabled multinationals to integrate distant operations and to ship components and products around the world in search of efficiencies. A decade later Harvard marketing professor Theodore Levitt would employ the term "globalization" to describe some of these revolutionary developments.[60]

Overseas Outsourcing

In this rapidly changing business environment, it is not surprising that large corporations sought to establish positions in all major markets and to achieve major cost reductions by either shifting their own production overseas or outsourcing assembly operations to Asian-owned subcontractors. Developing countries in East Asia with low labor costs and well-educated populations (Singapore, the Philippines, Taiwan, and Malaysia among others) appreciated the new opportunities and resolved to use export-led growth for rapid economic development. In 1971, for example, Malaysian prime minister Tun Razak offered foreign manufacturers generous incentives to assemble products in Malaysia and export them to high-income markets. Speaking to prospective U.S. investors in New York, Tun Razak declared that "Malaysia could be the answer to your problems of spiraling wages and increasing costs of production."[61]

Labor-intensive American industries responded, particularly makers of semiconductors, consumer electronics, and computer parts, with investments in tax-exempt, export-processing zones. Xinhua, the Chinese press agency, dismissed them in 1977 as "concessions where foreign capitalists make super-profits on local cheap labor." By 1980, management guru Peter Drucker was exhorting business leaders to pursue such production-sharing arrangements with "almost-developed countries" (ADCs) such as Brazil, Mexico, Taiwan and South Korea. These ADCs would supply the workers for labor-intensive manufacturing, with the developed countries providing materials and marketing expertise: "The almost-developed countries promise to change the economic map of the world as much in the next 25 years as the development of Japan . . . changed the economic map of the world in the 30 years after World War II." Interestingly, Drucker did not foresee China becoming a major market or producer of industrial goods in the next quarter century.[62]

During these early years of overseas outsourcing, trade expanded rapidly. As a share of U.S. gross domestic product, exports and imports of goods and services rose from 10.8 percent in 1970 (less than in 1929) to 20.5 percent in 1980 and 26 percent in 2000. But this trade expansion was unbalanced—imports rose much more rapidly than exports. There were several explanations for the widening trade deficit—including a strong dollar—but one of the most important involved a flawed trade policy. Eager to promote development and to strengthen developing countries against encroachments of the Communist bloc, the U.S. government encouraged production sharing and even embarked on a one-way preferential program of free trade designed to stimulate imports from developing countries. While 150 developing countries were eligible for the generalized system of preferences, ten rapidly growing developing countries obtained the bulk of the benefits (83 percent). These included Brazil, Malaysia, Mexico, South Korea, Singapore, and Thailand. Allowed easy access to the giant American market, these developing countries continued to restrict access to their own markets with a variety of trade and investment barriers. Undoubtedly, U.S. consumers and corporations benefited from overseas sourcing, as cheap imports flooded into the American market, but import-sensitive industries and workers complained loudly to Congress.[63]

Reacting to Free Riders

In response to these criticisms, Congress began to review U.S. trade policy more carefully. The Senate Finance Committee observed that for years the United States had "relied on a trade surplus to offset foreign aid, military expenditures abroad, as well as overseas private investment." But, in the early 1970s the trade surplus disappeared and the payments deficit widened. When European governments sought to convert accumulating dollar reserves to gold, the Nixon administration had little choice but to close the Treasury gold window in August 1971 and thus abandon the special gold-exchange obligations assumed at Bretton Woods. The resulting dollar devaluation had multiple roots—including Vietnam War–related domestic inflation and the emergence of new competitors such as Japan with state-of-the-art production facilities. But in the opinion of the Senate Finance Committee, misguided trade policies shared responsibility.

> Throughout most of the postwar era, U.S. trade policy has been the orphan of U.S. foreign policy. Too often the Executive has granted trade concessions to accomplish political objectives. Rather than conducting U.S. international economic relations on sound economic and commercial principles, the Executive has set trade and monetary policy in a foreign aid context. An example has been the Executive's unwillingness to enforce U.S. trade statutes in response to foreign unfair trade practices. By pursuing a soft trade policy, by refusing to strike swiftly and surely at foreign unfair trade practices, the Executive has actually fostered the proliferation of barriers to international commerce. The result of this misguided policy has been to permit and even to encourage discriminatory trading arrangements among trading nations.

The Finance Committee attributed much significance to the free rider problem. "The existence of many significant tariff and nontariff barriers in foreign countries and the very small reductions in tariffs of some industrialized countries in the Kennedy Round may be attributed to the realization by certain countries that they could automatically receive all the benefits of the trade agreement without paying any of the costs."[64]

On Capitol Hill, the end of the Kennedy Round produced a tidal wave of condemnation. Evidence of the widespread dissatisfaction came from the flood of quota legislation introduced and the reluctance of Congress to extend the president's trade negotiating authority. Organized labor sponsored the Burke-Hartke bill, the Foreign Trade and Investment Act of 1972, which would have imposed mandatory quotas on all competitive imports and radically changed the tax treatment of multinational corporations. Other evidence of congressional dissatisfaction with the Kennedy Round surfaced when the legislative branch refused to implement some of the key Kennedy Round agreements, particularly the antidumping code and repeal of the American selling price for certain chemicals. Not for six years did Congress offer the White House a new negotiating mandate and then on terms set by Chair Wilbur Mills of the House Ways and Means Committee and Chair Russell Long of the Senate Finance Committee. They insisted on a number of fundamental changes in the law to better safeguard domestic industries from import-related injury and to allow greater congressional and private-sector oversight of negotiations.[65]

From 1947 to the end of the Kennedy Round, Congress had insisted that trade liberalization not dislocate unnecessarily domestic industries and workers. The price for renewal of the trade liberalization program was the escape clause, permitting the withdrawal or modification of tariff concessions if imports surged and caused injury, or threat of serious injury, to domestic producers. Distrustful of executive branch free traders, Congress insisted on an open, transparent process for assessing claims for escape clause relief, one that involved an independent agency, the Tariff Commission. It had responsibility for recommending any import-remedy relief to the president.

In practice, the process seldom functioned as Congress intended—and did so only in election years or when the trade agreements program faced congressional reauthorization. The State Department viewed the escape clause as an impediment to trade liberalization and as an irritant to diplomatic relationships during the Cold War years. From 1951 to 1962, the Tariff Commission conducted 112 investigations, but only 15 industries actually obtained some type of relief. During the Kennedy Round negotiations, no domestic industry won relief, as a Tariff Commission loaded with free trade enthusiasts rejected thirteen successive petitions. But as it turned out, modifications to the escape clause enacted in 1974 brought only temporary changes. During the decade from 1975 to 1984, fifty-four industries filed for escape clause relief and eighteen (33 percent) gained some remedy from the process. Perhaps the most successful were the tariff on imported motorcycles that facilitated Harley Davidson's rejuvenation, and the Reagan administration's program of import restraints on steel products, which provided a breathing space for industry restructuring. By 1985, however, the escape clause was a dead letter. During the second Reagan administration, individuals opposed philosophically to trade remedies administered the statute. The Bush and Clinton administrations also assigned top priority to preserving the multinational system and the open American market, not to helping domestic industries deal with import-related competition more successfully.

The 1974 act also renewed for five years the president's trade negotiating authority. It did so by establishing the fast-track process for considering trade legislation. In return for regular consultation with Congress and private-sector representatives, Congress promised the executive to waive the usual congressional procedures and permit a vote on implementing legislation within ninety days. This agreed-upon procedure prohibited legislative amendments.

The act thus authorized U.S. participation in the seventh round of GATT negotiations, the so-called Tokyo Round. Unlike earlier rounds, these negotiations would emphasize nontariff barriers, which many trade specialists thought had replaced tariffs as the primary obstacles to expanding world trade. Multinational corporations, which increasingly set the U.S. trade policy agenda, were especially interested in removing foreign barriers to their activities. Mirroring these concerns, Congress stated the U.S. negotiating objective as attainment of "more open and equitable market access and the harmonization, reduction, or elimination of devices which distort trade or commerce." Emphasizing the need for reciprocal outcomes, not simply reciprocal tariff reductions, the act stressed that a principal U.S. objective was obtaining competitive opportunities for U.S. exports to developed countries equivalent to the opportunities afforded in the U.S. market, taking into account tariff and nontariff barriers and "other distortions." But, for developing countries, Congress would continue past practice and not insist on full reciprocity. On the free rider issue, Congress took a harder line. The Senate Finance Committee stated, "The United States should not grant concessions to countries which are not willing to offer substantial equivalent competitive opportunities for the products of the United States in their market as we offer their products in our market."[66]

Tokyo Round Promises

During the five years of Tokyo Round negotiations, which opened in September 1973 at a ministerial meeting in Tokyo and ended formally on April 12, 1979, ninety-nine countries participated—up from forty in the Kennedy Round. Twenty-nine of these were either not members or only provisional members. This group included Mexico, the Philippines, and Thailand as well as a number of African and Latin American countries.[67]

Advanced countries agreed to cut tariffs about 33 percent on industrial goods, and for the United States this meant reducing tariffs on dutiable manufactures from about 8.1 percent to 5.6 percent. Some progress was made in agriculture—particularly in opening the Japanese market—but the European Community blocked any effort to roll back the variable levy system. Although the Ford administration, sensitive to the interests of Midwestern Republican farmers, had pressed the Europeans for significant agricultural negotiations, the incoming Carter administration chose to subordinate this goal in order to break a negotiating impasse and restore momentum.

The Tokyo Round's principal outcome was an attempt to extend the GATT regime to cover nontariff barriers. Delegates approved a series of specialized, nontariff "codes" pertaining to subsidies and countervailing duties, anti dumping duties, technical barriers and product standards, government procurement, import licensing, customs valuation, and certain agricultural products. Reflecting a variety of philosophies and competing interests, these codes were intended to reduce the trade-distorting impact of domestic practices. The codes offered transparency, accountability, and dispute resolution.

Because of differing national philosophies, some, such as the subsidies code, blurred differences with vague language. Each depended on the follow-through of participant governments for implementation. The dumping and countervailing duty codes, for instance, appeared to extend government authority, while the code on government procurement represented an effort to deregulate certain types of trade and to provide nondiscriminatory national treatment to foreign suppliers.

Recognizing that the problems of nontariff barriers primarily interested high-income countries, the negotiators introduced the concept of code conditionality to address the free rider problem. To gain the benefits of a particular code, a nation had to sign the agreement and to accept the obligations. This represented a departure from the unconditional most-favored-nation principle underpinning the GATT since 1947. U.S. Trade Representative (USTR) Bob Strauss explained the rationale for the new approach to President Carter: "It is difficult to maintain a consensus for open trade if such countries continue to refuse to accept international discipline over their export subsidy practices." Also, he added: "We could not obtain congressional approval of the new subsidy code if a large number of countries were excluded from the discipline of the code (giving them a 'free ride')." In effect, Strauss was saying that congressional dissatisfaction with the asymmetrical results of prior negotiations had compelled U.S. trade negotiators to insist on reciprocity among code signatories.[68]

In 1979, as at the end of previous negotiations, U.S. officials boasted about gains and sold the agreement to Congress on the basis of the anticipated export opportunities. Once again U.S. leaders indulged in overselling a GATT agreement. President Carter called the Tokyo Round results an "obvious advantage to American exporters" and stated that "obstacles to American goods going overseas will be removed or drastically reduced." Strauss's deputy, Alonzo McDonald, advised Congress that "the Tokyo Round result is potentially the most significant development in world trade since the GATT was established over 30 years ago." In particular, he identified the government procurement code as a major victory for the United States: "We have estimated that the code will increase U.S. exports by between $1.3 and $2.3 billion over the next three to five years and U.S. job opportunities by between 50,000 and 100,000."[69]

Using the new fast-track procedure, Congress swiftly approved the accords with little discussion or dissent. The Trade Agreements Act of 1979 passed the House 395 to 7 and the Senate 90 to 4. The only substantial opposition came from Wisconsin cheese producers. But, recalling past White House efforts to pad trade agreements with optimistic forecasts, some in Congress remained skeptical of the stated advantages. Said Long's Senate Finance

Committee, "The benefits to the United States from the various nontariff agreements negotiated in the MTN depend very heavily on the vigorous insistence by the United States that its rights be secured and that other countries carry out their obligations." In the absence of such insistence, the committee said, the agreements "will become largely one-way streets whereby the United States assumes obligations without reciprocity." Consequently, Congress amended Section 301 to give the president broad authority to enforce U.S. rights unilaterally under Tokyo Round agreements. The 1979 act directed the chief executive to take steps to "retaliate against unjustifiable, unreasonable, or discriminatory acts, policies, or practices that affect U.S. commerce."[70]

What was the long-term significance of the Tokyo Round? Some supporters of the multilateral process saw the results as "the most significant round of trade negotiations in history." They argued the substantive codes extended the GATT system to nontariff barriers and established the foundation for other substantive and organizational changes in the Uruguay Round of the 1980s. Trade law specialist John H. Jackson of the University of Michigan waxed enthusiastic about the far-reaching scope of the nontariff codes. "The willingness of nations to yield 'sovereignty' . . . on such subjects as government procurement, is impressive," he said.[71]

But a decade after they went into effect, the six nontariff codes had little formal acceptance outside the European Community, Japan, and the United States. As of December 31, 1990, merely 40 percent of GATT members (40 of 100) subscribed to the code on technical standards, a relatively innocuous agreement, that negotiators sought to broaden in the Uruguay Round. Only twelve countries adhered to the controversial code on government procurement, while twenty-five adhered to the codes on subsidies and dumping.[72] For the most part, developing nations declined to participate in any agreements that might tie their hands or handicap domestic producers. In light of promises made by Carter administration officials about export opportunities, the government procurement code proved the biggest disappointment. According to the AFL-CIO, "the U.S. opened up $18 billion in procurement opportunities to foreign suppliers, while only $4 billion was seen by U.S. suppliers." The General Accounting Office reported to Congress that these expectations were not realized because of the limited coverage included in the code, the small membership, and the reluctance of members to comply fully. The national procurement policies of France, Italy, and other countries remained significant barriers to American exports. As it turned out, the United States had opened up four times more of its government market than all other code signatories combined.[73]

Negotiation and implementation of the Tokyo Round accords occurred during difficult economic times. Oil-exporting nations succeeded in driving up petroleum prices after the 1973 Mideast War, and this imposed major adjustment burdens on all oil importers. Inflation surged, growth slowed, currencies fluctuated, and budget deficits swelled. Oil-importing developing countries were severely impacted, and the resulting debt-overload crisis disrupted world trade patterns. Viewed from a quarter century afterward, it seems that supporters of the multilateral system pursued a successful holding action during the Tokyo Round. They continued to reward free-riding developing countries with tariff concessions. New Asian competitors and other developing countries were not obliged to offer substantially equivalent concessions or to bind tariffs. But by introducing reciprocity to the code negotiations, U.S. negotiators allayed some congressional concerns and thus kept enough legislative support for the trade liberalization process. These efforts would bear fruit in the 1980s and in the Uruguay Round.

During a retrospective session on the Tokyo Round negotiations, held in October 1998, members of the U.S. delegation offered widely divergent interpretations. While some gave themselves passing grades for saving the multilateral system, John Greenwald, a Treasury representative, suggested a failing grade. He argued that U.S. negotiators did not resolve trade problems with Japan or East Asia, had obtained few concessions from Europe, and had done little to liberalize agricultural trade. Another trade policy maker, Howard Samuel from the Labor Department, suggested that the Tokyo Round results "fostered an even greater . . . disaffection and cynicism on the part of industrial workers . . . who felt their interests had been sacrificed in the process."[74]

After the Tokyo Round, the globalization process and actions of the oil cartel continued to transform the environment for trade policy decisions, and the U.S. trade deficit widened. When serious negotiations began in the Tokyo Round in 1975, the United States still bargained from some strength, despite dollar devaluation. It had an $8.9 billion merchandise trade surplus and a current account surplus of $18.1 billion, both the largest in a thirty-year period extending from the 1960s to the mid-1990s. During these Tokyo Round negotiations, the U.S. surpluses disappeared, replaced in 1978 with a $34 billion trade deficit and a $15 billion current account deficit. Higher energy costs initially exacerbated the deficits, but during the 1980s the deficit continued to grow and its composition changed. In 1987, the trade and current account deficits peaked at $159.6 billion and $168 billion, respectively. The deficit with OPEC had fallen dramatically to only $13.7 billion from $41.5 billion in 1980, but the trade deficit with Asia (nonexistent in 1975) amounted to $101 billion as imports of automotive and consumer goods soared. As multilateral tariff reductions continued to open the American market and as improvements in transportation and communications facilitated international business dealings, Asia increasingly became reliant on the huge American market, and U.S. consumers on Asian products.[75]

Once again the GATT negotiations produced asymmetrical results. Tokyo Round tariff reductions lowered already low U.S. average duties on dutiable products from 8.2 percent to 5.7 percent, but did little to strip away nontariff barriers and open Asian markets to U.S. exports. The Carter administration had promised Congress that vast export markets would develop for American products as GATT members harmonized and eliminated nontariff barriers. In retrospect, this was largely wishful thinking. In 1985, when the USTR began to publish the first of its annual volumes reporting on foreign tariff and nontariff barriers, thirty-four major U.S. trading partners restricted or managed trade in one form or other. Problems with standards, procurement, subsidies, and investment policies, among other nontariff barriers, severely handicapped U.S. exporters. A separate Congressional Research Service survey of 521 U.S. companies and trade associations identified 751 specific foreign trade barriers to the export of U.S. goods and services. This study, said a House Commerce subcommittee, found a "clear and incontrovertible pattern" in which "U.S. firms are systematically excluded from exercising their comparative advantages in the home markets of virtually all of our trading partners." But foreign competitors "expand sales, generate investment capital and acquire new technology behind protectionist barriers, and bring these unfairly acquired advantages to the relatively open U.S. market to the severe disadvantage of domestic companies." Similarly, the Senate Finance Committee expressed concern that the Tokyo Round negotiations and efforts to implement them "have not had the effect of improving the American standard of living as intended." It added: "One-way trade is not good for this country, and it is not good for the world either."[76]

As the trade deficit widened in the early to mid-1980s, many economists chose to advance a different explanation. They blamed a strong dollar and inadequate domestic savings. With inadequate domestic savings, higher interest rates were required to finance a burgeoning federal budget deficit, and higher interest rates thus made U.S. exports less competitive in foreign markets. From a $40.7 billion deficit in FY 1979 the budget deficit grew rapidly to $207.8 billion in FY 1983. To finance the growing budget deficit, the Treasury turned to Japanese buyers, enticed by high U.S. interest rates. In 1978 the Japanese replaced the British as the leading foreign holders of marketable Treasury bonds and notes. Heavy Japanese buying of U.S. securities helped prop up the dollar and finance the growing bilateral deficit. It also helped to keep the yen weak, and this undervalued currency assisted Japanese export competitiveness. In 1985, for instance, Japanese investors bought $20.4 billion net in Treasury and other U.S. government bonds. That year the bilateral deficit was $43.5 billion. In effect, the U.S. budget deficit helped keep interest rates high, and the attraction of higher rates kept the dollar strong and the yen weak, benefiting Japanese exporters and American consumers, while harming U.S. producers and workers in import-competing industries. From an $8.6 billion trade imbalance in 1979, when the yen was relatively strong, the bilateral U.S.–Japan deficit rose to $21.6 billion in 1983 and $56.9 billion in 1987, when the overall merchandise deficit peaked at $160 billion. In 2002, the United States ran a $507 billion merchandise trade deficit and in 2003 a $582 billion deficit.[77]

Capital flows were an important part of the story, but many experienced business leaders with firsthand experience competing for sales had a different explanation for the stubborn trade imbalances. Their interpretation focused on the impact of divergent government philosophies and policies. A Congressional Research Service study highlighted these differences. In the United States "free trade has been the overriding ideology guiding U.S. trade policy." Under this theory, market forces determine what each country would produce and trade, while government should, ideally, act as a neutral referee and "not actually use trade policy to promote the competitive position of U.S. industry." By contrast, the study concluded that "free trade ideology has not served as a strong guide for the overall trade policies adopted by the major U.S. trading partners." Japan's resurgence occurred "behind a protectionist wall," and other East Asian countries, such as South Korea and Taiwan, had "successfully copied" the Japanese model of "using controls over trade and investment flows to promote a strong export sector and to acquire technology." Discussion of whether the foreign protectionist policies were completely successful or not misses a critical point: "Closed foreign markets, restrictive investment practices, and subsidized exports can all produce serious economic hardship for individual U.S. producers and workers." The President's Export Council also emphasized the significance of industrial targeting, in which foreign governments and their domestic industries coordinated in attacking key foreign export markets. Japan, South Korea, Taiwan, Brazil, and West Germany were among the major competitors cited as employing such tactics.[78]

Despite mounting controversy and recession, American leaders during the 1980s continued efforts to lead the world trading system toward the laissez-faire ideal. The global recession of 1981–1982 created dislocations and high unemployment in Western Europe and the United States. The developing country debt-overload crisis, exacerbated by a hike in oil prices and the fall in global demand for many commodities, contributed to a decline in world trade. Subsidized steel producers in Western Europe and some developing countries sought to adjust by boosting exports to the United States. Japanese motorcycle makers and semiconductor makers did the same. The result was a tough test for the new antidumping and countervailing duty laws, written to implement Tokyo Round obligations. These laws, while cumbersome, costly, and legalistic, sometimes required the Reagan administration to impose a variety of import restraints. White House economic adviser William Niskanen later described Reagan trade policies as "strategic retreat." Although the president's goal was more free trade, he said that adverse circumstances compelled the administration to impose "more new restraints on trade than any administration since Hoover." Actually, this greatly overstated President Reagan's use of trade law remedies. The bottom line was that U.S. imports rose 99 percent during his administration, while exports grew only 43 percent.[79]

As it turned out, Reagan's occasional resort to safeguard relief produced some significant gains for domestic industries and workers. The administration's program of bilateral steel restraints bought time for domestic industry to downsize, modernize, cut costs, and become more competitive. The most successful example of escape-clause adjustment occurred on Ronald Reagan's watch. In September 1982 Harley-Davidson, the last American motorcycle maker, was in desperate straits as Japanese motorcycle imports cut into profits and market share. After an International Trade Commission investigation, Reagan imposed high tariffs. Soon, Harley came roaring back. Within five years it was competitive and could even ask the government to lift the remaining import duties. President Reagan, the long-term exponent of free trade, went to the Harley production facility in Lancaster, Pennsylvania, and effused: "Like America, Harley is back and standing tall." He noted that "where U.S. firms have suffered from temporary surges in foreign competition, we haven't been shy about using our import laws to produce temporary relief. . . . You here at Harley-Davidson are living proof that our laws are working."[80]

FTA Blitz

Meanwhile, USTR Bill Brock, a former Republican senator from Tennessee, pressed the free trade agenda that appealed to multinational business and the Washington trade policy elite. Knowing from his years in Congress that the best way to contain protectionist pressures was to have ongoing multilateral negotiations, he urged GATT members to move forward with negotiations to improve the Tokyo Round codes and include other issues such as services, trade-related investments, and intellectual property under GATT supervision. But with Europe in a deep recession he found little interest at the 1982 Geneva ministerial in further negotiations. Consequently, the United States began a two-track approach to freeing trade. On the one hand, it began to pursue bilateral free trade agreements and on the other it urged GATT members to authorize negotiations.

The bilateral path led first to a free trade agreement with Israel in 1985, then to one with Canada in 1987, and then under President George Bush to the regional North American Free Trade Agreement (NAFTA) in 1992–1993 with Mexico and Canada. Presidents Bill Clinton and George W. Bush subsequently would push the regional approach with promises to extend free trade to the Western Hemisphere and to Southeast Asia in the twenty-first century. At a time in the mid-1980s when Congress was under enormous constituent pressure to restrict imports, free trade with Israel had political and strategic appeal. Economically, the case was less compelling. In 1985 this tiny middle-income country had a population of 4.2 million and a per capita gross national product only 40 percent of U.S. levels. In 1980, Israel sent 17.2 percent of its exports to the U.S. market some 6,000 miles away, while 52.2 percent went to Western Europe. Import statistics reflected a similar pattern. Europe supplied 52.2 percent of Israel's imports; the United States, 19.3 percent. During the November 1983 visit of Israel's prime minister Yitzhak Shamir, President Reagan had promised to negotiate a free trade agreement (FTA), and the administration did so after obtaining negotiating authority from Congress in 1984. The agreement proposed to eliminate tariffs and nontariff barriers on virtually all trade between the two countries by 1995. This first FTA also included items not covered in the GATT, such as trade in services, trade-related performance requirements, and intellectual property. But Israel retained substantial nontariff barriers and levies on agricultural items, and the United States did so on textile and apparel imports.

What were the results of this first bilateral free trade agreement? Two-way trade increased 51 percent in four years from 1984 to 1988, but in this period Israel's deficit with the United States turned into a strong merchandise trade surplus, reversing a trend that had existed since Israel declared independence in 1948. By 2002, the deficit had widened to $5.4 billion. On a per capita basis, the trade deficit with Israel was one of America's largest. The FTA appears to have increased the share of Israel's exports destined for the U.S. market from 17.2 percent in 1980 to 41.9 percent in 2002. The share of Israel's imports from America remained virtually unchanged—19.3 percent in 1980, 18.5 percent in 2002. The data seemed to indicate that U.S. trade officials had again oversold the gains from a trade agreement. In effect, Israel's export surplus on trade with the U.S. financed its purchases of products from Europe made by America's competitors.[81]

President Reagan's second FTA initiative—the Canadian agreement—represented another attempt to fulfill nineteenth-century aspirations for a single North American market. The two countries share a 3,000-mile border, speak a common language, and have similar governmental institutions, laws, and business practices. Moreover, they are mutually dependent, mature industrial economies with similar income levels. Each was the other's best customer. Canada sold 76 percent of its exports to the United States in 1985, while Canada took 26 percent of U.S. exports, more than the entire European Community.

Previous efforts to integrate the two economies had failed, mainly because of opposition from Canadian manufacturers concerned about competing with larger, U.S.–based competitors. In the 1980s, that mood changed. Dependent on access to its neighbor's market, ten times the size of the home market, Canadian business grew alarmed over increasing U.S. use of countervailing and antidumping remedies and fearful that the European Union might turn inward. To remain competitive and to benefit from economies of scale, Canadian firms needed more secure access to the American market. For the United States, the attraction of an FTA with Canada included an opportunity to strike a blow at nontariff barriers and investment restrictions and to establish rules regarding services, intellectual property, and subsidies that might impact multilateral negotiations.

The final agreement, formally signed on January 2, 1988, provided for elimination of tariffs and nontariff barriers by January 1998. In the controversial agricultural area, all tariffs would be eliminated during the ten-year period and nontariff barriers would be reduced. The FTA retained the 1965 U.S.–Canada Automotive Products Trade Agreement, which provided for a limited form of free trade beneficial to existing producers. Other provisions concerning government procurement were intended to serve as an impetus for the "multilateral liberalization of international government procurement policies to provide balanced and equitable trade." The FTA also established effective and expeditious dispute settlement procedures, which included use of binational dispute resolution panels. While each country would continue to apply its own antidumping and countervailing duty laws to imported goods, a new procedure provided for a special binational panel to review appeals.

Certain sensitive issues were not resolved in the negotiations. These included Canada's desire to preserve and maintain its unique cultural heritage. As a result, publishing and communications were generally excluded from nontariff provisions of the FTA. Nor was there agreement on financial services or on subsidies.[82]

Viewed from a decade after the negotiations, the U.S.–Canadian FTA appears to have had some adverse impact on the U.S. merchandise trade deficit and current account. The bilateral deficit in goods widened after implementation of the agreement, reaching $52.3 billion in 2002. U.S. surpluses on services and investment income only partially offset that amount, and the current account deficit for 2002 amounted to $34.6 billion. Because the two countries have a long, open border, trade account statistics contain discrepancies and must be used cautiously. Also, since the FTA negotiations did not produce fixed exchange rates, subsequent exchange depreciation enabled Canada to accumulate merchandise trade and current-account surpluses with the United States. In addition, a network of Canadian restrictions on the importation of foreign films, recordings, wine, poultry and eggs, dairy products, and grain hampered efforts of U.S. exporters to benefit from the FTA.[83]

NAFTA Oversell

The most controversial bilateral free trade initiative involved Mexico. Unlike Israel and Canada, which have much smaller populations than the United States, Mexico is a relatively large country (85 million estimated population in 1990) with a per capita gross national product of $2,360, about one-tenth of the U.S. level. Unlike Canada and the United States, which have similar political and legal systems with checks and balances, Mexico has a strong presidency, one dominant political party, and a long history of public corruption. After joining GATT in 1986, Mexico moved unilaterally to reduce its tariffs and to attract foreign capital needed to stimulate domestic growth and provide jobs for a rapidly growing population. Its leaders hoped to attract European capital and technology to offset the influence of American investors. But the collapse of the Soviet Union and the liberalization of Eastern Europe forced President Carlos Salinas de Gortari to look northward. In President Bush, an adopted Texan and former business associate of Salinas's father he found an American president receptive to a FTA.

In February 1991, leaders of the United States, Canada, and Mexico jointly announced their intention to pursue a trilateral FTA intended to liberalize trade in goods and services, foreign investment, protection of intellectual property, and dispute settlement. The two presidents and the prime minister of Canada initialed the North American Free Trade Agreement (NAFTA) text at a ceremony in October 1992, a month before the U.S. presidential election.

Tariff eliminations were a small part of the overall deal, since by 1992 average U.S. duties on imports from Mexico were 3 percent and Mexican duties on U.S. products about 10 percent. Far more important were the investment provisions. Until NAFTA, Mexico had strictly regulated foreign investment and prohibited or limited investment in many sectors. Generally, foreign ownership had been limited to 49 percent in a company. Activities in some 141 areas—including transportation equipment, transportation services, petrochemicals, mining, and automotive parts—remained subject to government regulations. NAFTA, while making exceptions for activities in a few key sectors reserved to the Mexican state, encouraged the liberalization process. It ensured that foreign investors would receive national treatment, prohibited expropriation except for "public purpose," and provided in those cases for prompt compensation at market prices.

Another important goal was mandatory dispute settlement. NAFTA provided for a five-member arbitration process and for binational panels to review antidumping and countervailing duty determinations. While the FTA considered a range of issues outside the GATT framework, some of the more innovative provisions related to the movement of professional workers and to rules of origin that operated against investors from outside North America.[84]

After the presidential election, President Bill Clinton revisited the NAFTA agreement, negotiated modest side agreements involving labor and environmental issues in an effort to placate some opponents, and submitted the agreement to Congress under fast-track procedures on November 4, 1993. Many Democrats, including House Majority Leader Richard Gephardt, opposed NAFTA, together with the AFL-CIO and consumer-advocate Ralph Nader. Businessleader Ross Perot was the most strident opponent; he predicted a "giant sucking sound" of jobs moving south of the border. The U.S. House of Representatives approved implementing legislation on November 17 by a 234 to 200 vote, although a majority of Democrats opposed. Three days later, the Senate approved 61 to 38.[85]

During the NAFTA debate, proponents engaged in overselling the benefits of a trade agreement. On the employment issue, Treasury Secretary Lloyd Bentsen and Trade Representative Mickey Kantor told the Senate that "there will be 200,000 more export jobs, which pay 12–17 percent higher than other jobs in our economy, in the next two years if the NAFTA comes into being." Secretary of State Warren Christopher called NAFTA a "turning point" in relations with Mexico that was in the "overriding national interests of the United States." Rejection of NAFTA, he said, "will seriously damage our relations with Mexico and erode our credibility with the other nations of the hemisphere, and, indeed, of the world." A former Republican secretary of state, Henry Kissinger, also supported NAFTA as the prelude to a regional Western Hemisphere–wide organization "dedicated to democracy and free trade" that "would be a first step toward the new world order."[86]

NAFTA passed Congress, but it produced few of the promised economic gains. While cross-border trade expanded rapidly, largely to take advantage of less expensive Mexican labor in assembly plants, the U.S. merchandise trade surplus ($4.9 billion in 1992) with Mexico evaporated after devaluation of the peso. The bilateral trade deficit soared to $40.6 billion in 2003, and America's merchandise deficit with NAFTA partners was $95 billion, larger than the chronic deficit with Japan. Not surprisingly, U.S. direct investment in Mexico soared as industry moved plants southward. In 1992, the United States had $13.7 billion invested in Mexico, of which $9.6 billion was in manufacturing. Nine years later, in 2001, American firms had invested $52.2 billion, of which $19.7 billion was in manufacturing. U.S. companies employed 729,000 Mexican workers. North of the Rio Grande, the textile and apparel industry was one of the largest losers. It hemorrhaged 740,000 jobs eight years after implementation of NAFTA, though some of these losses were attributable to other multilateral negotiations.[87]

Mexico's gains from NAFTA proved transitory. A decade later, the garment firms and electronics manufacturers that had gone to Mexico under NAFTA were migrating again. Having gained experience operating outside the United States, business leaders found the appeal of cheap Asian labor irresistible as they struggled to cut costs and remain profitable during difficult economic times. In Mexico labor cost five to six dollars per day, but in China millions lined up to work for two dollars a day, or less. Multinational giant General Electric shed 3,500 jobs in Mexico as it announced plans to purchase $5 billion of Chinese goods by 2005. In the age of globalization, low-skilled, labor-intensive industries raced around the world in search of the cheapest labor. Outsourcing expanded rapidly, impacting white-collar and professional workers as well as factory jobs.[88]

Uruguay Round "Victory"

The series of FTA negotiations energized the next installment in America's multilateral trade liberalization strategy. Concerned that the United States had embarked on a bilateral course, which could splinter the GATT system, Europe relaxed its objections to new multilateral negotiations during the Reagan years. Big business and financial interests also pressed for global trade negotiations, fearful that the debt-overload crisis of less developed countries (LDCs) could lead to a 1930s-style collapse of world trade and finance, in the absence of multilateral efforts to liberalize trade.[89]

In September 1986, a GATT ministerial at Punta del Este, Uruguay, authorized the eighth round of negotiations. This one, the Uruguay Round, would focus on efforts to improve GATT rules, particularly those pertaining to agriculture, subsidies, safeguards, dispute settlement, and non-tariff measures. The last item included several topics not raised in the Tokyo Round—services, intellectual property, and investment measures. In essence, the GATT was moving far beyond its initial mission of tariff liberalization to an expansive role establishing and overseeing the ground rules for international business activities.

The Uruguay Round negotiations moved slowly and did not conclude until 1994, during the first Clinton administration. To reach another "successful" outcome, the United States again abandoned its quest for major concessions in agriculture, opposed strongly by France. One hundred eleven countries signed the final act in Marrakech, Morocco.

The agreement established the World Trade Organization (WTO), a permanent organization to serve as a forum and a vehicle for implementing trade agreements, to replace GATT. The package also contained thirteen different agreements covering trade in goods and agreements on agriculture; sanitary and phytosanitary measures; textiles and clothing; technical barriers to trade (standards); trade-related investment measures (TRIMs); antidumping, customs valuation, preshipment inspection, rules of origin, import licensing procedures, subsidies, and countervailing measures; and safeguards. In addition, there was a general agreement on trade in services (GATS); an agreement on trade-related aspects of intellectual property rights (TRIPs); a dispute settlement understanding; a trade policy review mechanism; and four plurilateral trade agreements covering government procurement, civil aircraft, dairy, and bovine meat. The plurilaterals, however, did not involve all members, only signatories prepared to implement their obligations. The final act also set a further negotiating agenda to include financial services, basic telecommunications services, and civil aircraft, but these matters were left largely unresolved.[90]

The key to the final agreement was a deal between developed and developing nations. The former agreed to phase out restraints on textiles and apparel and to improve market access for developing world agricultural products, in exchange for extending the multilateral system to cover intellectual property, services, and TRIMs. Large transnational corporations based principally in the Northern Hemisphere chaffed at local-content restrictions in host countries and sought greater freedom to expand and sell in the most efficient way possible. Wall Street, the insurance industry, and telecommunications providers, among others, wanted national treatment in developing markets. The software, recording, and pharmaceutical industries demanded improved protections for patents and copyrights. Responding to these petitions, governments in high-income countries effectively traded off import-competing, labor-intensive industries for their expanding, high-tech industries, as they had done repeatedly in past talks.[91]

To sell the complex agreements to Congress, the Clinton administration presented rosy estimates of American export gains. Trade Representative Mickey Kantor forecast that the pact would contribute a minimum of $1 trillion in additional income to the U.S. gross national product over ten years. This estimate, which was 525 percent greater than the next largest estimate by the Organization for Economic Cooperation and Development (OECD), appeared to reflect wildly optimistic gains from the sale of financial and business services, telecommunications, and public procurement in developing markets. The USTR also claimed that the agreement would create "at a minimum, hundreds of thousands of new jobs" and that "every billion dollars of exports supports 17,000 new jobs at home—jobs that pay an average of 17% more than non-trade related jobs."[92]

Big business was ecstatic. Jerry Junkins, chair of Texas Instruments and spokesperson for the Business Roundtable, said that the agreement "provides a much improved set of rules for the world trading system." The agreement "will make it more difficult for countries to impose investment restrictions that distort trade and inhibit job creation." He predicted that the accord "will create hundreds of thousands of high-wage, high-skill jobs in the United States." The U.S. Chamber of Commerce and the National Association of Manufacturers agreed.[93]

Among the most controversial aspects of the package were the new World Trade Organization and mandatory dispute settlement. In the WTO, the United States obtained only one vote, despite its role as the leading trading nation. The European Union, which negotiates in GATT as a single bloc, received fifteen separate votes (one for each member nation). With an additional ten members entering in 2004, Brussels would wield an even larger bloc. More important, developing nations controlled over 80 percent of votes in the WTO and thus held more than the three-quarters majority needed to interpret WTO legal provisions. Even though the WTO, like its predecessor the GATT, sought to operate by consensus, the organization, once dominated by the leading trading nations, seemed destined to become another instrument for advancing Third World causes, like UNCTAD.

Further evidence of the emerging influence of developing nations occurred in September 2002, when Supachai Panitchpakdi, a former deputy prime minister of Thailand, became the WTO's director general. The first Asian and representative of a developing country to head the trade agency since GATT was established in 1947, Supachai espoused an agenda to "to boost the power of developing countries in the trade body while castigating those developed countries which suppress the voices of their less-developed counterparts."[94]

For the United States and other industrial countries, the WTO regime brought many changes. Instead of relying on diplomacy or on unilateral action, to enforce rights under the trade agreements, the WTO process gave primacy to the rule of law and invited litigation making use of the mandatory dispute settlement process. Governments would bring their complaints against other members to Geneva, and panels of trade experts would hear the cases in private with little public scrutiny. Members were obliged to implement the panel decisions or to pay heavy penalties. As it turned out, the new dispute resolution process contained a number of flaws. For one thing, members asked the panels to resolve highly contentious political issues, such as Europe's opposition to beef hormones, its discrimination against Central American bananas in order to benefit former African and Caribbean colonies, and America's export-subsidy, tax credit program for large corporations. Another flaw of the new system involved the lack of judicial restraint. The panelists attempted to impose judicial solutions on agreements riddled with ambiguities, resulting from the absence of agreement in the negotiating process. As Alan William Wolff, a former deputy U.S. trade representative observed, WTO panels "are not permitted to expand the obligations and right of the parties beyond their clean commitments . . . [but] that is exactly what the panels do—settle disputes outside of their legal authority to do so."[95] With the major trading powers—the United States and Europe—unwilling to implement controversial decisions, it was unlikely that smaller nations would yield national interests to legal rulings from Geneva.

Transnational businesses saw the WTO structure as an opportunity to integrate the world's largest market—China—into the WTO system, allowing them to gain access to 1.2 billion new customers and to some of the world's cheapest workers, many earning less than two dollars per day. This goal coincided with China's interest in attracting large flows of foreign investments to create millions of job opportunities for a restive public eager to acquire a higher standard of living. Membership in the WTO would enhance China's prestige, assure it access to the world's most lucrative export markets, and help it to acquire advanced technologies. Determined to retain political power and thus to avoid the fate of their Soviet counterparts, China's Communist leaders resolved to work with foreign capitalists to transform China and make it the world's workshop of the twenty-first century.

After China negotiated terms of WTO accession in 2000, big business joined with the Clinton administration to sell the agreement to Congress. Samuel Maury, chair of the powerful Business Roundtable, described the deal as "the economic equivalent of tearing down the Berlin Wall." He insisted that it was the "most significant market access agreement in U.S. history" and made "China play by the rules and gives America access to a market that encompasses over 20 percent of the world's population." Michael Bonsignore, chair of Honeywell, a transnational with $25 billion in revenue and 120,000 employees worldwide, said that Honeywell's business in China "is approaching half a billion dollars in revenue" and indicated that "a substantial portion . . . is direct exports from the United States." He asserted that normal trade relations with China served the "clear interest of America's workers, farmers, exporters, and consumers."[96]

Despite all the buoyant salesmanship about enhanced market access, the Uruguay Round and China's accession to the WTO produced few miracles for American exporters. The merchandise trade deficit continued to grow, widening from $176.6 billion in 1994 to $581.6 billion in 2003. Particularly significant was the negative swing in trade of advanced technology products from a surplus of $22.6 billion in 1994 to a deficit of $27.4 billion in 2003. The deficit with China increased from $29.5 billion in 1994 to $124.0 billion in 2003—as imports continued to rise more quickly than U.S. exports.

One important reason for the mushrooming deficit involved globalization. Intense competition in an open global marketplace prompted corporations to shift production and jobs to locations with the lowest costs. General Electric (GE), the firm frequently named "the world's most respected company," accelerated its expansion in cheap-labor countries like India and China. In GE's annual report for 2002, chair Jeffrey Immelt proudly announced its strategy for China: "To capitalize on its market growth while exporting its deflationary power. We have a vision for China: $5 billion in revenue and $5 billion in sourcing—'5 x 5'— by 2005." Every $5 billion in outsourcing meant $1 billion in cost savings for GE. Three years after Honeywell's Bonsignore told Congress that China's entrance to the trading system would boost opportunities for American workers, Honeywell had thirteen factories and a global research center in China. In April 2003, it announced the shift of its thermal-controls business from Rhode Island to China and Mexico, entailing one layoff of another 374 U.S. workers. One resident interpreted the result this way: "After 50 years of bountiful profits made by providing the U.S. military with equipment, all paid for with the U.S. taxpayers' money and the blood of U.S. youth (many who died in Korea fighting China; I am a Korean War veteran), Honeywell is moving its Rhode Island operations to China and Mexico, and throwing 374 U.S. taxpayers out of work. Is this a great country or what?"[97]

U.S.–based manufacturers tended to blame the asymmetrical trade relationship with East Asia on currency manipulation and closed markets. During 2002 and 2003, when the euro gained some 40 percent against the dollar, making European exporters less competitive in the American market, the currencies of major Asian competitors remained tied to the dollar at artificially low levels. The Coalition for a Sound Dollar, representing more than sixty trade associations with 95 percent of U.S. exports, blamed China, Japan, South Korea, and Taiwan for manipulating exchange rates to their undervalued currencies in violation of obligations to the International Monetary Fund. Together these four countries had a $200 billion surplus with the United States in 2002 and accounted for some 40 percent of the U.S. merchandise trade deficit.[98]

It was also apparent to U.S.–based businesses that the promised export gains from improved foreign market access and protection of intellectual property negotiated during the multilateral Uruguay Round had not materialized. In the telecommunications area, a U.S. government report found serious barriers to U.S. carriers—in Japan, the Philippines, China, and many other countries. Officials also concluded that advancing technology gave "pirates . . . new ways to undermine intellectual property rights." In Brazil, the largest Latin American market for sound and video recordings, copyright piracy cost U.S. firms $777 million in 2002. The European Union's moratorium on biotechnology imports cost U.S. corn growers $200 million annually. Regarding China, USTR reported "incomplete or delayed implementation of WTO commitments," "significant barriers to U.S. agricultural exports," "lack of effective intellectual property (IP) rights enforcement," discriminatory tax policies, cumbersome licensing requirements, and "standard-setting without regard to scientific basis." USTR also stated that a broad range of tariff and trade restrictions had kept American exports flat to India for the preceding five years. Japan, which had long managed its trade with the United States, continued to employ a variety of "market access barriers" to "limit opportunities for U.S. companies trading with and operating in Japan, our third largest trading partner."[99]

Bilateral and Regional FTAs

Frustrations with the legalistic WTO process and the inability, or unwillingness, of trading partners to implement their market liberalization obligations did not dim the American elite's faith in free trade. If anything, frustrations with the multilateral process only strengthened enthusiasm for accelerating bilateral and regional initiatives. So did the fractious WTO meeting of December 1999 in Seattle, where bitter north-south divisions and public demonstrations thwarted efforts to reenergize the WTO process. Determined to keep the trade liberalization process alive, the Clinton administration focused on rallying support for hemispheric free trade by 2005 and similar arrangements with Association of Southeast Asia Nations (ASEAN) countries. And it chose to negotiate a free trade agreement with a small, but strategically located, Middle East country. The proposed agreement with Jordan (population 5 million) had national security and political dimensions and thus could be presented to Congress as an instrument to promote peace and provide jobs in the Middle East. Also, to appease activists and disenchanted labor leaders, the Clinton administration inserted environmental and labor clauses that political supporters hoped might serve as a template for future agreements as well as benefit Democratic candidate Albert Gore in the 2000 presidential election.

Although cool to Clinton's clauses, big business strongly backed bilateral and regional trade initiatives to improve market access—especially in services, harmonized standards, enhanced transparency, and reduced risks associated with operations in developing countries. The globalization of business activity had moved faster than international efforts to define the rules of the global marketplace. At the turn of the twenty-first century, there were some 65,000 transnational corporations with 850,000 foreign affiliates. They had 54 million employees and sales of $19 trillion, more than double world exports in 2001. Nearly 50 percent of American trade—imports and exports—involved transactions among units of multinational corporations. Investment flows, far more than trade, drove the globalization process. According to UNCTAD, over an eleven-year period the stock of outward foreign direct investment increased from $1.7 trillion to $6.6 trillion.[100]

With the rising importance of capital flows in the 1990s, Wall Street and the U.S. Treasury pressured the International Monetary Fund (IMF) to push developing countries to adopt capital-account convertibility—that is, to remove controls on short-term and portfolio investments so that developing country markets and borrowers could benefit from greater competition. China and India resisted the advice, but Thailand, Indonesia, South Korea, and other emerging competitors yielded to the so-called "Washington–Wall Street consensus." As the East Asian financial crisis of 1997–1998 demonstrated, that was a catastrophic mistake. The countries that regulated hot-money flows—Malaysia, China, and India—survived with minimal damage, while the liberalizers were forced to devalue and accept controversial IMF structural adjustment plans that imposed substantial hardship on their economies and societies. Despite IMF claims that free trade in capital was associated with high economic growth, subsequent analysis has demonstrated that the advice was badly flawed for developing economies with inadequate institutions and regulatory mechanisms.[101]

Although technological innovations in transportation and communications had enabled global production networks and supply chains, business still chafed at the political risks associated with foreign operations. It wanted improved access for service providers and protection for intellectual property in emerging markets at a time when piracy was growing rapidly. In March 2002, the U.S. Council for International Business reminded U.S. Trade Representative Robert Zoellick that "investment abroad is still a risky business. We often face underdeveloped legal systems and judicial systems that are not independent or impartial." With the infant WTO an apparent casualty of verbal gridlock, business leaders favored results-oriented bilateral initiatives.[102]

President George W. Bush believed fervently in free trade, and his enthusiasm dovetailed with the practical needs of big business for investment-protection agreements. In his first two years, Bush's trade representative, Robert Zoellick, succeeded in winning congressional approval for the Jordanian FTA and in launching a series of FTA negotiations with Chile, Singapore, Morocco, Australia, Central America, and southern Africa. These commercial negotiations frequently had national security dimensions. Australia, a partner in the Iraq war but a competitor in agricultural markets, inserted itself on the FTA negotiating list, while New Zealand, an opponent, was ignored. Colombia, which supported U.S. action against Iraq's dictator Saddam Hussein, sought an FTA accord as a reward. When Chile opposed the United States in the UN Security Council, the Bush administration sidetracked a completed FTA, rushing forward instead with a similar agreement for Singapore, an ally in the war against terrorism.

These bilateral agreements carried the free trade label, but they were much more. The 800-page pact with Singapore contained twenty-one chapters dealing with a wide range of issues, including duty eliminations, rules of origin, intellectual property rights, financial services, telecommunications, customs administration, competition policy, government procurement, electronic commerce, temporary entry of workers, and dispute settlement. In effect, these were also investor-protection agreements, potential templates for international business activities in the age of globalization. Critics accused the Bush administration of continuing to press the special interests of financial service providers by insisting on provisions that restricted use of capital controls and of using the unequal power of bilateral negotiations to advance both an ideology and economic interests.[103]

Perils of Globalization

As the twenty-first century opened, Americans no longer lived in a national market insulated from the world by border restrictions and natural barriers, such as time, distance, and lack of information. Six decades of trade liberalization, along with innovations in telecommunications and transportation, had integrated global markets—and exposed workers in high-income countries to the pressures of global competition. Until the late 1990s, the harsh winds of global competition impacted mostly low-skilled, blue-collar workers and their dependents, but with the rapid growth of business outsourcing, skilled and professional workers faced similar disruptions. For example, Deloitte Research, a unit of Deloitte Consulting, a global management firm, reported that the world's hundred largest financial services companies expected to transfer 2 million jobs offshore by 2008, saving the companies approximately $1.4 billion each. Another management consulting firm, Forrester Research, has forecast that 3.3 million white-collar jobs and $136 billion in wages would shift overseas in the next fifteen years.[104]

In the late nineteenth century, many American exporters of farm and manufactured products viewed the China market as a great commercial opportunity. By the early twenty-first century, it was evident that China, India, and other low-cost-labor countries had become magnets for high- and low-skilled American jobs as manufacturers and service-providers raced to establish a presence with research centers and manufacturing plants. The expectation of U.S. trade negotiators in the Uruguay Round that America would export high-value goods and services proved ephemeral. As a result, America's trade gap continued to grow, approaching 5.0 percent of gross domestic product, and the American nation imported several billion dollars daily from international lenders to finance its import-dependent lifestyle. To prolong the life of high consumption, we were mortgaging future generations.

Such chronic asymmetries do not occur in the textbook free trade theory that American leaders continued to invoke to justify such circumstances. That theory assumed no permanent imbalances. In classical international trade theory, a price-specie flow mechanism removed trade imbalances automatically. Nations did not manipulate exchange rates, as China, Japan, and some other Asian trading partners have done, to boost exports and impede access to their own home markets. Current practices depart from international trade theory in several other ways. Adam Smith in his famous *Wealth of Nations* presumed that nations specialized in production and exchanged goods. As economist Paul Craig Roberts has observed, Smith did not contemplate a situation in which "U.S. firms relocate their capital and technology in China and India and employ labor in those countries to produce the products that U.S. firms sell in the U.S. markets." This is not international trade, Roberts concludes. Rather, the United States "is using Chinese labor to produce for U.S. markets."[105] Also, Smith and the other classical economists assumed that capital, labor, and technology did not cross borders and exploit absolute advantages associated with cheap labor. The classical economists assumed, too, that dislocated workers were rapidly reemployed in the home market.

It is appropriate to ask whether the global supply chain model, based on free trade, is sustainable and appropriate for twenty-first century circumstances. Certainly, it enables transnational corporations to obtain parts from the least expensive suppliers, to assemble them where labor is cheap, and to transport them quickly to factories and customers around the world. Global supply chains are highly efficient in producing and distributing goods, but they are also fragile and vulnerable to noneconomic shocks like war, terrorism, and epidemics. Even Adam Smith, the great free trader, appreciated the paramount need to defend the nation state, although it might require some departure from free trade. In *The Wealth of Nations* Smith wrote that "defense . . . is of much more importance than opulence."[106]

The terrorist attacks on the World Trade Center and the Pentagon in September 2001 as well as the recent severe acute respiratory syndrome (SARS) epidemic in China underscore the dangers of a world with few borders and barriers to the easy movement of terrorists and the rapid transmission of disease. Adopting David-versus-Goliath tactics, terrorists can use unsophisticated weapons, and unconventional delivery systems, to attack the soft underbelly of capitalism—the global supply chain. With some 12 million containers and trucks entering the United States every year, there is a real danger that terrorists could load containers with weapons of mass destruction, causing far more casualties than the attacks on September 11. The attacks could include assaults on transportation facilities, such as bridges, or the energy supply chain. Attackers might also indulge in cyberterrorism, aimed at corporate security or access to financial records and credit cards—made easy by the outsourcing of these activities to low-paid workers in developing countries. Another lethal scenario involves an assault on the global food supply chain, perhaps by tainting fruit or meat with harmful pathogens. In response to such threats, the United States and other targeted countries are increasing border security and introducing a variety of advanced technologies, including high-tech cargo seals, tracked by satellites. But so long as the imperatives of the rapidly functioning global supply chain—and the need to move merchandise and perishable products quickly from suppliers to consumers—take priority over careful inspection and regulation at the border, Americans assume high risks for the sake of short-term consumer gains.[107]

The SARS pandemic awakened transnational corporations to the dangers of over dependence on a single foreign supplier. U.S. importers of footwear, apparel, and electronics found their business operations held hostage by invisible microbes. Wal-Mart's global sourcing office is located in Guangdong province in China, the epicenter of the SARS disturbance, where Wal-Mart hoped to procure some $15 billion in merchandise. Public health officials suggest that SARS may prove only a "dress rehearsal" for other rapidly traveling epidemics that could rattle the global village. Some public health experts say that China, with millions of people living in close proximity to pigs and ducks, offers a natural breeding ground. As the *Washington Post* reported, "More than ever, we are a species on the move, abandoning countryside for closely packed cities, and boarding planes, trains and buses that can swiftly transport a SARS virus, flu virus, or mosquito infected with West Nile or dengue virus far afield."[108]

In light of the unusual and uncertain circumstances that characterize present-day world trade, it is appropriate to ask whether the doctrine of unrestricted (and unilateral) free trade still makes sense. To answer this question intelligently, we must review carefully the best accumulated insights of economists on trade policy. When and in what circumstances can free trade really improve the mutual welfare of nations and their peoples?

3

Free Trade

Static Comparative Advantage

RICHARD L. BRINKMAN

In the previous chapter, Alfred Eckes has drawn attention to the fact that the "age of globalization" is upon us. Mainstream economists tend to conceptualize and explain globalization as an evolving and conceivably borderless world, fed by the dynamics of liberalized markets and new forms of transportation and information technologies. Inexorable and irrepressible forces have come to dominate the global economy allegedly beyond human alteration and control, which is seen as "increasingly irrelevant" (Yergin and Stanislaw 1998, 13–134). But what humankind has created, humankind can also reform and control.

Given that the current form and structure of globalization appear as a function of the heavy hand of Multinational Corporate (MNC) power, globalization might best be called megacorporate globalization. Megacorporate globalization, characterizing the post–World War II period, constitutes a signal, defining feature of our current economic epoch. The process of megacorporate globalization and its results are debated in a large and growing literature. There is no consensus in the literature concerning the conception of globalization, let alone its merits. This lack of agreement is explained, in part, by the fact that globalization constitutes a multivariate complexity. Another consideration is that the globalization process is not dealt with by a universal or agreed-upon paradigm of economic analysis and theory.[1] In the context of globalization, the theory of international trade that is applied becomes of utmost importance. Empirical facts do not speak for themselves but require relevant concepts and theory for analysis and explanation.

In the overall globalization debate, two recent books—*The Commanding Heights* by Daniel Yergin and Joseph Stanislaw, and *Globalization and Its Discontents* by Joseph Stiglitz—illustrate the point that conception and theory determine analysis and policy derivatives. These two books polarize and dichotomize the debate in the context of mainstream predilections split between many neoliberals, exemplified by Friedrich Hayek, Milton Friedman, Jeffrey Sachs, and Lawrence Summers, on the one hand, and a liberal Keynesian viewpoint offered by Stiglitz on the other. Yergin and Stanislaw argue that neoliberal theory and a laissez-faire policy orientation currently constitute the "commanding heights" in control of the globalization process. Neoliberals argue that the results of globalization, nurtured by the dynamics of a free market process and technological advance, have been benign. While governmental participation in the past might have proved beneficial, such is no longer the case, especially in assaying the role of government from the vantage point of economic efficiency, as measured by the control of inflation and by the "generation of wealth, not the subsidizing of employment" (Yergin and Stanislaw 1998, 99).

By comparison, Stiglitz questions the merits of the Washington Consensus and market fundamentalism in relation to the neoliberal free market ideology. The invisible hand described by Adam Smith is not that visible in that a self-regulating market process apparently exists only in the minds of economic theorists (Stiglitz 2002, 73–74, 222, 248). Keynesian economics and an associated positive role for government are not dead but very much in need and relevant today in dealing with the dynamics of globalization. Nations in East Asia, where the neoliberal policies put forth by the International Monetary Fund (IMF) and the World Bank were avoided, have succeeded in what has come to be called the "East Asia Miracle." By comparison, in Latin America and Africa, where neoliberal policies have been applied, the results have proved negative. Keynes's baby, the IMF, has incorrectly been transformed and now embraces policies primarily oriented toward market conditionality, and austerity programs. The basic Bretton Woods institutions are now directed toward constraining inflation and balancing budgets more than toward employment and macro-stability, the original Keynesian policy goals. Stiglitz argues that governmental participation is relevant and necessary not only for economic development but for social justice as well (Stiglitz 2002, xv, 218, 246). There is a need to move "toward globalization with a more human face" (p. 247).

Debate is one thing; political reality as to the policy actually in place is another. It appears, whether rightly or wrongly, that neoliberal outlooks dominate recent policies directing the current globalization process. International trade is obviously related to globalization and, given control of the "commanding heights" by the neoliberal free market ideology, the policy derivative is that of unrestricted free trade. What are the origins of free trade theory and policy? This chapter argues that the free trade theory from which the policy of free trade is derived is based upon "whopper" assumptions and comprises faulty logic in its errors and omissions. This critique will not be based upon the heterodox views of Friedrich List, Henry Carey, Gunnar Myrdal, or Raul Prebisch but rather will place primary emphasis on the dynamic theory of trade provided by Adam Smith. In the last analysis, that wise old Scot might just be the wisest of all, after all!

Origins of Free Trade: Theory and Policy

In the 1840s, Britain, having innovated the Industrial Revolution and acquired absolute cost advantages, decided that policies of free trade, not protection, would better serve national interests. Since Britain now enjoyed broad industrial supremacy, Britain's need was no longer to protect the economy from foreign manufacturing, but rather to open more global markets for expanding British industrial production. Adam Smith has been widely credited with pioneering economic theory in support of free trade. Yet Smith's support for laissez-faire was not so rigid as to prevent him from backing nation-building policies.[2] In addition to promoting national defense as "more important than opulence," and the "act of navigation" as perhaps the "wisest of all commercial regulations," as Jacob Viner noted, Smith also made "concessions to the mercantilistic policy of regulation of the foreign trade" (Smith 1937, 431; Irwin 1991, 111). Of course, Smith wrote the *Wealth of Nations* during the 1770s in a milieu of widespread mercantilism.

It is often maintained that the advocacy of free trade in Britain during the 1830s and 1840s was supported by the comparative cost theory.[3] Ricardo's cloth/wine arguments served as the foundation for what later came to be called the "pure theory of trade." Historically, this theory, in turn, has been used to justify and rationalize a policy derivative of free trade. This theory was in place during the formative period of the Bretton Woods institutions. Given the respective hegemonic positions of Britain (1840s–1880s) and the United States (1940s–1970s), both nations embarked upon policies allowing the extreme of one-way or unilateral free trade. Unfortunately, one-way free trade policies did not maintain their respective industrial-maritime predominance. Accordingly, support for such unilateral free trade policies, in disregard of global asymmetries and nonreciprocity, waned as each country lost ground against more protected rivals. Both countries delayed considerably in recognizing their vulnerability, which was manifest in growing global economic asymmetries.

By the later 1970s, however, an American economic malaise was recognized even among the orthodox (Haberler 1979). While causality and cures might be debated, the empirical facts indicative of economic malaise and maladjustment could not. After an apparent turning point, circa 1973, U.S. rates of economic growth became anemic in comparison to the historic long-term trends (Madrick 1995). This provided evidence of a conceivable American long-term economic decline. In addition and as an explanation, many economists came to conclude that our problems were structural in nature (Bernstein and Adler 1994). Troubling economic indicators appeared in such areas as productivity decline, balance of payments deficits, international indebtedness, and a decline in real wages.[4] Consequently, the apparent need for industrial renewal and a restoration of global competitiveness spawned the industrial policy debate. Given the current economic quagmire and malaise, that debate still appears relevant.

From Adam Smith and the works of David Ricardo, John Stuart Mill, and Alfred Marshall, to the contributions of Eli Heckscher, Bertil Ohlin, and Paul Samuelson, orthodox trade theory in support of free trade has experienced significant changes, refinement, and narrowing.[5] The standard story that unfolds in the textbook and mainstream literature is that Adam Smith argued the case for free trade based on natural absolute advantage. It has also been argued that absolute advantage constitutes a logical impossibility and should be ignored or even discarded (Brandis 1967, 169, 174). In what constitutes a big error of omission, the literature dealing with absolute advantage has largely ignored Smith's opinion that absolute advantages could also be acquired (Smith 1937, 425–426). But if a nation had absolute advantages, whether acquired or natural, why would or should that nation engage in international trade?

In answering this question, Ricardo explained "what" was traded in terms of the "doctrine of comparative costs," as relative cost ratios, which in turn came to serve as the basis for determining relative comparative advantages among nations.[6] Mill offered an explanation of the "international price" at which goods were exchanged in terms of reciprocal demand. Marshall, in *The Pure Theory of Foreign Trade*, provided a base for analytic synthesis, and his general equilibrium theory offered a more rigorous foundation for theory. Gottfried Haberler introduced "opportunity costs" to replace the classical and Marxian labor theory of value and its associated measure based upon labor costs. The orthodox pure theory was added to by the works of Heckscher, Ohlin, and Samuelson, explaining "why" a given nation had a comparative cost advantage based upon comparative cost ratios. Theory also evolved to direct more attention to the results or "gains" to be derived from a policy of free trade (Samuelson 1939).

To understand Adam Smith one must appreciate the gradual, evolutionary process that spawned the Industrial Revolution and from which these ideas sprang. The process of trade itself served a dynamic function and catalytic role in culture evolution in the later Middle Ages. It can be argued that the expansion of trade constituted a significant factor in the breakdown of the feudal system. After a long era of feudal stagnation from the fall of the Roman Empire up to the epidemic of bubonic plague (1349–1350), came a stage in economic and culture evolution designated as a Commercial Revolution (circa 1350–1750) (Packard 1948; Deane 1965, 51–68). And it was that overly restrictive "mercantile system" of the early modern period (1550–1750) that Adam Smith attacked in the *Wealth of Nations*.[7] The Commercial Revolution can be conceptualized as "early capitalism" or, using Rostow's classification, as a stage of "preconditions" allowing for the subsequent "take-off" into modern economic growth and industrialization (Rostow 1968). A seed bed nurturing the ultimate flowering of what later came to be called the Industrial Revolution (circa 1750–1850), the Commercial Revolution was interrelated to many technological inventions of the period, both social and material, such as the compass, larger sailing ships, banking, double-entry bookkeeping, improved iron making, and the greater use of coal. Of all the advances made during this period in material technology, the printing press was one of the most important. The printing press was instrumental in the innovation of one of the greatest social inventions of all time. We speak here of the invention of the method of invention, a social technology better known as the institution of science. This science-based process of invention became institutionalized during the period that Kuznets has designated as a "scientific epoch" (Kuznets 1973).

The science being nurtured during the period was not confined simply to material culture, but spilled into nonmaterial (social) culture as well. Enter Adam Smith, the *Wealth of Nations*, and the modern science of economics. By comparison, earlier mercantilist writers are viewed as pamphleteers seeking personal gain and mercantile profits. The theory behind mercantilist policies is allegedly sparse and not really representative of a unified matrix (Marshall 1927, 719–720). By contrast, Smith offered a path for policy to be predicated on "scientific" inquiry. As assessed by Max Lerner in his introduction to Smith's work: "Like all great books, *The Wealth of Nations* is the outpouring not only of a great mind, but of a whole epoch. The man who wrote it had learning, wisdom, a talent for words; but equally important was the fact that he stood with these gifts at the dawn of a new science and the opening of a new era in Europe" (Smith 1937, v).

But crucial to the mercantilism that evolved during the Commercial Revolution was the nation-state. "The emergence of national states governed by rulers who exercised sway over large areas, was perhaps the most important political development of the early modern period" (Heaton 1948, 221–222). And from this new structure of social organization, the nation-state, came forth the policies later referred to as mercantilism. The actual policies included state corporations, franchises or guild privileges, substantial excise taxes, tariffs on imports, overseas colonies, and favors to domestic as opposed to foreign artisans, merchants, and shipping activities.

Though crude and somewhat oppressive, mercantilist policies did work in terms of state building.[8] And this meant *nation*-state building. This integrative process served as a sine qua non for the first Industrial Revolution (Deane 1965). Mercantilist policies had an impact even beyond that of state building in that they also served as policies of transition into modern economic growth and industrialization.[9] However, it was not the domestic policy of laissez-faire, nor its international extension as British "free trade," that served to foster the Industrial Revolution. Rather, it was the policies of mercantilism and the emergence of science during the later Commercial Revolution that fostered a "scientific epoch" and, ultimately, led to the dynamics of modern economic growth. Government played an active and decisive role.

It was after the British Industrial Revolution, when the nation-state, Britain, achieved a measure of global hegemony, that freer trade was innovated with the repeal of the Corn Laws in 1846. Similarly, for the United States, it was the Hamiltonian internal improvement and external tariff policies embedded in the American System and protectionism that promoted national unification and power, and industrialization (Mitchell and Mitchell 1947, 310–315, 328, 334–336). Like Britain, the United States acquired absolute advantages and industrialization through protectionism, rather than through policies of freer trade. Again, only after achieving global industrial and economic hegemony did the United States, like Great Britain, embark on policies directed toward freer trade during the 1930s, though mainly after World War II, and manifest in the Bretton Woods institutions.[10]

What then is Adam Smith's framework? Wealth for a nation resides in production, not gold. Production rests on labor productivity, which is based on the division of labor. Specialization, inherent in the division of labor, is promoted by a larger market size. A larger market size is partly related to the accumulation of capital, but a larger market size is also a function of trade. The policy orientation that held the whole system together was a general laissez-faire. And as recognized by Jacob Viner, free trade is synonymous with international laissez-faire.[11] The operation of an invisible hand, as a self-regulating economic process, was assumed to provide for economic growth and development. There are three basic legs to Adam Smith's theory of international trade: absolute advantage, the vent-for-surplus, and, the productivity doctrine (Myint 1958).

Why nations trade particular items and what nurtures relative or comparative trade advantages and allows for lower costs are functions of "absolute advantage," not comparative cost ratios, as Ricardo later maintained. A static conception of absolute advantage, based upon natural conditions, is the one usually offered in textbooks and mainstream, orthodox literature. "By means of glasses, hotbeds, and hotwalls, very good grapes can be raised in Scotland, and very good wine too can be made of them at about thirty times the expense for which at least equally good can be brought from foreign countries" (Smith 1937, 425). "Smith finds the fundamental basis for foreign trade, viewed *statically* in what has since been called absolute advantage" (Bloomfield 1975, 475; italics added).

As delineated earlier and of great significance, however, although often mitigated to the point of being ignored, especially in the textbook literature, is that Smith also claimed that absolute advantage was not based only upon natural and static conditions. Absolute advantage can also be *acquired* via the evolutionary dynamics of economic development in the movement toward industrialization. "Whether the advantages which one country has over another, be natural or *acquired*, is in this respect of no consequence." (Smith 1937, 425–426; Irwin 1996, 119; and Bloomfield 1975, 458; italics added).

Contrary to conventional wisdom and textbook mythology, Adam Smith actually placed the domestic economy and its advance over the international: "According to the natural course of things, therefore, the greater part of the capital of every growing society is, first, directed to agriculture, afterwards to manufactures and last of all to foreign commerce" (Smith 1937, 352, 360, 423; and Irwin 1996, 84). And further, that acquired absolute advantage rests with the industrialization of the domestic economy: "Most opulent nations, indeed, generally excel all their neighbours in agriculture as well as in manufactures, but are commonly more distinguished in the latter than in the former" (Smith 1937, 6; Bloomfield 1994, 111; 1975, 457). Once having acquired absolute advantages inherent in the processes of modern economic growth and industrialization, it is then prudent for a nation to compete in global markets, and from this to gain the benefits of a larger market size, improved productivity, and further technological advances.

Certainly, this has been the historic path pursued by Britain and the United States. The Japanese pursued a similar development path, applying policies of a developmental state, which has also served as the model pursued by the "tigers" of East Asia.[12] "In short they adopted the Japanese approach—'competing out and protecting in,'" and thereby "insulating their domestic economies . . . from foreign competition" (Yergin and Stanislaw 1998, 159, 180).

But assuming an absolute advantage in both industrial and agrarian pursuits, whether natural or acquired, why then should a nation engage in trade and import goods produced less efficiently abroad? This question was alleged to be outside the boundaries of Smith's matrix. It led to the introduction of Ricardo's doctrine of comparative costs. By comparison, the framework of comparative costs explains that it is possible in some circumstances to

benefit from importing a good that is more costly in its production abroad—
a possibility supposedly overlooked by Smith, but recognized by Ricardo.
Ricardo's static theory of comparative cost ratios will be discussed and critiqued later in this chapter.

The second leg of Smith's theory of trade, the vent-for-surplus theory,
was stressed by Hlya Myint as perhaps more relevant and the better framework to be applied in relating classical trade theory (Myint 1958). In allowing a vent-for-surplus production, exports and free trade permit a nation to
advance and improve its position on its efficiency locus, better known as the
production-possibility or transformation curve. The vent-for-surplus reasoning accounts for a movement from unemployed to fully employed resources
at zero opportunity costs. The vent-for-surplus theory, however, also can serve
to support the dumping of surplus goods abroad, with frequent disruptive
impacts upon other nations.

But the reasoning in support of freer trade offered by Adam Smith was not
merely confined to a static analysis embedded in absolute advantage and the
outlet-for-surplus theories. Smith, importantly, provided a dynamic theory of
international trade in the context of acquiring absolute advantages, but also
with the "productivity doctrine." Laissez-faire and broader trade are a dynamic
force that, by widening the market and scope for the division of labor, raises
the skill and dexterity of the worker, encourages technical innovation, over-
comes technical indivisibilities, and generally enables a trading country to enjoy increasing returns and economic development (Myint 1958, 318–319).

The freer trade position of Adam Smith has historically been submitted to
a whole variety of criticism and limitations. These views have also evolved
over time but include attacks originating from Alexander Hamilton, Friedrich
List, Raul Prebisch, and Gunnar Myrdal, among others. Trade theory, more
relevant to the dynamics of development, will be dealt with specifically in
the next chapter. Another critique relates to the oppressive results of an unrestricted free trade policy. Mercantilism was critiqued for its colonization and
because benefits accrued mainly to the mother country. With classical free
trade, all nations were supposed to benefit. In actuality, however, the end
result was sometimes more colonialism, and even on a larger scale. Colonialism, like imperialism, was often associated with the policies of free trade.[13]
The earlier colonialism of mercantilism paled by comparison to the imperialism of the late nineteenth century. And in turn, to some viewers the colonialism of the nineteenth century might pale in comparison to the "new
colonialism" of the current period. The pattern that emerged in the nineteenth century was that the "relatively most efficient in industrial production
(by good fortune Britain) would continue to industrialize while the most
relatively efficient hewers of wood and drawers of water would go on doing

just that" (Dowd 1993, 17). This pattern of international specialization has been strongly supported by the specialization inherent and rationalized in the statics of Ricardo's theory based upon relative cost ratios.

Pure Theory of Trade

Attention has been drawn to Adam Smith's dynamic theory of trade, including the concept of acquired absolute advantage and the productivity doctrine. In this context, a comparison will be made between Smith's dynamics and Ricardo's statics. And in this comparison it appears that the wise old Scot was indeed, and without equivocation, the wiser of the two. It is the Ricardian framework, the static "doctrine of comparative costs," that has given rise to *The Pure Theory of Foreign Trade* (Marshall 1949). The epithet "pure" theory, according to Bhagwati, is derived from the work of Marshall, which postulates a separation of "trade" theory from "monetary" theory.[14] In the Marshallian offer-curve framework, exports paid for imports and there was no possibility of international borrowing. Ricardo also postulated balanced trade and "maintained that international capital movements did not take place" (Robinson 1980, 138). Given this awesome assumption, that exports and imports are in balance, balance of payments problems currently proving so onerous to the United States, simply would not exist.

Over time, as the theory of comparative advantage evolved, neoclassical economists developed a variety of ancillary analytical tools in their attempts to argue the correctness of free trade policy. "The pure theory of international trade has been most thoroughly refined in terms of *static* general equilibrium analysis" (Meier 1968, 10; italics added). Haberler's introduction of opportunity costs during the 1930s served to substitute for the classical tradition, which focused on a measure based on labor productivity and a labor theory of value. Over time, the maturation of the pure theory of trade, in its evolution, produced the current standard textbook treatment, which includes a composite mix of several additional tools. Among them are the production-possibilities curve, Marshallian offer curves, and an indifference map to serve as a basis for value theory.

From these abstract, esoteric tools of neoclassical economics, a basic analytical and methodological sequence follows (see Figure 3.1. Marshallian Offer Curves and the "Engine of Growth"). Its overall composition constitutes the "pure theory of trade." *What* is traded is a function of the domestic terms of trade. The domestic rates of exchange are derived from a given nation's production-possibilities (P-P) or transformation curve. These domestic rates of exchange are then used to determine a nation's relative comparative cost advantage. Among the production functions in the Edgeworth-Bowley (E-B) box diagram, the efficiency locus, so achieved, provides for the derivation of a nation's P-P curve. But the P-P curve is important not only in determining the relative cost ratios as the domestic terms of trade. In the framework of the neoclassical pure theory of trade, the P-P curve serves a very important function in relation to the conception and meaning of economic growth and development.

Crucial to the pure theory of trade is the demonstration of the "gains" to be derived from international trade and further that the "gains" be shown as an improvement in human welfare. How then to distribute the "gains" from trade in relation to the processes of economic growth and development? Certainly, an assumed gain would be that trade, more correctly free trade, would promote development for both nations engaged in trade. This is especially important and relevant to an agricultural or less developed country (LDC) nation. Therefore, what conception of development does the pure theory of trade offer? "We can now extend the analysis to development problems by first interpreting a country's development in terms of outward shifts in its production frontier."[15] These shifts, in conjunction with an indifference map, are used to indicate the welfare aspects of economic development, the "gains" supposedly wrought in the crucible of free trade.

Meier's neoclassical conception of economic development is essentially synonymous with the comparative statics of economic growth. And this "growth" is then made to be the conceptual equivalent of economic development. But how, then, in the matrix of neoclassical theory is the outward shift of the P-P curve explained and, thereby, the realization of economic development (in a more complete, institution-building sense)? The domestic terms of trade (DTT) are derived from the P-P curve (efficiency locus) and are used to determine the ratios of exchange between, for example, cloth and wine and thereby to determine the "what" that is traded. Comparative costs do not determine the international price or the international terms of trade.

John S. Mill answered this question with the conception of reciprocal demand. Enter Alfred Marshall and the offer-curve analysis. The equilibrium position obtained from the offer-curve analysis provides for the derivation of the international terms of trade (ITT). This new rate of exchange is of great importance in the context of the pure theory of trade and is demarcated in Figure 3.1 A as the line ITT. The ITT is not based upon labor productivity, or actual increases in economic growth and development. The ITT represents price changes as new rates of exchange, offering an improvement over the DTT for both nations. This has a "real income effect, the same *as if* there had been an outward shift in its production frontier" (Meier 1968, 20; italics added).

Especially to be noted, therefore, is that the newly formulated ITT serves

Figure 3.1   **Marshallian Offer Curves and the "Engine of Growth"**

A. Marshallian Offer Curves

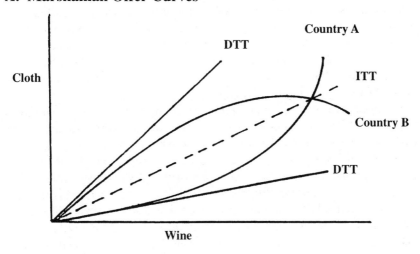

B. Gains from Trade: "Economic Development"

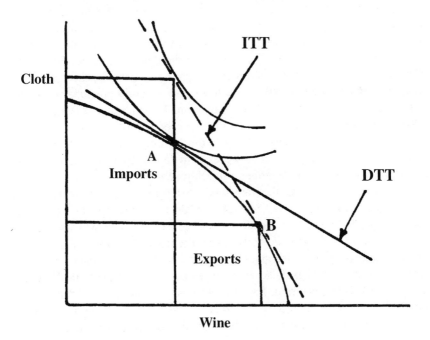

the same function, *as if* there had been a real shift in the production frontier, when in actuality all that has occurred is a change in price, manifest in the newly originated ITT. Reciprocal demand (not the dynamics of technological change) is assumed to be causal in promoting economic development through the newly formulated ITT, which serves the same function *as if* the production-possibilities curve had shifted outward, when in actuality it had not. Increased specialization in the production of more wine simply results in a movement along the given P-P curve, but not in an actual outward shifting of the curve (see Figure 3.1B).

Changes in resources, factor inputs, or technology (the basis for an actual or real outward movement of the production frontier) are assumed not to have taken place and are taken to be given. Other things remaining the same, it becomes necessary to show how the introduction of international trade, as the isolated and independent variable, promotes growth (development) that is the outward shift of the P-P frontier. The *as if* shift is accomplished via a newly formulated ITT. Consequently, what the analysis shows is that a favorable change in the ITT (price changes) is the conceptual equivalent as *an assumption of economic development*, given the offer-curve methodology. Price changes are equated with economic development as an explanation of the "gains" from free trade.

Price changes and static economic efficiency of given and existing resources, in the context of a given structure, have always constituted the major concern of neoclassical economic analysis. The upshot of the pure theory of trade manifests and continues this focus in the context of international prices and the improved terms of trade, not the dynamics of development. The paradigmatic boundaries and predilections demarcated by the analytical tools of the neoclassical pure theory of trade, consequently, preclude an analysis of the dynamics of economic development. The pure theory of trade, by focusing on the gains that accrue from the production of more and more wine or cloth, offers a restricted, static function of trade as an "engine of growth." The relevant question, however, is to demonstrate how trade serves a dynamic function as an "engine of development."[16]

And finally, to round out the framework, "why" did a nation have a relative cost advantage to begin with? The Ricardian "doctrine of comparative cost," as theory, explains "what" was traded but does not really explain "why" a particular nation has such a relative cost advantage. The Heckscher-Ohlin model offers an explanation in terms of the quantitative supply of labor and capital, the basic factors of production. These factors serve to demarcate the basic analytical boundaries of the E-B box diagram. The efficiency locus of the E-B box determines the P-P curve, which, in turn, is used to determine the domestic terms of trade.

"Heckscher's innovation was to attribute disparities in comparative costs and hence in the pattern of trade, to dissimilarities in factor endowments. . . . Ohlin recognized the revolutionary nature of Heckscher's brilliant idea, married it explicitly with general equilibrium, neoclassic theory" as the pure theory of trade.[17] The Heckscher-Ohlin (H-O) theory evolved into what has come to be called the Heckscher-Ohlin-Samuelson-Jones theory of international trade (Flam and Flanders 1991, 1–30). The neoclassical analytical circle from causality to results, starting with the E-B box diagram in the orthodox pure theory of trade, was thereby given its logical completion with the introduction of the H-O model.

Of the two basic theorems of the H-O model to be explicitly stated, one was associated with an explanation as to why a nation had a relative cost advantage in the production of a given commodity. The second explicit theorem of the H-O model was related to an explanation as to why a free market system of laissez-faire, with its international concomitant of free trade, tended to provide for factor-price equalization. Factor-price equalization is not to be equated with a tendency toward an international leveling or equalization of GNP per capita, rather means that factor payments, per se, in a specific area of production or country would move toward equality. The conclusion reached was that all nations would improve their positions in terms of economic growth and welfare, *but not necessarily equally.* The question then becomes, is the pure theory of trade sound in terms of its internal conceptual orientation and logic, and especially, in terms of its basic and underlying assumptions?

Static Comparative Advantage under Siege: Errors and Omissions

The static theory of comparative advantage has experienced criticism for many decades. In 1937 Viner noted that, historically, the theory had been under attack: "Never widely accepted on the Continent, the doctrine is clearly on the defensive everywhere" (Viner 1965, 438; Irwin 1996, 2002). The cannonade continues today with increased intensity, only now there are more cannons with increased firing power. William Lovett's article "The WTO: A Train Wreck in Progress" expresses and analyzes the reality of the situation (Lovett 2000). The WTO and the ancillary Bretton Woods institutions are having negative impacts on labor and the environment, to the point of nurturing riots. The intensity of the riots, starting with the Battle in Seattle (December 1999) and spreading elsewhere (Prague, Davos, Genoa, and Cancun) has be interpreted as a leading discontent, portending "a war against globalization" (Stiglitz 2002, 3). A fundamental critique is that unrestricted, yet incomplete, free trade policy ignores and discounts the obvious global asymmetries that exist today. "The resulting global asymmetry, in which diminished states and augmented markets serve only private, economic interests, damages not only a well-functioning democratic civic order but a well-functioning international economic order as well" (Barber 2001, xxvii). And whereas global realities indicate the need for greater reciprocity, the actual policy recommended by pure free traders moves in the direction of unilateral free trade for the United States. "The economist's case for free trade is essentially a unilateral case: a country serves its own interests by pursuing free trade regardless of what other countries may do" (Krugman 1997, 113).

Unilateral, unrestricted free trade takes a head-in-the-sand view of reality. This outlook assumes that one policy prescription for the United States is immutable and will work for all nations in all times and all places. It has been conceptualized as a "one-size-fits-all" approach (Stiglitz 2002, 34, 47–48). To assume that a policy of unrestricted laissez-faire in tandem with a self-regulating market will resolve all of the current global maladies is analogous to believing in that old snake-oil medicine sold in the Wild West of the past. Complete laissez-faire does not work even in the far less complex arena of the domestic economy, let alone in the heterogeneous complexity of international cultures at different stages of development that characterizes the asymmetrical global economy. Samuelson is correct: "undiluted laissez-faire died before Queen Victoria died" (Samuelson 1970, 820). But given the neoliberal resurgence, perhaps this is better stated, "should have died with Queen Victoria."

The crucial flaw usually cited is that the pure theory of trade rests upon a foundation of "magnificent assumptions," which can also be classified simply as "whoppers" (Salvatore 1998, 110):

1. Only two nations, two commodities, and two factors of production (labor and capital) exist.
2. Production functions are homogeneous; all nations use the same technology.
3. One commodity is labor intensive (X) and the other capital intensive (Y) in both nations.
4. Commodities in both countries are produced under constant costs.
5. There is incomplete specialization in production in both countries.
6. Tastes are the same in both countries.
7. Perfect factor mobility exists within nations; immobility exists internationally.
8. There is perfect competition in commodity and factor markets.
9. There are no transportation costs, tariffs, or other obstructions to free trade.
10. All resources are fully employed in both nations.
11. International trade is balanced.

It is an understatement to say that these assumptions are necessary in order to rationalize the theory. Therefore, to void the assumptions is to void the theory. In that the Heckscher-Ohlin model is predicated on a quantitative base of factors in explaining comparative costs for a given nation, the assumption of immobility of factors must be made in order for the theory to hold. But even in the latter part of the nineteenth century, when the static framework of Marshall's pure theory was being formulated, reality and the empirical record revealed large migratory flows of capital, labor, and technological diffusion. The assumption of full employment had a similar problem. Periodic fluctuations in business activity produced high levels of unemployment, quite apart from the massive unemployment of the Great Depression.

It appears that every one of the eleven basic assumptions stretches any semblance of credibility and relevancy to the real world. But one that deserves special attention, as related to the dynamics of economic development, is the assumption of homogeneous production functions. In plain English, this means that technology everywhere is assumed to be the same. This assumption is founded on the further assumption that since knowledge is free and accessible to all, every nation gets its fair and equal share. And since knowledge constitutes the fountainhead of technology, all nations have homogeneous production functions. All of which then further assumes that all nations are at the same level of economic development, and ignores the great technological and developmental asymmetries that exist among, for example, the United States, Japan, Somalia, and Ethiopia—not to mention the obvious asymmetries in the comparative levels of technology and development that exist between the United States and its Mexican next-door neighbor.

How, then, to explain such flawed assumptions offered in support of the pure theory of trade? Marshall perhaps provides the answer. "A politician is compelled to seek his allies among those who desire the same ends as his; and therefore political influences on economic studies are not always wholesome" (Marshall 1927, v). Perhaps the economists who originated the pure theory of trade placed the cart of politics and the policy of free trade before the horse of relevant, systematic, and scientific inquiry. It is duly noted in the literature that for many economists the Ricardian theory of static comparative advantage served as an underlying rationale for the politics of the free trade battle that ultimately resulted in the repeal of the Corn Laws in 1846 (Condliffe 1950, 203–236; Cunningham 1904).

It is far more publicly palatable and practical for power elites to have their policies directed and rationalized by systematic "scientific" inquiry rather than by political maneuver organized by blatant political interests and power. It is no wonder, then, that Viner states, "many of the best expositions of the classical theory of international trade were made in the course of discussion of proposals for legislation, and that, *Hansard*, the record of the British parliamentary debates, is not a bad source from which to learn what classical theory of international trade was and that it . . . was formulated *primarily with a view to its providing guidance on questions of national policy*" (Viner 1952, 15; 1965, 437; italics added). In their desire to implement the free trade policy agenda and to prove the validity of their theory, maybe orthodox economists lost sight of empirical economic realities, especially in relation to their underlying, fictional assumptions.

And while the list of the eleven assumptions is long and strikingly irrelevant to the real world, more could be added, such as the assumption of rational *homo economicus*. Another extremely important assumption, and one not usually given its warranted attention, is that economic growth as a simplistic outward shifting P-P curve is assumed to be the conceptual equivalent of the complex cultural processes of economic development (recall Meier 1968, 22). But as Schumpeter and Myrdal among others have observed, economic growth is not synonymous with economic development (Brinkman 1995).

Static Versus Dynamic

A central issue deserving of further explication relates to the static nature of the pure theory of trade. And while the list of the eleven assumptions could be expanded to include additional assumptions, another big error resides in the assumption that the world is static and fixed rather than dynamic and evolving. At best, a shifting P-P curve demonstrates "comparative statics," not a dynamic analysis. Assuming "comparative statics" to be a conceptual equivalent of a dynamic analysis would be tantamount to assuming that shuffling a deck of cards, or moving marbles around in a fish bowl from one equilibrium position to another, over time, constitutes a dynamic process. Change has taken place, a new equilibrium has been achieved, but nothing has really been transformed. The structure being analyzed is still the same. Not only heterodox economists, but supporters of the pure theory of trade, themselves, concede the point that the pure theory of trade constitutes a static framework.[18]

An evolutionary analysis, relevant to the dynamics of development, is demarcated by structural transformation of the social and the cultural (Dugger and Sherman 2000, 7, 121). Structural transformation is essential for a dynamic and evolutionary analysis of the economic process. A dynamic analysis is characterized by institutional transformation and adjustment (Kuznets 1930, 432). This perspective is expressed by LDC nations: "[D]eveloping nations attack traditional theory as static and irrelevant to the development process. They view traditional trade theory as involving *adjustment* to existing conditions, while development requires *changing* existing conditions" (Salvatore 1998, 331). Consequently, a dynamic process relates to a metamorphosis and transformation of structure. This important and relevant distinction has been noted by Frank Knight: "One of the major errors of the classical tradition [is] that it failed, and still largely fails to make a sharp and correct theoretical distinction between the working of a system under given conditions and, including the movement towards equilibrium, changes in the given conditions or content of the system itself."[19]

While Knight's critique might accurately be directed at others representing the classical paradigm, it is not applicable to the contributions of Adam Smith. As noted previously, Smith did offer a theory of trade that included the dynamics of acquired absolute advantage as well as the productivity doctrine. And while other economists writing in the neoclassical tradition searched for the Holy Grail in the form of a dynamic theory of trade, Adam Smith had already provided what should have been accepted as a seminal contribution. Ironically, a common critique raised in praising the virtues of a pure theory of trade is that Adam Smith was a poor theorist whose free trade theories lacked "analytical rigor" (Bloomfield 1994, 109). In making the theory more "rigorous," practitioners of the pure theory of trade obfuscated and avoided any realistic understanding of the dynamics of international trade interrelated to the processes of economic development. That Great Britain and the United States, in the past, and Japan, more recently, achieved positive trade balances and improved global competitiveness resulted from acquiring absolute cost advantages. Their greatest surges of growth and development were predicated on policies of protection, not free trade. It is absolute cost advantages that cut the competitive edge, not comparative cost ratios. Such cost ratios are fictitious and relate to intuitive reasoning. They lack empirical reference as any basis to serve as a measure for the whole of the trading process.

In the past some economists have argued that the theory of absolute advantage constituted a logical impossibility and should be ignored and discarded (Brandis 1967, 169, 174). More recently, however, arguments have been presented to promote "A Rehabilitation of Absolute Advantage" (MacDonald and Markussen 1985). "Our hypothesis is thus that absolute advantages *dominate* over comparative advantages as determinants of trade flows" (Dosi, Pavitt, and Soete 1990, 148–151). That Britain once exported textiles and dominated the global economy and trade in the hegemonic Pax Britannica of the nineteenth century was not a function of relative or comparative costs, but rather, and obviously, the result of that British innovation, the first Industrial Revolution. The patterns and expansion of trade that ensued relate to the dynamics of technological evolution, which in turn reflect absolute cost advantages.

It appears that Ricardo's static theory of comparative advantage shunted classical trade theory off a potentially dynamic track, laid by Adam Smith, onto a static track leading to a way station. Smith was clearly wiser than David Ricardo. The "law of comparative advantage" served to support a global colonial structure based upon specialization of production. This specialization between the center (industrial producers) and periphery (agricultural producers) was enthusiastically endorsed, later, by neoclassical economists writing in the Ricardian tradition of the pure theory of trade.

Given Adam Smith's dynamics and triumph over the statics embedded in the pure theory of trade, it is appropriate to ask whether the neoliberal predilections toward laissez-faire and free trade are the best policies to pursue. Are we to assume that unilateral, unregulated free trade is the best policy to promote absolute advantages for the LDC world as well as for the advanced countries (ACs)? In fact, a basic message of this book is that a policy of one-way, nonreciprocal free trade and its damaging, asymmetrical results generally retard and inhibit a nation's drive toward economic development and human progress. Certainly this realization did not escape Hamilton, List, Myrdal and Prebisch, among many others. Nor has it escaped the leaders of East Asia.

If the United States is to compete in the globalization game of competitiveness and nurture a sound trade policy, it needs to innovate more relevant theories of trade to serve as concomitants to economic development and human progress. The question now becomes whether the neoliberal policies currently at the "commanding heights" and oriented toward laissez-faire and free trade will promote the achievement of acquired absolute advantages as a sine qua non for competing in the evolving global marketplace.

4

Dynamics of Absolute Advantage and Economic Development

Richard L. Brinkman

The question now becomes—how does a nation acquire absolute cost advantages? Would Adam Smith's advocacy of policies oriented toward laissez-faire and free trade, as the neoliberal predilections also assume, suffice? Other than comparing Smith to the Ricardian statics embodied in the "law" of comparative advantage, what if one were to interject other competing alternatives offered by heterodox economists as a basis for comparison? Would Adam Smith, then, still be the wisest of all, overall, after all? An answer to this question would require a better understanding of the processes of economic development. In evaluating "gains" from trade, a major concern relates to the impact of trade on economic development. According to Gerald Meier: "Dominating all issues. . . . Can foreign trade have a propulsive role in the development of a country?" (Meier 1968, 215). The problem of advancing and sustaining economic development relates to the not only less-developed countries (LDCs), but also is of concern for the ongoing development of mature nations.

Globalization does not simply start or stop at the water's edge, but also significantly impacts a nation's domestic economy, as well. But the static, pure theory of trade, with its "as if" assumptions related to shifting production-possibilities (P-P) curves, hardly constitutes a model for any meaningful or in-depth, rigorous analysis of economic development. Trade theory needs to incorporate a better understanding of the cultural complexities and evolutionary processes relevant to a theory of economic development. The process of globalization, dominating our current economic epoch, manifests an evolutionary dynamic of development as transformation.

Structural Transformation: The Secretary-Lawyer Analogy

The analytical conundrum, in applying a static framework to a dynamic process, is illustrated by the secretary-lawyer analogy. Granting that a lawyer has an absolute advantage in both legal and secretarial work, (but discounting the gender references which some might feel to be offensive today), Milton and Rose Friedman conclude as to the merits of specialization, that "both he and the secretary are better off if he practices law and the secretary types letters" (Friedman and Friedman 1980, 45). This view is widely supported in the literature. The conclusion, based upon comparative advantage and intuitively obvious, is that a lawyer would be better off by specializing in legal work and having the secretary specialize in typing and secretarial work (Bloomfield 1994, 111). Of course a lawyer would be irrational to opt for doing secretarial work, after acquiring absolute cost advantages by becoming a lawyer and achieving the higher income and perks that presumably go along with being a lawyer.

The problem, in assuming that the lawyer had absolute advantages in both legal and secretarial work, was also the problem addressed by David Ricardo with the "doctrine of comparative costs."[1] But do the conclusions and logic based upon the static assumptions, inherent in the theory, necessarily follow? Case 1, from Table 4.1, Statics and Dynamics of the Secretary-Lawyer Analogy, illustrates a situation in which the lawyer has an absolute advantage in both legal and secretarial work. It is assumed that the secretary and lawyer work one-half time at both legal and secretarial work for a total combined income of $80,000. After reading Ricardo and learning about comparative cost advantages, they both now work full-time, one specializing in "more productive" legal work and the other in secretarial. The logic of comparative cost ratios appears vindicated, in that total income increases from $80,000 up to $120,000. Both receive increases in income, though not necessarily equally. Case closed? Not quite!

The secretary might also have become a lawyer, if only the circumstances and chance tumblers of life had been different. Case 3 presents such an outcome. Given a dynamic solution, like structural transformation, the secretary in becoming a lawyer would have acquired absolute cost advantages and would now make $100,000. Total income for both, consequently, goes up to $200,000. Although American experience seems to be moving this way, admittedly we cannot all become lawyers. This is not to say, however, that all nations cannot achieve modern economic growth and thereby acquire absolute cost advantages as well, given the dynamics of structural transformation. If, further, we equate the lawyer with an industrial nation (Britain) and the secretary with an agrarian nation (Ricardo's Portugal or current LDCs), total world income as well as the income of individual nations would be advanced considerably via the dynamics of structural transformation. LDCs are cultures specializing in and locked into an agrarian (secretarial) stage of economic development. Such cultures are limited in economic capacity and characterized by low standards of living. LDCs locked into a traditional or agrarian stage of pre-Newtonian science experience a path of growth in the

Table 4.1

Statics and Dynamics of the Secretary-Lawyer Analogy (dollars/year)

	Nation (A) Secretary/ Agriculture	Nation (B) Lawyer/ Industry	
Static: Comparative advantage			
Case #1. Nonspecialization			
Secretary Wine/agriculture	10,000.00	16,000.00	
Lawyer	4,000.00	50,000.00	
Cloth/industry	14,000.00	66,000.00	80,000.00
Case #2. Specialization			
Secretary Wine/agriculture	20,000.00	* * * * *	
Lawyer	* * * * *	100,000.00	
Cloth/industry	20,000.00	100,000.00	120,000.00
Dynamic: Acquired absolute advantage			
Case #3. Rational-structural transformation Secretary Wine/agriculture	* * * * * *	* * * * *	
Lawyer	100,000.00	100,000.00	
Cloth/industry	100,000.00	100,000.00	200,000.00

Source: The empirical accuracy of the data is not necessary in order to validate the internal logic or conclusions derived therefrom—compare Ricardo (1912, 81–83), as a basic exemplar of the intuitive and deductive logic and methodology.

form of an "S" growth curve like the sigmoid, logistic, or Gompertz (Rostow 1960). Growth, as a quantitative increase of more of the same, such as more cotton or wine, is ultimately manifest in an asymptotic ceiling of stagnation.

Given the logic of comparative cost ratios, the lawyer employs the secretary and buys (imports) those services, even though produced less efficiently. In this "fallacy of composition," what seems logical for individual behavior is then transferred to the well-being of a whole nation. This logic supposedly explains why it would be rational for a nation to import goods even though they are produced less efficiently abroad. Inefficiently produced usually means production at higher costs and, consequently, at higher prices. Granting ceteris paribus assumptions, the "doctrine of comparative costs" consequently suggests that it would be logical to import goods that are more expensive and cost more. This is an irrational, not rational, conclusion. Does this mark the final folly of the rational species Homo economicus? To assume that wheat costing $2.00 per bushel, having been produced less efficiently abroad (an absolute disadvantage), would be imported, even granting a more efficient domestic producer (having an absolute advantage) offering wheat at $1.50 per bushel, defies the basic logic contained in downward-sloping demand curves. Do Californians import BMWs by comparing cost ratios between automobiles versus wine, or simply because the given absolute price of the BMW, ceteris paribus, represents a better buy?

Again, granting ceteris paribus assumptions, acquired absolute cost advantages are more important in determining the flow of goods between countries than are relative cost ratios. What Britain produced and exported, in the form of textiles, was not based upon relative cost considerations between cloth and wine. Rather, Britain acquired absolute cost advantages from having been transformed through the innovation of the Industrial Revolution. Like the lawyer, Britain achieved an absolute advantage in both agricultural and industrial production.[2] Therefore "what" is produced and sold in international markets resides in the dynamics of development, rather than relative price ratios.

By comparison, international specialization based upon static comparative cost ratios offers a danger of sclerotic stagnation and economic stagnation in a "staple trap." It follows that "[r]egions or nations which remain tied to a single export commodity almost inevitably fail to achieve sustained expansion" (North 1961, 3).[3] Consequently, nations need to experience broad economic development in order to acquire absolute cost advantages and move beyond the limitations related to natural absolute advantage. The dynamics of development as to conception and theory, not a static framework of specialization, serves as a necessary concomitant to a warranted and scientific theory of international trade. "[T]he nineteenth-century theory of international division of labor . . . is hardly tenable" (Kuznets 1968, 3, 80). Another institutional economist concurs: "As theory, the free trade doctrine is untenable" (Myrdal 1957, 143). As a result of applying the theory as a policy of free trade, which results in international specialization (such as secretaries and lawyers), the rich nations via processes of circular and cumulative causation become relatively richer and the poor nations relatively, and even in certain cases absolutely, poorer.

Dynamics of Economic Development: Concept and Theory

As many social scientists argue, today, "Globalization is not working for many of the world's poor. It is not working for much of the environment. It is not working for the stability of the global economy" (Stiglitz 2002, 214; Korten 1995; Greider 1997; and Barber 1995). To currently argue that problems associated with adequate rates of economic growth have been solved; that the needs for labor and jobs and ecological sustainability are being met; that unregulated capital movements are benign; that the U.S. balance of payments is improving; that the transition from Communism to market economies has been smooth; that the development of LDCs is being promoted; and that global harmony and peace prevail, as provisioned by the current structure of globalization, constitutes a bit of a stretch, even for sanguine social scientists. The Battle in Seattle and the continuing "war against globalization" suggest growing public disillusion. The globalization debate and the portending societal crisis for the future are predictable given a continuation of the current neoliberal policy orientation.

It is arguable, however, that the "problem is not with globalization but how it is being managed" (Stiglitz 2002, 214). Neoliberal ideology and predilections, or "market fundamentalism," offer, from the stratosphere of "the commanding heights," one style of management. The free marketeers, Friedrich Hayek, Milton Friedman, Jeffrey Sachs, Lawrence Summers, and Keith Joseph, argue that laissez-faire and free trade policy governing the globalization process, sans government intervention, will produce a salubrious solution. The underlying assumption is that the operation of a self-regulating market will ameliorate problems and imbalances. Stiglitz's book, *Globalization and Its Discontents*, in support of the Keynesian mainstream and development process, provides a good offset to currently fashionable neoliberal ideology.

However, there is need to go beyond the Keynesian paradigm as a critique of current globalization and move into the more heterodox arena of economic thought, which can be especially relevant to a theory of economic development. The paradigm of Keynesian economics is also static, and perhaps too orthodox, and too conservative. The supposition of a self-regulating market may warrant a stiffer critique than Stiglitz offers. George Soros argues that "market fundamentalism is today a greater threat to an open society than any totalitarian society"; "The development of a global economy has not been matched by the development of a global society" (Soros 1997, 45; 1998, xxii; 2002, xx, xxix).

Karl Polanyi stands out as a leading social scientist in this genre of thought (Polanyi 1944; Baum 1996; Mendell and Salée 1991; Stanfield 1986). This point of view, stressing the antagonism between the application of an alleged self-regulating free market system and its incompatibility with a viable, functioning society, is increasingly being referred to in the globalization debate.[4] Polanyi's warning of a collapse of society seemed to have been borne out in the disruptions of the 1930s. In analyzing the globalization process taking place today, with some similarities to the 1930s, are we witnessing a case of Polanyi, déjà vu?

To further delve into questions raised by neoliberals, Keynesians, and heterodox economists, there is a need to formulate a better theory of economic development and evolution as a concomitant to a dynamic theory of trade. Given the complexities involved in the globalization process and economic development, the formulation of such a theory should be predicated on an interdisciplinary and holistic methodology. What constitutes the dynamics of the process, who or what has the power to control it, how is this being done, and for which purpose?

The economist Gunnar Myrdal offered a conception of economic development that included the dynamic processes of structural transformation. The social and cultural are not taken as given or fixed parameters by Myrdal, but treated as qualitative, "non economic" variables. Myrdal's conception—"the movement of the whole social system upward is what all of us in fact mean by development"—is clearly outside the neoclassical paradigm limited to an outward shift of the P-P curve and Marshallian offer-curve analysis (Myrdal 1974).

Myrdal's conceptualization, of the substantive nature of the process of economic development, coincides with the seminal anthropological conception of culture "as that complex whole," offered by Edward Tylor in 1871 (Kroeber and Kluckholm 1952). Consequently, it is culture that constitutes the substantive grist for the mill of the process of economic evolution. Humankind's culture comprises what grows and develops in the process of economic evolution (Brinkman 1992). Material technology as aspects of material culture—bridges, boats, buildings, and technology—as capital and consumer goods, along with their social concomitants, advance as an integrated whole in the overall dynamics of cultural evolution.

But if a culture simply grows quantitatively, does it also experience development? Schumpeter clearly drew a distinction: "Nor will the mere growth of the economy . . . be designated here as a process of development. For it calls forth no qualitatively new phenomenon" (Schumpeter 1983, 63). Orthodox economists, by comparison, in discussing not only trade theory, but growth theory in general, often assume that growth and development "are in essence synonymous" (Meier and Baldwin 1959, 2; Meier 1968, 22). But why not assume that economic growth is the conceptual equivalent of development? For if an economy, nation, or culture achieves the level of approximately $20,000 GNP per capita, is not such growth also indicative of development? Culture does not mark time and stand still in a static mold or given structure but, rather, evolves over time. And though evolution comprises the processes of both growth (as reproduction and replication) and development (as transformation and metamorphosis), it is the latter process that dominates the dynamics of structural transformation and is manifest in big improvements in productivity.

But as culture evolves, how then to demarcate or describe its transformation? Sociologists identify the evolutionary and structural transformation of culture in the form of a sequential pattern of "logistic surges" in which one S curve is superimposed on another.[5] The result is manifest in an accelerated evolution of culture. Empirically, this pattern of "logistic surges" appears in the overall culture as the stages of economic development. This sequential pattern also appears in parts of the whole, such as of transportation technology and energy transformation, as cases in point (Hart 1946).

Humankind achieved growth in the speed of travel to the current level of 20,000 miles an hour not by growing more feet or running faster. That speed was achieved through a sequential, structural transformation of transportation technology from foot travel to space rocketry. Similarly, the pattern prevails for culture as a whole. Humankind did not achieve $20,000 GNP per capita levels of income by "growing" more hoes and plows, or more bows and arrows. Humankind achieved the $20,000 level through a sequential, structural transformation manifest in the stages of culture evolution from "hunting and gathering" to, ultimately, an "Industrial Revolution" characterized by modern economic growth (Easterlin 1996, 16).

Ongoing growth within the confines of a given structure cannot continue indefinitely. A dugout canoe cannot grow to the size of the *Queen Mary*, nor a tepee into a skyscraper. "Growth of a university from 5,000 to 50,000 students is clearly not just a linear increase in size but a massive upheaval in structure as well" (Bell 1973, 174). Given the "principle of similitude," ongoing, *sustained* growth implies a need for ongoing structural transformation—that is, the process of economic development.[6] Growth, as the quantitative, comprises processes of reproduction and replication, whereas development, as the qualitative, relates to processes of structural transformation and metamorphosis. Consequently, there can be only limited "growth" without development; the two concepts are not synonymous, as neoclassical trade theory and as most mainstream economists lead us to believe (Clower, Dalton, Hawitz, and Walters 1966; Brinkman 1995, 1992).

Economic development entails a process of sequential, structural transformation fed by the dynamics of technological advance. According to Schumpeter, "Add as many mail coaches as you please, you will never get a railway thereby" (Schumpeter 1983, 64). Similarly, the antebellum South pursued agrarian specialization in the production of more and more cotton, a "staple trap." Such specialization, ultimately to be manifest in a sigmoid curve of growth, led to a sclerotic reinforcement of slavery and the plantation system. Such a culture was not suitable for modern economic growth and served to retard its innovation. Comparable systems of serfdom or slavery, and their embedded illiteracy, resist a science-based technology characterizing modern economic growth (Kuznets 1973, 247). This is the plight of LDCs (secretarial) that specialize in agrarian production. Such static specialization explains the structural rigidity of Rostow's traditional societies, as stated earlier, and places a ceiling on their capacity to continue to grow and develop.

More cocoa beans, or more wine produced by Portugal (the Ricardian case), in the promotion of a staple trap of narrow specialization, may retard the structural dynamics characteristic of economic development. The "magnificent dynamics" associated with the process of economic development, constitute the basic heterodox position associated with the contributions of Hamilton, List, Myrdal, Prebisch, and others (Baumol 1951, 6, 11–51). But their contributions are neglected in the textbook literature, especially in the field of international economics. By comparison, John S. Mill's claim that "foreign trade . . . sometimes works sort of an industrial revolution in a country whose resources were previously undeveloped" falls flat (Mill 1911, 351).[7] Merely increasing production is not synonymous with economic development, which by comparison constitutes a sequential pattern of logistic surges in which one structure gives rise to and is transformed into the next—that is the "principle of similitude" as delineated by Daniel Bell and Talcott Parsons (Brinkman 1995).

In the literature, economic development is usually relegated to the category of technological advance. "Economic development is fundamentally a product of technological change. . . . Yet traditional economic models provide little help in understanding this process" (Dosi, Tyson and Zysman, 1989, 19). To Kuznets, modern economic growth was spawned in a crucible of a "scientific epoch." Science-based technology constitutes the key to the understanding of the dynamics propelling modern economic development and growth. The additions to human knowledge are of major significance and importance in shaping the course of modern economic growth. And modern economic growth, in turn, is characterized by increases in production, social transformation, and a global spread.[8]

Kuznets's emphasis on the advance of science appears on firm ground in that technology is universally conceptualized as applied knowledge. And technology constitutes the dominant variable invoked by economists to explain the dynamics of development and evolution. A conception of technology, consequently, is crucial. Both Kuznets and Myrdal, among others, understand technology to include both the material and the social.[9] The steam engine as material technology also required a concomitant factory system, railroads, and shipping in order to function. Thus, technology should be seen in holistic terms, comprising both material and nonmaterial culture. Such a cultural conception of technology explains why some cultures (civilizations)— potentially including the United States—rise and fall and/or stagnate.[10]

The construct of social organization as social technology serves as a necessary condition in the control of material technology. This explanation of the process of economic development and the dynamics of cultural evolution, and Kuznets's emphasis on the advance of useful knowledge and technology, provide a framework upon which to build a dynamic theory of relative or comparative advantage. A nation's relative or comparative advantage to another nation is based not upon relative cost ratios (David Ricardo) but rather upon acquired absolute cost advantages (Adam Smith). The problem concerns how, then, to relate international trade to a theory of the production and accumulation of useful knowledge and technology. Such dynamic theory is outside the paradigm of the simplistic, though "rigorous," Heckscher-Ohlin model and the static, pure theory of international trade. Consequently, it is no wonder that the static theory of comparative advantage is currently under siege (Thurow 1996, 65–74; Irwin 1996, 2002). This is manifest in myriad attempts to formulate "new" theories of trade. "The need for a new paradigm" appears warranted (Porter 1990, 1–30).

New Theories of Trade: Toward Dynamic Comparative Advantage

Economic development does not simply lead to a more efficient allocation of given resources within a given structure (Arndt 1981, 463). The "principle of similitude" mandates a transformation of structure. To understand the dynamic processes of development, one must understand structural transformation, especially of social institutions. Essentially this process relates to the achievement of acquired absolute advantage and constitutes a prerequisite for the formulation of a dynamic theory of international trade. Consequently, the neoclassical paradigm that equates an outward shift of the P-P curve with the process of economic growth (assumed to be synonymous with economic development), as argued above, appears an overly simplistic abstraction, and far too primitive as a conception of economic development.

This is recognized by "new" theories of trade appearing in the literature that attempt to incorporate "new" theories of economic growth and technological change into a dynamic theory of trade. Of special interest is that this literature comes not simply from heterodox economists, but from neoclassical and mainstream economists themselves. For example, Robert Solow employed technology as an exogenous variable (Solow 1957). Solow's theory, itself, came under siege by other mainstream economists who directed attention to the origination and innovation of theories incorporating technology as an endogenous variable. These new trade theories are associated and interrelated with the contributions of Maurice Scott, Paul Romer, and Robert Lucas, in their new theories of growth (Grossman and Helpman 1991, 22–42; Aghion and Hewitt 1998; Brinkman and Brinkman 2001). However, while making an attempt to step into the "black box" of technological change, they apparently "forgot to bring a flashlight'" (Brinkman and Brinkman 2001, 509).

Thus, in attempting to make technology endogenous, Scott offered a conception of technology that is equated to that of gross investment. "Indeed, with my definition of investment, separation is strictly meaningless," he wrote, and "inventions are best regarded as a form of investment" (Scott 1989, 95, xxxii; Aghion and Hewitt 1998, 2, 99). This conception tends to obliterate a distinction between technological accumulation and technological advance. Alternatively, however, because technological advance is fundamentally predicated on the evolution of science and useful knowledge, this process might be "quite unrelated to the terms of factor supply" (Abramovitz 1993, 237). Rather than manifesting new forms of technological innovation, capital accumulation may simply represent a quantitative growth process in the replication of a technology already in existence.[11] Further, these so-called new theories of growth still carry forward the underlying neoclassical assumption that mere growth is synonymous with development (Lucas 1988).

Consequently, through a magical conceptual sleight of hand, given the assumption that economic growth is synonymous with development, theories and policies of economic growth are assumed, ipso facto, to be also theories and policies of economic development. There is no need to engage or formulate a theory of development that would include the dynamics of cultural evolution and all the complex variables that this entails. The emphasis of Grossman and Helpman upon technology and the role of knowledge, the diffusion of knowledge, and making trade theory permeable to a "dynamic evolution of comparative advantage" is consequently highly commendable (Grossman and Helpman 1991, 177–205). However, given their neoclassical orientation, the Heckscher-Ohlin conclusions reached by Grossman and Helpman are somewhat predictable: "Strikingly, we found that long-run patterns of specialization and trade are determined solely by countries' relative factor endowments" (Grossman and Helpman 1991, 206).

Yet other economists emphasize that "comparative advantage based upon the factors of production is not sufficient" and that "insufficiency of factor advantage in explaining trade is widely accepted" (Porter 1990, 12, 16). Unfortunately, some attempts at "new" trade theory still end up with the same old paradigmatic blinders contained in the "flawed" Heckscher-Ohlin matrix and theory.[12] "[S]uch new trade theory pushes the limits of traditional thought . . . but it still reflects many of the assumptions and foundations of such thought . . . the theory is centrally concerned with the problem of the optimal allocation of resources" (Dosi, Tyson, and Zysman 1989, 11).

But the fact that a nation has an abundance of capital, as a factor input, and consequently absolute advantages in the production of knowledge and technology, is not fixed or given by nature. Capital and its accumulation (abundance) is not a function of natural absolute advantage but is predicated on advances that lead to acquired absolute advantage. Capital is a social product and as such in its accumulation is functionally related to a given stage and level of culture accumulation and evolution. An LDC nation can consequently make the transition from capital scarcity to capital increases and abundance via economic development in the process of acquiring an absolute advantage. This point also negates the incorrect and static assumption of fixed quantitative amounts of capital inherent in the Heckscher-Ohlin model. Therefore, once again, it is the stage of economic development that determines relative absolute cost advantages, manifest in what is traded and trade patterns, not relative comparative cost ratios. This dynamic position is consequently more in line with the contributions of Hamilton and List rather than that of Ricardo, as well as some more attempts to formulate "new" trade theories by Grossman and Helpman.

Trade between Somalia and Ethiopia, the agrarian (secretarial) LDCs, for example, is naturally limited in product diversity and volume. In terms of "what" is traded between LDCs and ACs (advanced countries), how can a traditional LDC country have the option to specialize and export a product that it is technologically incapable of producing and for which a comparative cost ratio is nonexistent? The "what" that is traded by advanced countries has much wider diversity as to product content and volume. In explaining trade patterns, the largest volume of trade takes place between the mature industrial countries, rather than between mature nations and LDCs, or among LDCs themselves. Those trade patterns are explained by absolute cost advantages rather than comparative cost ratios. Consequently, if more trade is the desideratum, this goal can be achieved not by specialization and nurturing more trade between industrial nations in the center and LDCs in the periphery, but rather by having all nations achieve modern economic development.

By comparison, Friedrich List related trade theory and trade patterns to a stage of economic and cultural development. The stage methodology is still widely ignored in the current literature of mainstream trade theory. But the level or stage of economic development is of central importance to an explanation of a nation's acquired absolute advantage. In contrast, Ricardo's static comparative cost doctrine is based on a limited insight that is ahistorical, nonevolutionary, and unrelated to economic development or changing structures of technological capability.

Ricardo's static view was historically reinforced by the practitioners of the free trade orthodoxy; heterodox views were largely ignored. But this was a mistake. In this context, Marshall noted: "But killing the messengers did not kill the hostile troops of which the messengers brought record . . ." and therefore the arguments were never properly refuted (Marshall 1927, 759–762). Heterodox messengers of dynamic concerns—for example, the concerns embodied in the infant industry argument—were essentially ignored. The infant industry argument of Hamilton and others, although initially ignored, was finally accepted, much later, by Mill and Marshall. Similarly, while the infant industry argument was ultimately recognized as a limitation on free trade policy, the message and messengers in support of an evolutionary framework and more active development policy are still being ignored in the current orthodox literature, textbook or otherwise, in dealing with trade theory.

Jacob Viner has been recognized, and deservedly so, for his scholarship and erudition in the fields of international economics and the history of economic thought. Inexplicably, however, in explaining the relation of trade to development, Viner apparently failed to recognize fully that the path of economic development, to its most advanced level, involves modern economic growth and industrialization. Viner tends to mitigate the role played by industrialization, conceptualized as the movement out of agriculture into industrial production, as one of the defining characteristics of modern growth (Kuznets 1973). "That agriculture is not necessarily associated with poverty becomes obvious when one considers Australia, New Zealand, Denmark, or Iowa and Nebraska" (Viner 1952, 62–73, 144). Economists "should insist that scarce resources shall be allocated to their socially most productive use, and wasting resources on romantic dreams is not such a use" (1952, 73). But Iowa, California, New Zealand, Denmark, and so on, are not mainly agricultural cultures. They are efficient in agricultural production because they constitute integral parts of regions that have utilized modern technology extensively and that have industrialization as a general characteristic. Thus, as even Viner stressed, there is not "any marked backwardness in the technology of the agriculture of Denmark, New Zealand, of England or of Iowa" (144).

A key to a rational trade policy is that it be based upon and interrelated to the dynamic forces inherent in the processes of economic development. Mill and Marshall apparently accepted this logic. It was the Industrial Revolution that enabled Britain to acquire absolute cost advantages and in the process accounted for British hegemony and trade dominance during the nineteenth century.[13] In fact, the advance toward modern economic growth and industrialization for Britain, the United States, Japan, South Korea, Taiwan, and so on has been based upon protection, and governmental promotion of industrialization. Modern economic growth was not achieved via a laissez-faire-oriented, unilateral free trade policy. This position is recognized by Yergin and Stanislaw, who point to the Japanese model that in turn was followed by other nations in Asia.[14] The epicenter of modern economic growth shifted from Britain to the United States, in turn accounting for U.S. hegemony and Pax Americana in most of the twentieth century and the ensuing high volume of U.S. trade. The epicenter of modern economic growth, conceivably, may now be shifting to Asia. It is mainly the internal development process and the achievement of acquired absolute advantages, and higher levels of productivity, that account for the volume of what is traded as well as the improved global competitiveness of developing nations. In this context it, has been the role of the developmental state to serve as the catalyst for the domestic achievement of modern economic growth and industrialization.[15]

Those nations who have benefited most from globalization "recognize the role that government can play in development rather than relying on the notion of a self-regulating market. . . . Government can, and has, played an essential role not only in mitigating these market failures but also in ensuring *social justice*" (Stiglitz 2002, 218). Consequently, the bottom line: Adam Smith was decidedly wiser than Ricardo and the practitioners of the pure theory of trade.

Hence, trade policies currently following the neoliberal paradigm, especially one-way, unilateral free trade policies, which obviously lack reciprocity, can operate negatively and retard economic development and prosperity, as Britain and the United States have come to realize. In rationalizing the benefits of unrestricted free trade, orthodox economists have become too limited and unrealistic.[16] The pragmatic dictum of Chinese leader Deng Xiaoping should prevail: it does not matter if the cat is white or black as long as it catches mice (Yergin and Stanislaw 1998, 194–216). The cat of government can play a strong role in the economic process. Orthodox economists, who espouse unilateral free trade, ignore asymmetrical global structural imbalances, the chronic U.S. trade and current account deficits, and so on, all of which is indicative of a long-term malaise and maladjustment currently characterizing the global as well as the American economy. To assume that the global economy is doing well because of increased, but unbalanced, trade fails to address how that "growth" has been achieved and distributed. That is, it ignores who really collects the bounty from the current globalization process as it is now being organized.

Toward Improved Trade Policy

Periods of anomalous results and maladjustments are indicative of cultural lags. Culture evolution does not advance as a synchronized or integrated whole. Some parts of culture accelerate faster than others and as a result produce periods of socioeconomic maladjustments (Brinkman and Brinkman 1997). One basic cultural lag that we now face pertains not only to trade policy, but also to the theory upon which such policy is based. "There need to be changes in institutions and mind-sets. The free market ideology should be replaced with analyses based on economic science, with a more balanced view of the role of government drawn from an understanding of both market and government failures" (Stiglitz 2002, 250). The current period of cultural lags and associated maladjustments requires more realistic theories of trade concomitant and relevant to the dynamics of economic development and culture evolution. Such theories would be a necessary condition for the formulation of a rational trade policy that would ameliorate and resolve the current economic problems that America faces. There is a need for a new game plan, a new logistic surge in the evolution of the science of economics, to address the new ball game being played in the global arena (Thurow 1996, 1–19; 1992, 259–299).

Basically, given the conception and theory of modern economic growth offered by Kuznets (1968), trade, if it is to serve a dynamic function in the domestic economy, must reinforce the advance of useful knowledge and technology. In this context, international trade serves as an umbilical cord of culture diffusion. There is a need to explore the gaps and analyze the vital links between trade, the environment, and culture (Lee 2000). The question then becomes who and/or what controls that advance of knowledge and technology. And, further, whose benefit does that control serve?

From a political standpoint, unrestricted U.S. free trade policies, especially on a unilateral basis, are becoming more difficult to sell. Even after being inundated by a multinational corporation (MNC) media blitz, presidential hype, and public relations overkill, we still find that "free trade gets an unfriendly reception" in the United States and in the groves of academe (Hammonds 1997, 34; Irwin 1996, 2002). Polls abound which indicate negative attitudes toward complete free trade vis-à-vis the negative impact on jobs, wages, and the environment.[17] Consequently, other than free-trade-oriented textbook writers, who really endorses an unrestricted free trade policy orientation?[18] Another way of phrasing the same question is: Who benefits from a unilateral free trade policy? The obvious answer appears hard to avoid—megacorporations and their lobbyists, an increasingly influential network of interest groups and elites.

It is the contention of John K. Galbraith that "economics divorced from consideration of the exercise of power is without meaning and certainly without relevance" (Galbraith 1983, xiii; 1973). It is impossible to inject MNC political power into a Marshallian, offer-curve framework. An increasing number of books draw attention to the political clout of MNCs.[19] Currently, many argue that the larger MNCs are as big and as powerful as nations. This power is translated not only into economic power, administered prices, and market control, but into political and legislative power as well. The simplistic market-versus-the-government debate, the focus of Yergin and Stanislaw, goes back to the days of mercantilism and the *Wealth of Nations*. It serves as a red herring to divert attention away from a basic issue. A fundamental issue for the current phase of megacorporate globalization resides in the domain of sovereignty.

This issue is addressed, currently, in a large literature juxtaposing nation-state sovereignty to that of the MNCs. Article XVI of the WTO and Chapter 11 of NAFTA certainly add credence to the fact that the sovereignty issue dominates.[20] And which source of power bears responsibility for such legislation and treaty provisions—the power of the tooth fairy or the MNC? Given this obvious battle over sovereignty and power, it is hard to agree with the claim that those who raise the sovereignty issue are "intellectually bankrupt" (Burtless, Lawrence, Litan, and Shapiro 1998, 26, 95, 118, 127). However, should not one expect that U.S. MNCs would use their power to promote "protectionist" trade policies *for their interests* as a means to maximize U.S. corporate profits? But why, then, do the MNCs use their political muscle to favor a unilateral, free trade policy orientation? Because asymmetrical, one-way free trade allows MNCs to relocate production to cheap labor markets.

The problem of MNC power dominating the current globalization process needs further analysis and explanation. Chief executive officer (CEO) profits are currently integrated into the whole of the process of megacorporate globalization, constituting Myrdal's framework of a vicious circle (Brinkman and Brinkman 2002). With American technological superiority during the immediate post–World War II, Bretton Woods era, it was widely assumed that even the unilateral opening of American markets, regardless of nonreciprocity, would still produce favorable results for the American economy (Atlantic Institute 1970). This overly optimistic attitude, as stated in Chapter 2 of this study, was especially apparent in the legislation passed during the Truman and Kennedy eras. However, it has become increasingly evident since the 1970s that as the world economy became more and more internationalized, the United States has not been meeting the increased global competition (President's Commission on Industrial Competitiveness 1985). The U.S. share in global markets has declined, and since the late 1970s the United States has suffered serious merchandise trade imbalance problems, indicative of maladjustment and economic malaise, from which the country has yet to recover. In fact, the most recent trade deficits are the largest ever experienced in the whole of American economic history.

The predominant reengineering or structural change taken by corporate America to meet the globalization challenge appeared in policies directed toward cutting labor costs, the lowering and stagnation of real wages, part-time work, moving plants abroad, outsourcing and downsizing, a "race to the bottom," union bashing, cutting back on entitlements, cutbacks and even loss of pensions, underfunding of health and education, and so on. These jump-start policies, embedded in the ideology of neoliberalism, were sold to the American public as a pain necessary for gains to be accrued in reestablishing global competitiveness. This austerity objective for working Americans appears egregiously obscene given the "gain" reaped by CEO greed, the celebrated Enron debacle being one case in point among the many. Rather than pursuing the "high road," as noted by economist Dan Luria, policies embracing a "low road" of wage-cost reduction ensued (Madrick 1995, 78–83). The linchpin of this policy was provided by the MNC orientation toward unilateral free trade and the use of cheap foreign labor. This outsourcing, called a "race to the bottom," is predicated on a potentially enormous untapped global supply of cheap labor (Tonelson 2000; Korten 1995, 229–238).

The next phase of this policy evolution is manifest in the results derived from "low road" policies. The empirical record here of "pain" is clear in that real wages stagnated or even declined in certain instances. This contradicted the goals and policy recommendations set forth by the President's Commission on Competitiveness. Attempts at a restoration of American global competitiveness should not be predicated on a reduction in American standards of living (President's Commission 1985, 6). Yet this is what has happened, as reflected in the very title of Alan Tonelson's book: *The Race to the Bottom: Why a World-Wide Worker Surplus and Uncontrolled Free Trade Are Sinking American Living Standards.* The impact on American standards of living has been manifest in a stagnation of real wages, loss of jobs, redistribution of income to the rich, reduction in entitlements, degradation of the environment, and so on. An alternative "high road" solution would have been to invest in skilled American labor as an asset to be developed through improvements in productivity, not as a burden or cost to be reduced. And as noted in Chapter 2 of this study, outsourcing has afflicted not only the unskilled but also the skilled, an issue discussed and debated in the literature (Davis 1999). Exporting service and professional jobs, and relying on skilled foreign labor, diminishes American labor productivity and negatively impacts our whole educational structure. But the basic result and upshot of such "low road" policies has been, of course, to increase corporate profits in an attempt to satisfy CEO greed.

These newly founded globalization policies are also interconnected to the stock market. The increase in stock prices resembled a sophisticated sort of

Ponzi scheme. Corporate profits were now reflected in an increase of stock market prices. The scenario here is all too well known. The impact of corporate profits so achieved fueled a bullish stock market bubble. Unfortunately, the ensuing speculative excesses were orchestrated between Wall Street and corporate CEOs. The speculative bubble was doomed to burst. This vicious circle is now clear and within our grasp. In contradiction to the Adolph Berle and Gardiner Means thesis, arguing that corporate managers, rather than owners were in control, are we now witnessing a return to control by stock owners? (Brinkman and Brinkman 2002). Are we now experiencing what is referred to in the literature as "investor capitalism" (Useem 1996)?

The basic issues involve corporate excesses, such as "golden parachutes" and CEO bonuses and benefits that are tied to stock prices. A bonus allowing for stock to be purchased in the future at today's prices often results in a bonanza for corporate CEOs. An increase in stock prices, predicated on increases in profits, and in turn predicated on cost reduction, has an appealing logic for corporate CEOs. Policy concern is now directed by CEOs to cost reductions, however achieved. Such cost reductions come at the expense of labor and the environment rather than as a result of technological advance and increases in productivity. Accounting books are being cooked. CEOs have now broken the crust of a legal pursuit of profit maximization. CEO policies have now dipped into an abyss, a deep and dark reservoir of criminality. Can anyone surmise that globalization policies, so orchestrated, are working for the betterment of human welfare?

This situation constitutes a "virtuous" circle for the corporate CEOs and the elite top 3 percent benefiting from the profits and wealth redistribution now taking place in the United States. For everyone else, especially the upper middle class, the middle class, and the poor, the circle is vicious. Current revelations of CEO greed and selfishness no longer border on the obscene but now engage criminality. Even J.P. Morgan, hardly a stereotypical friend of labor or altruist, felt that a ratio between salaries and wages in the neighborhood of 20 : 1 was fair and adequate. Currently, Germany has a ratio of approximately 20 : 1 and Japan 16 : 1. The United States, led by corporate America, now has a ratio approximating 400 : 1. The "search for excess" has dominated the recent American economic landscape, often with rapacious results (Crystal 1991). And all of this CEO greed and exploitation was taking place while hard-working Americans were being downsized, experiencing a loss of jobs from outsourcing. And further, all of it fed the megacorporate globalization process led by a neoliberal paradigm of free markets and free trade.

With all this widespread "pain" for working America, the upper middle class, the middle class, and the poor, there has been insufficient "gain," and American competitiveness and economic renewal have yet to show any fundamental recovery.[21] U.S. balance of payments deficits are at their highest levels in American economic history. Long-term rates of economic growth, rather than short-run cyclical upturns, are still sluggish. A continued policy orientation toward unilateral, nonreciprocal free trade will only exacerbate the current American and global economic malaise. Free trade promulgated as policy—not tnat anyone abroad really wants it or intends to practice it— can be translated into an avoidance of warranted regulation of MNC power and low-road policies. The government, as humane referee in the economic process, is thrown out in the free trade bathwater. Unrestricted, one-way laissez-faire in trade policy becomes very costly negligence, reinforcing America's long-term economic decline.

A neoclassical synthesis, emphasizing exchange rate depreciation coupled with restrictive monetary and fiscal policy, is not sufficient.[22] Exchange rate realignment only constitutes a short-run palliative or Band-Aid solution. It has obviously proved ineffectual in eliminating U.S. competitiveness problems and deficits. The need is for structural change and trade policy reforms. Ongoing, unresolved trade and current account deficits will ultimately be translated into a reduced American economic growth, more structural unemployment, and risks of growing asymmetrical results—with increased social discord, as Polanyi déjà vu.

In conjunction with the concept of cultural lag, McClintock has presented the institutional view that "international trade is a dichotomous process in which technology tends to outpace the ability of institutions to adapt to the new exigencies" (McClintock 1996, 240, 242). The ongoing processes of acquired absolute advantages require the rebuilding of industrial strength in connecting trade to the dynamics of economic and cultural evolution. The opening of the American economy on a nonreciprocal basis promoted the current American economic malaise. Consequently, current U.S. policies oriented toward perpetuating unilateral free trade and indifferent to reciprocity hold back and retard American economic recovery and development. And it is technological advance, embedded in the processes of economic development, that in turn serves as the fountainhead for increases in productivity— the key for improving global competitiveness.

But the overall goal is not simply economic efficiency, increased rates of productivity, improved competitiveness, and the advance of economic development. Economic advance and sustainable development provide a necessary, though not sufficient, condition for ongoing human development and well-being. How should we make the evolutionary economic process sustainable so as to also promote basic human needs and rights? There is need for a broader "human development strategy." Significant work in this area, dating back to the early 1990s, is being done, suggested by the United Nations Development Programme (Griffin and McKinley 1994).

There is a need to address more realistically the issues of U.S. living standards, jobs, education, health, and environmental sustainability. The process requires a more participatory democracy, of, by, and for all the people and not simply for a privileged few. The process also requires skillful government rather than a mystical laissez-faire ideology, be it domestic or international (Schafer and Faux 1996, 321–333). What unilateral free trade advocacy really serves to accomplish is to grant greater license to MNC power.

Currently flawed trade policies based upon flawed trade theory produce flawed results. How then to implement a rational trade policy? And, especially, how then to address the current dominant problems in the areas of trade asymmetries, manifest in trade deficits and imbalances, and the lack of reciprocity embedded in our current trade policies?

What the Cuomo Commission annunciated in the early 1990s still holds true today: "The debate on trade policy has been constricted by a narrow, often ideological focus on rules of trade *rather than results for the United States.* An ideal set of 'free trade' rules guarantees neither trade balances for the United States nor prosperity for the world. . . . Our ultimate goals remain the same, more trade, more competition, more access to U.S. producers, the only difference is how to get there" (Cuomo Commission 1992, 200, 202).

5

Rebalancing U.S. Trade

William A. Lovett

Stubborn trade imbalances challenge America's role in the global economy. These imbalance and asymmetry problems grew serious in the 1980s and 1990s. Between 1981 and 2003, the United States suffered a total of –$4,000 billion in accumulated trade deficits, and –$3,500 billion in current account (balance of payments) deficits. As a result, the United States transformed itself from the world's largest creditor nation (+$325 billion) to become the biggest debtor country –$3,000 billion in these years. Because of weak U.S. trade policy, the United States suffered a net loss of at least 10 to 12 million manufacturing jobs, substantially distorted economic growth, and painful demoralization in some areas. With stronger, reciprocity-based trade policy, U.S. GNP could have been 10 to 20 percent higher.[1] Instead, weak U.S. trade policies increased structural unemployment and long-term poverty and aggravated crime. Enhanced inequalities and social conflict followed for many communities. In addition, the U.S. industrial, technology, and mobilization base has been weakened by this failure to enforce reasonable balance and reciprocity and by all these excessive and really unnecessary trade and current account deficits.

Also, many U.S. environmental, labor, and consumer interests insist that important U.S. trade concessions, especially in the GATT 1994 and WTO agreement, undermine generations of hard-fought progress in setting high standards for U.S. environmental protection, wages, and regulatory supervision.[2] Thus, weak U.S. trade bargaining eroded responsible safeguards for the environment, workers, and consumer protection in the United States and abroad. The problem is that multinational corporations (MNCs) can now move their plants to low-wage, poorly regulated, and minimally protected areas with complete freedom under GATT 1994. Environmental, labor, and consumer interests complain that wage freezes, reduced standards, and weaker protection are the inevitable result. From their perspective, only if imports can be limited from areas with weak environmental protection or minimal safeguards can we restore confidence in U.S. environmental standards and consumer laws and attain more reasonable wages and salaries in U.S. manufacturing. A new, reciprocity-based U.S. trade policy is needed for these purposes, and to restore overall balance in U.S. trading relationships.

U.S. industrial decline and job losses (watches, photographic equipment, clothing, shoes, appliances, and other consumer industries) were already occurring from the late 1940s to the early 1970s. This decline could be traced to previous trade concessions, and a failure to enforce reciprocity in the GATT rounds between 1947 and 1967. But in those years, the United States at least maintained overall trade balance (or modest trade surpluses), most of the time. Thus, while Americans accepted somewhat less overall industrial and economic growth as part of their Cold War strategy, and conceded industrial expansion to key allies and trade partners (especially Germany, Switzerland, Scandinavia, France, Italy, Japan, Taiwan, and Korea), the overall balance of U.S. trade between 1947 and 1974 suggests that the United States was living within its means from a merchandise trade point of view.[3] Although the United States invested a bit more abroad between 1958 and 1974 than it "earned," this extra outlay to promote industrial expansion and growth among U.S. allies, *and to support naval, ground, and air forces in defense of free world interests*, was largely welcomed by most of America's friends abroad.[4]

But the subsequent years (1975–2003) have brought serious and recently, large U.S. trade and current account deficits (Tables 1.1A /B and 1.2). Certainly it seems fair to say that the United States has been living beyond its means, in an external account sense, since the mid-1970s and particularly so from the early 1980s to 2003. Unfortunately, as a result of accumulated U.S. structural trade concessions, in the Kennedy Round, Tokyo Round, and Uruguay Round (along with the NAFTA and WTO agreements), the Americans created for themselves a very bad problem of entrenched asymmetries and trading imbalances.

To be sure, increased U.S. budget deficits, especially between 1983 and 1996, did aggravate the nation's external account and trade imbalance problems (Table 1.3). But the direct and more substantial cause of these large, chronic external deficits was U.S. trading policy. For the sake of Cold War–alliance politics and defense of free world interests, the United States simply accepted these trade imbalances without much protest. Why? Clearly Cold War politics was at work, but also U.S. trading policy was influenced, to an increasing degree since the 1960s, by major multinational corporations and banks. So far as U.S. trade policy making was concerned, big business (the MNCs) has become the main constituency on the details of America's economic relations with foreign countries.[5]

This situation—chronic, excessive U.S. trade and current account deficits—cannot continue much longer. Sooner or later, large and sustained imbalances of payments must be eliminated by countries suffering them. Eventually, all nations are forced to live within their means from an external accounts perspective. Somehow U.S. imports must be cut back and/or U.S.

exports increased (or some blend of the two must occur). By what adjustment process should this reconciliation be accomplished?

Alternative Solutions

Three strategies (or some combination) are available to the United States for its external imbalance predicament:[6] (1) substantial dollar devaluation and a likely weakening of the dollar's role as the major reserve currency, (2) a more reciprocity-based U.S. trade policy that emphasizes bilateral and regional relationships and enforces reasonable balance in U.S. trading, and (3) comprehensive renewal of U.S. technology, manufacturing, and export expansion.

Dollar Devaluation

Currency realignment is a normal adjustment process (in the era of floating exchange rates since 1971). Most countries must accept devaluation of their currencies when they suffer large and/or chronic external deficits. And, in fact, the United States already did suffer some long-term dollar devaluation as against *the strongest* currencies (Swiss franc, German deutschemark, and Japanese yen) (Table 1.4). But why has not dollar devaluation completely eliminated U.S. external deficits in the 1990s? One reason is that key export surplus countries (especially Japan, China, and other Asian nations) would not allow their currencies to appreciate sufficiently. In other words, they were afraid to weaken their exports into the United States. A substantial part of the continued U.S. trade deficit into the late 1990s and beyond might be explained this way. Thus, while the Japanese yen appreciated by 300 percent between 1983 and 1995, later the yen had fallen, from 1 dollar/80 yen in April 1995 to roughly 1 dollar/ 120 yen. But the yen appreciated recently, and reached 1 dollar/106 yen by early 2004. Secondly, the dollar remained the most reliable reserve currency in the world (especially as against currencies of developing countries). Large capital inflows keep coming into dollar accounts, U.S. government securities, and the U.S. stock and bond markets.[7] No other currency and capital market has had comparable size, reliability, or prosperity in which to allow foreign investors to park their medium-term assets. Only the euro of the European Union could become a serious rival for the dollar as a reserve currency and challenge U.S. capital markets as a convenient parking place for secure investments of liquidity. All this explains why the normal process of exchange rate realignment did not proceed to completion between the 1990s and the beginning of the twenty-first century. Key export surplus countries are afraid to let their currencies appreciate sufficiently, and heavy foreign capital inflows prop up the dollar because of its unique reserve currency attractiveness.

To what extent, then, can the United States expect to utilize dollar devaluation (or currency realignment) as the cure for its structural trade imbalance problems? So far, at least, although the dollar declined greatly from 1971 (in the era of floating exchange rates), U.S. trade imbalance problems gradually got worse (Tables 1.1A/B, 1.2, and 1.4). Even the Plaza Agreement, an orchestrated, two-year effort (1985 to 1987) to bring the U.S. dollar down from an excessive, unsustainable level failed to eliminate the U.S. structural trade deficits. Some improvement occurred in U.S. trade balances during the late 1980s, but not enough. In fact, asymmetrical openness (with the United States more open than most foreign markets) continued from the mid-1980s onwards, and it got worse as a result of GATT 1994 and the WTO agreement (Tables 1.1A/B, 1.2). NAFTA was sold in 1993 as a mutually balanced trade expansion deal. But after the Mexican peso devaluations of 1994 to 1995, the U.S. trade deficit with Mexico increased dramatically.[8] And, most recently, when Southeast Asian nations (Thailand, Philippines, Malaysia, and Indonesia) developed large export surpluses into the United States like Mexico in 1990 to 1993, these "new tigers" became hot emerging markets for foreign investment. But speculative excess again led to overinvestment, significant losses, and a corrective reaction. Devaluations and stock market declines followed for Thailand, Indonesia, and, to a lesser extent, Malaysia and the Philippines.[9] Thus, these new industrial countries retrenched imports, and hopes for bigger exports from the United States have been set back substantially; continued trade surpluses with the United States from Southeast Asia will be hard to eliminate quickly.

Accordingly, significant relief for the U.S. balance of payments does not seem likely soon. Many U.S. interest—banking, securities, insurance, importers generally, and MNCs relying on foreign parts or components—also would be upset by any big U.S. dollar devaluation. And politically, large-scale dollar devaluation would greatly weaken any incumbent presidential administration, whether Democratic or Republican. Devaluation does not seem realistic now as the main vehicle for U.S. external account adjustment. The United States must use other channels to correct and eliminate its large trade and current account deficits.

Reciprocal Trade Policy

The United States should recognize that the major and continuing source of its external deficits is a lack of effective trading reciprocity.[10] Although the United States began to open its markets under Reciprocal Trade Agreements (see Chapter 2), in fact, American trade negotiators generally accepted less than full reciprocity. As a result, asymmetries and trade imbalances developed between the United States and many of its trading partners. Some asymmetries still

operate between the United States and the EU, especially in more heavily subsidized EU agricultural markets, quicker access to EU antidumping settlement
relief, and more extensive industrial and regional subsidies in the EU. But,
apart from agriculture, the United States, EU, Canada, Australia, and New
Zealand are fairly open to each other, and trade has been substantially balanced most of the time (Table 1.2).

With Japan, unfortunately, trade remains unbalanced. This pattern has
persisted since the early 1980s. Although Japan dropped its tariffs to low
levels after the Tokyo Round (1975–1979), foreign manufactured imports
are disfavored under restrictive Japanese marketing customs, and through a
mix of language, cultural loyalties, and administrative guidance. U.S. manufactured exports to Japan are much smaller than U.S. manufactured imports
from Japan. And, as a result of asymmetrical policies with respect to foreign
companies, Japanese enterprises are allowed a much bigger role in the United
States than American companies in Japan (Table 1.2), U.S.–Japan trade has
been out of balance for nearly twenty years, with U.S. trade deficits averaging $50 billion or more annually since 1985.

With respect to new industrial countries (NICs), like Taiwan, South Korea,
China, Thailand, Malaysia, Brazil, and Mexico, U.S. markets are open. But
NICs generally employ substantial tariffs (averaging between 15 and 35 percent), extensive subsidies,[11] nontariff barriers, and restrictive regulations; some
NICs use exchange controls and/or capital market regulation, and most limit
access to their service markets. Intellectual property is often a problem for U.S.
companies, with extensive misuse by other countries without adequate compensation. For many NICs, therefore, it was only natural that export surpluses
would develop against the United States (Table 1.2). In 2002, U.S. trade deficits
were $111 billion with China, $70 billion with Japan, $40 billion with Mexico,
and $15 billion with Taiwan. Total U.S. trade deficits for Malaysia, Singapore,
Thailand, Indonesia, India, and Sri Lanka were $44 billion in 2002. In that year,
U.S. imports from all of Asia were $426 billion while U.S. exports to Asia were
$173 billion (with an all-Asia deficit of $253 billion). More recently, in less
developed countries (LDCs), similar asymmetries operate. But most LDCs have
not yet expanded their manufacturing and exports enough to have big trade
surpluses against the United States. Many would like to do so, hoping to emu-
late NIC success stories. So far, however, most LDCs are simply NIC wannabes.

Obviously, asymmetries distort investment and trade flows; they are the
main cause of United States structural trade deficits. Multinational corporations naturally locate manufacturing plants and service activities in lower-
wage, convenient, protected, and often subsidized national settings. If major
U.S. markets are completely open to the output of favored foreign operations, we have established a major, systemic bias toward deindustralization

and outsourcing in the United States, and toward relocation of U.S. manu-facturing, industrial technology, and engineering capabilities. Unfortunately, this has been the growing (though not intended) impact of U.S. industrial-trade policies over the last fifteen to twenty years. If the United States per-sists in this unequal, perverse policy, the inevitable consequence will be further erosion in its industrial, technology, and prosperity base. Not only are such policies self-destructive economically, they undermine ultimately the country's mobilization base for national security purposes (and America's ability to stay at the forefront of military, naval, and communications technology).[12]

The United States accepted some erosion of its industrial-technology lead (after World War II) in helping its allies in the Cold War, when U.S. per capita incomes remained well ahead of those of most other nations. But circumstances have changed. Now the United States has lost its lead in many areas of industry and technology, and U.S. per capita incomes no longer exceed average OECD levels by significant margins. Furthermore, growing poverty pockets and dis-tress for the American low-middle class are very serious, deeply troubling prob-lems. No longer can the United States afford to subsidize its competitors in the global marketplace with nonreciprocal trading policies.[13]

So what changes in U.S. trade policy make sense? An urgent goal must be to restore effective, overall reciprocity. Fortunately, for *most* OECD coun-tries (apart from the EU's Common Agricultural Policy), something close to reasonable trade balance and mutually open markets prevails (Table 1.2).[14] Thus, for countries with reasonably balanced and/or open trade with the United States no significant change in treatment is needed.[15] The big imbalance prob-lems in 2002 were Japan, China, Germany, Mexico, Taiwan, Malaysia, Thai-land, Indonesia, India, and Sri Lanka (Table 1.2).

	US$ (billions)		
Country	*Exports to U.S.*	*Imports from U.S.*	*U.S. trade deficits*
Japan	125	51	−70
China	133	22	−111
Hong Kong	10	13	+3
Germany	64	27	−36
Mexico	137	97	−40
Taiwan	36	20	−15
Malaysia	25	10	−11
Thailand	16	5	−11
Indonesia	10.3	2.6	−7.6
India	12.5	4.1	−8.4
Sri Lanka	1.9	0.2	−1.7
	527.5	250	−277

Worst of all, certainly, are the China and Japan imbalance problems. But the other countries, also had large, disproportionate trade surpluses with the United States (although their trade volume does not bulk so large as Japan's or China's).[16]

Clearly, if U.S. trade policy makers had enforced overall reciprocity with important U.S. trading partners, these large, excessive, and now chronic U.S. trade deficits could have been limited. But, even though belated, strong U.S. reciprocity and balancing measures should now be imposed within a reasonable transition period, say three to five years.

More specifically, what is the best, most efficient way for effective U.S. reciprocity to be enforced at this stage? A new U.S. trade policy must set overall balance in its external accounts as a top national priority and a major goal for macroeconomic policy. Fortunately, all other countries in the world are forced to live under comparable external account discipline. So most countries will readily understand the U.S. predicament and accept the need for the United States to put its own house in order. They will, in many cases, enjoy a wry satisfaction that the mighty United States too must submit to the disciplines of world currency markets and the International Monetary Fund (IMF). A few countries, such as by Japan, China, Taiwan, and Malaysia, may plead special circumstances and try to justify their disproportionate trade surpluses. But U.S. trade policy must focus on the largest, most disproportionate, and longest lasting trade surpluses as needing correction. Countries (and companies) that collaborate should be given easy, flexible treatment. But nations (and corporations) that resist or stonewall should be dealt with more harshly, with shorter deadlines. Thus, cooperation with the United States in solving its external account problem must be rewarded; but antagonism, noncooperation, and recalcitrance should be discouraged with higher prices for access to U.S. markets.[17]

Here is how the new, reciprocity-based U.S. trade policy should work. From this point forward, continued access to U.S. markets should be governed by overall balance, reciprocity, and the need to eliminate, within a few years, U.S. trade and current account deficits. Countries already equally open to U.S. companies and exporters, and those maintaining something close to overall balance, would enjoy continued access to U.S. markets. But corrective action would be taken under U.S. trade laws to enforce reciprocity and achieve reasonable trade balance within a few years against countries that enjoy large or disproportionate trade surpluses with the United States, except for vital natural resources (e.g. petroleum). Their collaboration would be solicited, and greatly appreciated, but the United States should protect its vital national interests and achieve an overall balance in trade within a few years.

Against large, disproportionate trade surplus countries, consolidated action should be brought by the U.S. government under Section 301 of the U.S. Trade Act of 1974 (as amended) and GATT Article XII (Balance of Payments Relief). If appropriate, GATT Article VI (Countervailing Duties for Subsidies or Dumping with Injury) to U.S. producers should be enforced against some countries. Normal U.S. relief against large, disproportionate trade surplus countries should be a 10 to 15 percent import surcharge, continued until the disproportionate trade surpluses are eliminated.

The United States should no longer allow unconditional most-favored-nation (MFN) treatment to large, disproportionate trade surplus countries. A crucial implementing measure for the new reciprocity-based U.S. trade policy will be to suspend MFN treatment for all such countries (Japan, China, Taiwan, Malaysia, etc.) until these disproportionate trade surpluses are greatly reduced. Justification for this enforcement measure shall be based upon GATT Article XII (Balance of Payments); Article VI (Countervailing Duties Against Dumping and Subsidies); and Article XXI (National Security). Under U.S. trade law, the relevant statutory authority will be the Trade Act of 1974, Section 125 (presidential authority to terminate international agreements), Section 122 (balance of payments relief), Section 232 (national security), and Section 301 (unjustifiable trade practices and discrimination), and a new U.S. Trade Balance and Reciprocity Act (TBRA) outlining a congressional mandate for reciprocity-based trade policy.

Certainly the United States has economic justification for discontinuing MFN treatment for countries that accumulated and maintain large, disproportionate trade surpluses against the United States. Unconditional free rider privileges make no sense for nonreciprocal trading partners. But sound legal justification also can be employed under GATT Articles XII and XXI, because the United States needs to eliminate large, excessive trade and current account deficits for its long-term economic prosperity and national security interests. Asking U.S. trade partners to open markets without limiting their exports to the United States simply has not worked at all. This is why U.S. trade policy must now rebuild overall balance and reciprocity, and this reciprocity discipline should be focused on whatever countries happen to be running large and/or disproportionate trade surpluses with the United States[18]

But the United States must insist upon its legitimate freedom to charge import fees under GATT Article XII and U.S. trade laws (Sections 122, 125, 232, and 301 of the Trade Act of 1974, and if appropriate, U.S. antidumping and countervailing duty laws) against large, disproportionate trade surplus countries. Under no circumstances should GATT Article II (the unconditional MFN provision) be a constraint upon the new reciprocity-based trade policy. The United States could seek explicit amendment or interpretation of

GATT Article II (the MFN provision) to allow these reciprocity enforcement measures against countries with large, disproportionate trade surpluses. If the WTO does not accept this amendment or interpretation, the United States might have to withdraw from the WTO on these grounds—that is, the need for the United States to enforce overall reciprocity discipline in its trading policy. (Withdrawal from the WTO only requires six months notice to the UN Secretary General and Director General of the WTO.) (See the section headed Cleaning Up Legal Underbrush below.)

Industrial Rejuvenation Efforts

America's industrial and technology base has suffered erosion in some sectors, although others have been adequately cared for. Industries losing ground in the United States include parts of metallurgy, machinery, electronics, transportation equipment, textiles, fisheries, shipbuilding, and shipping. On the other hand, most of U.S. agriculture is still sound, aerospace was well financed through the Cold War, and computers, software, and applications flourished, although global competition has been increasing lately. Health care is well financed in the United States, and its pharmaceutical sector has been strong. Petroleum and chemical technology is highly developed in the United States, too.

In most really healthy industries, wherever located in the world, the strong companies are progressive and export-oriented, and ample research and development (R & D) investment continues (by the companies themselves and/or with government support). Weak or declining industries normally are not investing enough, lack government nurturing, lose technical talent, and often become defeatist through neglect.[19]

An important feature of declining industries, quite frequently, is strong support abroad, with government subsidies or scale economies, protected home markets (with higher prices and profits), and marginal cost discounting into the more open countries. Thus, maintaining healthy competitiveness in the open market countries is a serious challenge. While it is unwise to be overly protective and shut out foreign imports completely, a sensible compromise solution is likely to be the most productive. Such a compromise welcomes foreign joint ventures, especially for improved technology, and accepts rising imports on an average cost basis. But to avoid a total wipeout of the domestic industry, a blend of voluntary restraint agreements (VRAs) and substantial offsets to foreign dumping or subsidies may be needed. This requires subtlety, pragmatism, quick decisions by business and government, and fast-track import relief and settlements. But heavy, sustained high tariff protection is more often unwise and counterproductive.

Unfortunately, U.S. government-industrial-trade practice has tended to be simplistic. Frequently, in recent years, U.S. trade policy has reflected a naive, completely open, "unilateral free trade" mentality. By contrast, Japanese, European, and NIC practices (in the most successful nations) tend to strike a more skillful balance. Most U.S. trade policy makers frame their choices in a black-or-white "free trade" versus "protection" dichotomy. Furthermore, U.S. trade administrators, especially from the USTR, see the government's role as a neutral, hands-off, minimal function—solely to maintain the "integrity" of free trade. This outlook, while fashionable among postindustrial age writers in late twentieth-century U.S. politics, does not account for the collaboration, even, at times, the government-industry partnerships, that are common in Europe, Japan, and many new industrial countries.

All too often, U.S. trade negotiators failed to grasp the degree of teamwork, support, and nurturing supplied by foreign governments for their significant industries, companies, or entrepreneurs abroad. Thus, government procurement practices abroad still favor domestic companies; any other result is difficult to achieve. "Opening the market" assurances were given by foreign trade officials in the knowledge that not too much disruption from unwanted foreign imports could occur. In fact, these divergent outlooks between U.S. trade officials and foreign trade networks are a large part of the ongoing asymmetry problem (i.e., structural trade imbalances). The U.S. State Department, its various embassies abroad, and the Foreign Service officer establishment tend to favor the local ally-client state's interests, its export programs, and overall economic growth agendas. Few in the U.S. foreign policy, State Department, or USTR network see the object of U.S. trade practice as a tough, day-by-day struggle for export expansion, and fair market shares, requiring loyalty to U.S. industries, in which success is measured by eliminating U.S. trade deficits and, if possible, by achieving solid U.S. trade surpluses. Obviously, for balance and reciprocity-based U.S. trade policy to be implemented successfully, our network of administrators in the United States and abroad must really change its thinking, operational goals, and performance standards.

Also, successful industrial competitiveness and rejuvenation for the United States requires a more industry-friendly enthusiasm generally. Traditionally, Americans enjoyed an industrious, hard-working culture, which took pride in technical skills and ingenuity from the Revolution through World War II and on into the 1960s. More recently, however, significant elements of the U.S. industrial base have been viewed with disdain, or simply taken for granted. In a rather odd, selective way, some technical skills are glamorized—computers, "high tech," health care, finance, many professional services, lawyering, and even small-scale handicrafts. But basic industries, machinery, factories, chemicals, and manufacturing are viewed negatively by much of the public and the media.

To be sure, most modern people realize that far greater care, increased investment, and safeguarding are needed for the natural environment, especially in areas of the world where population growth and crowding are evident. But intelligent environmental policy realizes that broad prosperity, full employment, and social harmony still require ample industrial production. Yes, that output must be cleaner, respectful of the environment and better engineered. There should be a realistic view of total, long-term effects on our habitat. But general deindustrialization as a mind-set undermines general prosperity and employment.

So the United States must overhaul its industrial nurturing systematically and provide comprehensive support to productive, efficient, and environmentally respectful activities. The full range of engineering and technology should be exploited, with good teamwork between universities, R & D organizations, government, and industries. The externalities of a broad, complete technostructure are very substantial, greatly enhancing the potential for sustained success across the front of science and engineering. The most successful nations—the United States from the 1860s to the 1970s, modern Japan, the EU, and the most dynamic NICs (China, India, Brazil, Korea, Taiwan, etc.)—illustrate this approach.

The most important ingredients of a good, industry-friendly environment include (1) a healthy tax structure that encourages productive investment, and sustains vigorous enterprise teamwork; (2) a strong educational system that provides a solid foundation of literacy, math abilities, and technical potential, with upgrading for the more talented, higher-skilled professions in reasonable proportions; (3) healthy labor relations that encourage productive teamwork, job mobility, full employment, and industrial progress (not sluggishness or resistance to productivity improvements); (4) a good social insurance, pension, and health care system that makes the best of improving technology, builds upon healthy family life, and helps people to take better care of themselves (without undue waste, overpricing, or inefficiency); and (5) sound macroeconomic coordination, involving responsible fiscal, monetary, wage-price and external account disciplines (and the avoidance of substantial inflation, unemployment, disruptive slumps, heavy budget deficits, and large or chronic external account deficits).[20]

Unfortunately, modern politics (in many countries) makes implementation of these goals controversial, at least in some respects. But for countries at the top of their games, in their most successful eras, there is a general sense of progress. Rational compromises spread through the system (e.g., the United States, Scandinavia, West Germany, and Switzerland in the later 1940s to the 1960s, or Japan in the 1950s to the 1980s). Unfortunately, as countries falter they suffer more internal conflict, unemployment, stagnation, poverty, and demoralization. The quality of these compromises often erodes, leading to decline and reduced national teamwork.[21]

One way or another, industrial and technological progress is a prime feature of every successful nation. Governments should play an active, sustaining role in broadening this progress and overcoming sectors of backwardness with realistic aid and reforms. Responsible politics should include industrial prosperity, full employment, and strong environmental protection as a harmonious, mutually reinforcing agenda. Industries are not enemies of humane progress, they are essential ingredients of sound social policy—in every country of the world.

This is why most "backward," less developed countries set a priority on general industrialization and improved rates of economic growth. They learned from Britain's industrial revolution from 1750 to the 1880s, and the somewhat later industrial successes of the United States, Germany, Japan, and other nations, that encouraging a broad front of industrial progress generates rapid, self-sustaining prosperity. In most of these success stories, a substantial degree of tariff protection played a crucial, positive role. Government subsidies, bureaucratic awards, and central planning are a lot less productive most of the time. A key advantage of moderate to substantial import tariffs, set in place long enough so that investments in manufacturing plans and marketing operations can flourish (from infant industries into healthy, self-sustaining maturity), is that myriad independent business enterprises take faster, more productive decisions than a few top-level government officials. Industrial success requires a great deal of decentralized initiative. The beauty of general tariffs (whether at 15, 20, or 25 percent) is that domestic industrial expansion efforts can rely upon a reasonable, steady cushion or safeguarding from the bigger, stronger industries of the leading nations. For these reasons, most LDCs and NICs have been reluctant to give up the use of infant industry tariffs, and this outlook was recognized in GATT 1947, GATT amendments in 1965 (Articles XXXVI to XXXVIII), and GATT 1994 and the WTO agreement. Thus, trade asymmetries favoring developing nations have become strongly entrenched in the present multilateral trading regime. It is not realistic to believe that these tariffs and other restrictions to promote industrial progress will be abandoned any time soon by most LDCs and NICs.

But this leaves an awkward, interesting question for mature, somewhat stagnant industrial nations (like most OECD bloc countries today). If the mature nations lose too much ground and excessive deindustrialization occurs, should not they be allowed to use tariffs again, at least selectively, to rejuvenate their industrial base? Thereby, over the longer run, the redevelopment cycle could be started again and rejuvenation tariffs can be justified. Countries that have slipped back too far, with imprudent reliance on industries in LDCs and NICs, too much outsourcing and excessive imports, trade deficits, and chronic balance of payments problems, need a significant renewal of tariffs (like the LDCs and NICs used to catch up). The United States, in fact, may suffer this predicament to some extent already. Twenty years of increased, large, and stubborn external deficits suggest that, to some extent at least, rejuvenation tariffs are needed by the United States for its industrial renewal. Should not GATT 1947, the 1965 GATT amendments, and GATT 1994 be interpreted, reasonably, to authorize rejuvenation tariffs where too much industrial decline has occurred? Or, does not this logic suggest that unconditional MFN must have natural limits for countries like the United States, that gave up too much industrial ground by not insisting on more effective reciprocity? Certainly, as against trading partners with large, disproportionate and extended trade surpluses, this logic justifies moderate rejuvenation tariffs (in addition to remedies outlined previously in the section headed Reciprocal Trade Policy, above.)

Clinton-Perot: A Mandate Not Implemented

In 1991–1992 unease was developing among a majority of the U.S. public about slowed economic growth, reduced job prospects, and a decline in real wages (discounted for inflation). In spite of euphoria over Allied victory in the Gulf War (the defeat of Iraq's army and the liberation of Kuwait) and a surge of free world confidence after the collapse of Russian Communism (1989–1991), the American public mood turned pessimistic on the economic front. President George Bush had become overconfident, and during the presidential election campaign of 1992 three strong challengers hammered away at U.S. deficits, job losses, and reduced confidence among the middle class. They exploited a slump in the economy and raised serious objections to the conduct of U.S. foreign economic policy and the cumulative effects of industrial decline. For the majority of voters, it was evident that this country's kindness and Cold War politics allowed foreign exporters more access to the U.S. marketplace than Americans enjoyed in many markets abroad. The conservative populist, Pat Buchanan, attacked "King George" (Bush) in New Hampshire and later primaries on these issues, which hurt Republican momentum that year. Threatening an independent, third party ticket, Ross Perot, the moderate populist and billionaire, attacked excessive U.S. deficits and weak trade policy, urged health care reform for a broken system, and bitterly attacked NAFTA, saying that it would cause a "giant sucking sound" of U.S.

jobs moving south. And within the Democratic Party, Bill Clinton proved to be the most resilient, tougher campaigner. Clinton focused on "jobs, jobs, jobs" and "it's the economy, stupid" as his mantras, and he also promoted overhaul of the health care system. Meanwhile, Paul Tsongas and Warren Rudman (former U.S. senators) of the Concord coalition strongly attacked excessive and chronic budget deficits. All these political attacks reflected the widespread dissatisfaction with the sluggish U.S. economy, weak jobs performance, and concerns about U.S. trade policy.[22]

When Bill Clinton (43 percent) and Ross Perot (19 percent) defeated George Bush (38 percent) in the November 1992 election, a mandate seemed reasonably clear, at least up to a point. Americans wanted a stronger economy, more jobs, reduced deficits, health care reforms (cost reductions and broader coverage), and a tougher trade policy. Most Americans were alarmed about rising crime and wanted stronger action on that front, too. In the spring of 1993 Clinton enjoyed the normal, brief honeymoon for newly elected presidents, but this ebbed by midsummer. Meanwhile, fierce fights erupted within the administration over Clinton's economic and trade policies. An advantage for Clinton, at least initially, were Democratic majorities in both House and Senate.

But Clinton's economic policy gradually crystallized as a moderate, somewhat Wall Street–oriented view on the need to gradually reduce budget deficits, which would allow lower interest rates. Most of his economic advisers (Bentsen, Rubin, Rivlin, Altman, and Greenspan) urged that outlook, and they also supported freer trade. Although Clinton's U.S. Trade Representative, Mickey Kantor (initial campaign manager and leading fund-raiser) was not a trade policy expert, Kantor soon took a largely free trade line. Clinton quickly approved mild side agreements with Mexico on NAFTA, which supposedly dealt with import surges, labor rights, and environmental protection, but they did not seriously limit or alter the NAFTA agreements as negotiated by the Bush administration. Clinton's side agreements just set up more formalized mutual consultations for "problems" in these areas. And, more importantly, Kantor pretty much accepted the draft Uruguay Round GATT deal as negotiated by his USTR predecessor, Carla Hills. The only important change, at the last moment, was to rename the Multilateral Trade Organization (MTO) as the World Trade Organization (WTO). These U.S. trade negotiating decisions were essentially complete in the summer of 1993. In fact, Kantor had promised in the spring of 1993 that the Uruguay Round GATT negotiations would be completed by that fall. Unfortunately, this timetable eliminated any effective bargaining leverage to substantially improve upon the Dunkel draft deal. In this way, unfortunately, the Clinton administration gave away its best opportunity to substantially improve U.S. reciprocity.

The bigger questions for the Clinton White House were political. And this trade and job slump caused some real agonizing, especially over NAFTA. During the spring and summer of 1993, Clinton handled trade matters in a low-key way, allowing many Democratic congressional leaders to believe that his political commitment to NAFTA was weak and limited. In this context, House Majority Leader Richard Gephart and Whip Phillip Bonior took strong public stands against NAFTA, the AFL-CIO launched an expensive campaign against NAFTA, Jesse Jackson and Ralph Nader opposed NAFTA, and the majority of environmental organizations opposed NAFTA. By August 1993, Clinton faced a tough political dilemma. Should he let NAFTA "fail," which would weaken his prestige as an international leader, or should he divide his own party with a bitter fight over trade policy? Representative Newt Gingrich and the House Republicans offered to help Clinton pass NAFTA, knowing this would drive a sword of division into the belly of House Democrats. By September Clinton decided that he had to go ahead with NAFTA and make a strong effort for Congressional approval under fast-track procedures. Interestingly, the final Uruguay Round GATT deal was scheduled to be finalized shortly after the NAFTA vote. (Much more complicated, and hard for Congress and the public to understand, the Uruguay Round GATT deal was hardly mentioned by the administration, nor even much discussed by the NAFTA opposition. This lack of serious attention or debate proved to be a major U.S. trade policy blunder.)

As Clinton focused on the crucial House NAFTA vote (in mid-October 1993), Vice President Al Gore was selected by the White House to debate Ross Perot on prime-time TV, *mano a mano*. Polls reported that Gore "won" the debate. Interestingly, the somewhat cranky Perot was picked to personify the opposition to NAFTA, rather than Ralph Nader, Jesse Jackson, Pat Buchanan, Richard Gephart, or Phil Bonior. The administration's gamble paid off. Shortly thereafter NAFTA was approved by the House (although nearly two-thirds of the House Democrats still opposed it). Then Kantor announced that the Uruguay Round GATT agreement was signed. But little discussion, detailed analysis, or debate followed on the GATT deal. And, most interestingly, a special congressional vote on the Uruguay Round GATT deal under fast track was scheduled eventually for late November 1994, after the congressional elections.

Meanwhile, during 1994, political attention had shifted to the health care package, which had been carefully developed under the leadership of Hillary Rodham Clinton, with a great deal of fanfare and publicity. Unfortunately, the plans proved too complicated, required large new budget outlays, and featured threatening new regulations for health care providers, and yet they did not achieve substantial savings in the short run. Congress was never consulted adequately in preparing the package, and as the summer of 1994 wore on it became apparent that the Clinton health care overhaul effort had failed, with great embarrassment for the administration.[23]

But that summer and fall, Republicans under Newt Gingrich were mounting a strong national campaign to carry the House of Representatives. They proposed a "Contract with America" under which a ten-point agenda of balanced budget, fiscal, tax, family, crime control, and other measures would be pushed under a Republican Congress. To the surprise of most observers, Republicans carried in November not only the House of Representatives, but also the Senate.

In the immediate wake of that Republican midterm electoral victory, Congress reconvened (as previously agreed) to vote on the Uruguay Round GATT deal—now referred to as GATT 1994 and the World Trade Organization Agreement. Hardly any national debate, minimal congressional hearings, and only brief, conclusory "reviews" of the deal were offered by the USTR in support. So little discussion occurred in the media that it was evident that few press people were up to speed on the many technical issues dealt with by the Uraguay round (between 1985 and 1991).[24] There was almost no historical literature on U.S. trade policy in recent years, especially for the post–World War II era.[25] Intriguingly, Newt Gingrich had complained openly, in a House Ways and Means Committee hearing on June 10, 1994, about the lack of serious debate and literature on the Uruguay Round deal. He, quite properly, compared the U.S. decision on GATT 1994 and the WTO to Britain's entry into the European Common Market in 1973. Certainly, he said, the United States should be thinking through, systematically and carefully, the ramifications of the new GATT 1994 and WTO agreement. But few other members of the House expressed serious concern. In this context, it was not really surprising that Congress would give fast-track approval to GATT 1994 and the WTO agreement. The surprise, frankly, was that a third of the Congress, from both Republican and Democratic ranks, voted *against* GATT 1994 and the WTO agreement. Without much debate or leadership involvement, this congressional vote really reflected broad unease over U.S. trade policy and accumulated asymmetries.[26]

Department of Industry, Technology, and Trade (DITT)

Many experts on industrial development, engineering, and technological progress believe that governments have an active, continuing, and essential role to play in fostering these activities.[27] Certainly tax policies should encourage productive investments, and ample incentives for engineers, designers, production workers, and marketing organizations. Intellectual property, patents, trademarks, and copyright protection are valuable incentives, too. But government support for engineering schools, research and development projects, and scientific expertise has played a significant role as well. In periods of national emergency, like World Wars I and II, the Cold War, or severe economic dislocation (e.g., the OPEC I and II energy shortages, 1973–1980), government R & D programs, mobilization efforts, and coordination have been crucial. And, of course, long-standing U.S. tariff policies, from Alexander Hamilton's day through World War II, strongly nurtured U.S. manufacturing, mining, and agricultural industries. Other industrial nations, NICs, and LDCs have employed comparable industrial and technology encouragement policies, to the extent their resources and stage of development allowed.

The organizational structure used by the U.S. government was comparable to that used by other nations in fostering this industrial expansion and technological progress. Congress established and regulated the tax and tariff structure, with guidance at times from presidents. The War and Navy Departments were created initially, along with a Treasury Department. The Departments of Commerce (for business and industry), Agriculture (for farming), and Interior (for mining and resources) were set up later on to promote economic development. The Department of Labor was established to promote worker interests. During World Wars I and II, emergency industrial mobilization and coordination agencies were created, more elaborate for the longer World War II effort (1940–1945), including a War Production Board, Labor Board, and Office of Price Administration. Smaller ad hoc institutions were needed, among the most striking being the Manhattan Project (atomic energy research to develop the nuclear bomb). After World War II major demobilization of the armed forces occurred, although reorganization split off the Air Force (formerly the Army Air Corps) as a separate service. But the new Department of Defense and collateral agencies, including the National Security Agency and Central Intelligence Agency, and long-term procurement relations with many defense equipment suppliers (aerospace, naval, shipbuilding, electronics, computers, tanks and armored vehicles, lighter arms, and munitions of all kinds) took on important roles in sponsoring industrial progress, engineering improvement, and the maintenance (as far as possible) of a U.S. technical edge in most aspects of weaponry.

In defense-related sectors, the United States maintained a systematic industrial policy, at least through the Cold War era (1946–1991). The Department of Agriculture, farm lobbies, and their influence in many states supported efforts for progress, efficiency, and prosperity in that sector. And in the minerals sector, tax and other policies promoted production, emergency stockpiles, international investment, and adequate supplies for industry.

But for the rest of U.S. industry and manufacturing, little need was seen for government nurturing. World War II left America with a lead in many industries. This allowed U.S. trade policy to open its manufacturing markets (far more than other nations) as part of Cold War politics, helping allies and developing nations to prosperity by leading the way toward an integrated free world economy.

The chief instrumentality for this "trade, not aid" policy was a small section of U.S. trade negotiators in the State Department.[28] Later, as part of the Kennedy Round enabling legislation, these people staffed the new Office of the U.S. Trade Representative (USTR). Subsequently, the USTR became dominant over U.S. trade policy. Unfortunately, the USTR did not see itself as the guardian of trade reciprocity or overall balance in U.S. export/import flows. Quite the contrary, the USTR saw the use by the United States of its own trade laws to limit imports, enforce fair trade, or require effective reciprocity *as an interference with free trade*. Typically, the USTR accepted foreign pledges to gradually open their markets and reduce trade barriers abroad *as the equivalent* of U.S. openness. In effect, the USTR became the primary architect of asymmetries in U.S. trading relationships, further entrenched by the GATT 1994 and WTO agreement negotiated by the USTR. The USTR became a steadfast foe of any effective U.S. industrial policy, and insisted that it be the only significant voice in shaping detailed trade policy or negotiations (within the U.S. government).

Because of the USTR's institutional bias and track record on their view of free trade, it is evident that this agency would probably never accept or implement a new, reciprocity-based U.S. trade policy that emphasizes the goals of overall balance in U.S. trade flows. Therefore, the USTR should be abolished. The USTR and its culture are simply not consistent with a stronger, reciprocity-based policy.

Accordingly, all U.S. trade negotiation and oversight functions and responsibilities should be transferred to a new, larger, and stronger agency, the Department of Industry, Technology, and Trade (DITT).[29] Portions of the Department of Commerce, for the most part, should be the core of the new DITT, but energized with a new and stronger trade policy mandate. The DITT should take over most of the business, industrial, and trade-statistics-gathering responsibilities in the U.S. government (except for financial markets, which should be left to the Federal Reserve, SEC, and other financial market supervisors). Agricultural data should be left to the Department of Agriculture. A new mission statement must be developed for the DITT that emphasizes as national policy goals: (1) the promotion of U.S. industry, technology, and trade; (2) effective trading reciprocity and overall balance in U.S. export/import flows; (3) achieving fair shares for U.S. business, commerce, and industry in world markets; (4) careful monitoring and reporting on industrial developments in the world marketplace, observing technology trends, trade barriers of all kinds, and relative access to foreign markets by U.S. companies, investors, and workers; (5) skillful enforcement of U.S. trade laws and representation of the United States in foreign trade dealings (including working with the WTO, NAFTA, and other trade organizations); and (6) collaboration with other government agencies and departments that impact industry, technology, and trade, including the Environmental Protection Agency, the Federal Reserve, the Departments of Defense, Agriculture, Interior, Labor, and Treasury, and a new Maritime Department (which should take over the Maritime Administration and Maritime Commission presently in the Commerce Department).[30]

Thus, DITT becomes the new, predominant lead agency for U.S. trade policy (replacing the USTR). It will rival, and be a counterpart of, the Japanese Ministry of International Trade and Industry (MITI). DITT should (like Japan's MITI) have a coordinative role in representing the interests of U.S. industries, companies, communities, and workers. A clear commitment to U.S. trade reciprocity and overall balance in U.S. imports/exports will make it clear to all other nations that a new U.S. trade policy is installed. The United States will be friendly, fair, and evenhanded. But the United States will no longer accept the short end of the stick. America will no longer be the World Chump of trade.

In this regard, we must emphasize that a strong, coordinative role for DITT does not replace vigorous, dynamic U.S. companies and manufacturers as the primary vehicles of industrial success and prosperity. The function of DITT is *not to control or dictate*, but to aid, encourage, and promote U.S. manufacturers, plants, companies, and workers. Very importantly, DITT's mandate is also to offset the strong, widespread industrial support systems of many OECD nations, and the majority of NICs and LDCs. This offset responsibility is now generally neglected by the U.S. government. Under the ideologically biased worldview of the USTR, this lack of U.S. response was rationalized as a "commitment to free trade." The real, important, and continuing contribution of foreign industrial support systems was heavily discounted and minimized by naive free trade enthusiasts. Sadly, this mentality only helps to sustain asymmetries widely appreciated abroad, but not adequately understood by many in the U.S. government (especially within the USTR).

However, we must realize that the growing spread of MNCs, their subsidiaries, investments, and allies, does make it more complicated to trace relative market shares and influence. And MNCs, especially the large ones, have been taking a bigger share of world trade in recent years. Much of the growing volume of world trade, in fact, represents intracorporate (and interaffiliate) trading, investment, and financial flows. Routings through tax havens to divert profits into minimal or no tax environments add fog to the data problems, especially for capital flows, financial services, and royalty payments, particularly for intellectual property.[31] Nonetheless, some countries (e.g., Japan) are far more effective than others in making sure *that their multinationals* get a good, fair share of the transactional pie. Those nations get a higher yield in real benefits, market shares, and trade flows, of course, and enjoy faster overall, real GNP growth (with less risk of stagnation). Thus, the role for DITT must be actively pursued with savvy and long-term determination. In the modern global economy, DITT must be a permanent feature of sound, effective U.S. trade policy.

It is interesting that the first major proposals for a new U.S. Department of International Trade and Industry (DITI) came during the 1983 to 1985 period.[32] Secretary of Commerce Malcolm Baldridge proposed to transform the Commerce Department into a DITI as a necessary countermeasure to deal effectively with Japan's MITI and comparable industrial-trade policy efforts in other countries. (An earlier, more limited version of this effort was made under Secretary of Commerce Maurice Stans in early 1969, but President Richard Nixon chose not to press the matter after some congressional misgivings.) Not surprisingly, of course, the USTR lobbied strongly (though not too publicly) to head off this idea and prevent its implementation; it would have been a major threat to continued USTR dominance over the details of U.S. trade policy.

Cleaning Up Legal Underbrush

An essential chore for new, reciprocity-based U.S. trade policy is to clear away the legal underbrush that gets in the way. U.S. trade laws, so far as they go, are reasonably adequate.[33] The Trade Act of 1974, including Section 122 (balance of payments relief), Section 125 (presidential authority to terminate agreements), Section 232 (national security), Section 301 (unjustifiable trade practices and discrimination), Section 337 (actions against unfair trade practices, mainly involving intellectual property), along with the antidumping and countervailing duty for subsidy laws, makes sense. The main problem with U.S. trade laws has been great timidity in enforcement. Thus, for example, as part of their Uruguay Round "standstill" pledge in 1985 to 1991, U.S. trade negotiators promised that they would minimize the development of any significant import restrictions (or trade barriers) under U.S. trade laws.

Fortunately, the recent Uruguay Round Agreements Act of 1994, the U.S. implementing act for GATT 1994 and the WTO, made it very clear that U.S. trade laws prevail over the WTO agreement.[34] Even though explicit language in the WTO agreement expresses a contrary idea—that is, that the WTO agreement prevails over all national laws—the U.S. implementing act explicitly rejects this impact. Thus, an evident conflict has been created between U.S. implementing law and the text of the WTO agreement. The United States must insist that U.S. trade laws prevail, and if any WTO panel decision or interpretation fails to sustain this priority for U.S. law, the United States will promptly withdraw from the WTO.[35]

It is important also that the new reciprocity-based U.S. trade policy be enunciated in strong, fresh, and clear legislation that sets forth the goals of enforcing effective trade reciprocity and achieving overall balance in U.S. imports and exports. For these reasons, a new Reciprocity Trade Balance Act must be enacted as the charter and explicit mandate for the new U.S. trade policy. And the fundamental rationale should be clear, too. The United States respects the right of all nations to make the best deals possible in world trade. But now that the Cold War is behind us, a new U.S. trade policy is needed. The United States has widespread unemployment, underemployment, and growing income inequalities. Poverty, drug abuse, and crime are serious problems. Americans must take care of their own people. Full employment must be achieved. And all nations must discipline their external accounts and eliminate excessive trade and current account deficits. The United States must put its economic house in order.

New Realism Versus Holier Than Thou

An aspect of U.S. foreign policy that has been vexing, troubling, and alienating to many nations, including those well disposed to Americans, is a tendency to self-righteous and self-centered moralism. All too frequently, the United States proclaims a special wisdom and rightness in foreign policy, a superior commitment to democracy, human rights, and individual freedoms. "Be like us" is the implicit message. Accept U.S.–style free market institutions. Practice U.S.–style democratic politics. Observe U.S. social mores and conventions. Implement U.S. free trade policies, open your markets, and let MNCs into your markets on the same terms as domestic companies. Moreover, do not mistreat minorities, unions, workers, women, or children. And have free elections, with a free press (domestic and foreign) given access to everything. If you do not, well. . . you are uncivilized, mercantilist, and maybe even guilty of human rights violations.

Yet U.S. history hardly represents a clean slate on these issues. Slave labor came early in the British colonies (although already practiced by the Spanish, Portuguese, and French colonies, and elsewhere). Slavery in the United States continued into the Civil War (1861–1865). It took another century for U.S. national policy to proclaim discrimination on the basis of national origin, race, religion, or sex unlawful. Unionization of workers began gradually and was not clearly favored under U.S. law until the Wagner Act of 1935. Tariff protection in the United States was established policy from 1791 to 1945, although the country moved toward "reciprocal" free trade after 1934. The United States has been a leader in democracy, but its practice has been imperfect. And the liberalism of U.S. social mores, recent fashions in family life, and outlooks on sexuality are controversial even among Americans. The Western press and other media, while an inspiration to many people in the world, are seen as licentious and corrupting by others.

Condemnations by the U.S. government, prominent senators or representatives, elements of the American media, or special interest groups are often taken badly. Charges of hypocrisy are thrown back at Americans, based upon our own history or lack of consistency. To be sure, really brutal regimes, dictatorial and repressive governments, and extensive abuse and cruelties against their peoples and minorities generally deserve international criticism. But the United States (like other countries) lacks consistency in applying these standards to trading partners, friendly nations, and allied states. And the failure to be consistent, evenhanded, and fair with other countries is often resented. If this hectoring persists, the results are often counterproductive, frequently leading to political and economic alienation. Such pretentious, offensive moralism in the United States is bad, inept foreign policy.

Trading policies are better left to pragmatism and mutual interest among nations, at least for the most part. Certainly the overwhelming majority of states employ primarily mercantile, practical standards (commercial reliability, creditworthiness, and reciprocity) in their trade policies.[36] Rarely is there a strong consensus to sanction or outlaw a nation on moral or legal grounds (as there was, for example, after Saddam Hussein's conquest of Kuwait or during South Africa's apartheid regime). Sanctions may be needed, however, to deal with some dangerous adversaries or enemy powers (for example, those sponsoring terrorism or responsible for acts of aggression). But U.S. trade sanctions normally should be confined to hostile regimes, governments that have earned broad, and widespread condemnation among nations of the world, and countries with recent trade policies strongly in conflict with U.S. trade interests (such as large, disproportionate trade imbalances resulting from a lack of effective reciprocity).

A great advantage for a new, reciprocity-based U.S. trade policy would be its lack of moral pretentiousness. Reciprocity-oriented trading policies are the traditional and realistic norms of international relations. Every nation has the right and expectation to be treated fairly and equally by others. Most of U.S. history, from the Revolutionary American Republic through the New Deal's proclaimed reciprocal trade policy and into the post–World War II era, was dominated by this thinking. Treaties of Friendship, Commerce, and

Navigation were sought with most states. But the United States took for granted its right to impose tariffs, industrial development, and growth policies as it saw fit and respected the rights of other states to do the same. Thus, in the new U.S. trade policy environment, the United States can and should seek common ground in mutually beneficial trade relationships with most nations. And, within shrewd and effective limits, the United States should apply substantial pressures against allied and friendly states to achieve better balance and more effective reciprocity in import/export flows. But this is not a big deal morally. It is only common sense, normal and healthy business dealings. Realistic, sensible trading states understand that mutually beneficial, reciprocal trading, without disproportionate advantage to either side, is satisfactory and sustainable over the long haul.

Teamwork: Labor, Environment, and Consumers

In healthy countries with good, realistic teamwork and pride in their general prosperity, engineering progress, and mutual achievements, there is a harmony of interest between workers, industrial leaders, and consumers. And for our modern generation, an increasing awareness of shared enjoyment of the environment has become essential, too. But when industrial workers, labor organizations, environmental groups, and many consumer leaders are alienated against their own government officials responsible for trade policy, there is, at the very least, troubling disharmony.[37] Unfortunately, U.S. trade negotiators (especially the USTR) chose a course of dealings between 1985 and 2003 that often favored multinational corporations, but neglected the interests of domestic workers, wage rates, and overall employment. MNC's were encouraged, increasingly after the early 1980s, to outsource their manufacturing and other operations to lower-wage countries—that is, the lowest common denominators of cost and convenience.[38] This tended to undercut standards for environmental protection that had been developed since the late 1960s. Communities and labor organizations worried about losing jobs and their remaining industrial plants, accepted lower wages and less favorable benefits, and sometimes weakened environmental safeguards that could limit industrial activity and jobs in their localities.

During much of the 1980s, however, many U.S. companies and industries did try to get support from the U.S. government to limit disruptive imports and provide reasonable safeguard relief.[39] Steel products, machine tools, automobiles and trucks, textiles and clothing, shoes, and many other industries brought companies and working people together for these efforts under U.S. trade laws. And, to some extent, the International Trade Administration (ITA) of the Commerce Department, and the International Trade Commission (ITC), provided relief under U.S. trade laws. But the Uruguay Round GATT (1985–1993) negotiation, with the USTR's "standstill" pledge against new trade "restrictions," undercut a lot of this industry-labor collaboration. And the final Uruguay Round outcome weakened U.S. enforcement potential for countervailing duties against foreign subsidies, antidumping proceedings, and Section 301 and Section 337 actions and made it even more difficult to get effective safeguard relief.[40] Understandably, more American companies, like many MNC's, developed an "importer" mentality. Manufacturing jobs increasingly moved overseas to low-wage countries. This substantially weakened, over time, the teamwork between U.S. manufacturers and labor interests. By the mid-1990s, the U.S. government's trade policies (NAFTA, GATT 1994, and the WTO) signaled a general lack of concern for U.S. workers and a preference for investor and MNC interests.

What about consumer interests? Consumers share interests with business investors, producers, and working people. The incomes that consumers spend come from domestic industries, export sales, the service sector (including federal, state, and local government), and America's overall share of world trading activities. Unfortunately, the U.S. share in global output has been declining for the last generation. In other words, combined incomes of American teamwork have been sagging. Thus, "United States, Inc." has often not done so well *in economic growth rates* as "Japan, Inc.," "Taiwan, Inc.," "South Korea, Inc.," and so forth (see Table 1.4). Also, from low levels of income, China, India, and Southeast Asia were making rapid progress for their consumers from the mid-1980s through most of the last two decades.

And what about shifting incomes among consumers? Data on U.S. worker wages, family incomes, and the redistribution of wealth showed a troubling pattern. The average U.S. real wage declined between 1973 and the mid-1990s (Table 1.6).[41] The people in the top 10 percent of the income and wealth scale improved their share, while middle and lower classes lost ground.[42] Some middle-income families held their own by working longer hours, and more women now work full-time. But single-earner families fell back, for the most part, and lost real income. Industries like manufacturing, which used to employ a large part of the higher-wage people, declined, with net losses in higher-wage jobs. Lower-paid service jobs cannot make up all of the difference. And some service sector expansion may be unsustainable, with big increases in the share of GNP going to health care, insurance, lawyering, and the criminal justice system. Even so-called free trade enthusiasts were conceding, by the late 1990s, that while the global economy brought some gains to "winners," substantial numbers of "losers" had accumulated. A majority of the American people are now doubtful about the benefits of free trade.[43]

Unease about the global trading system was spreading internationally in the late 1990s.[44] Europe was divided and troubled about high, chronic levels of unemployment. Europeans suffered overloads in their social welfare states and increased inequalities as in the United States. Many experts project more EU defensiveness as a result. Eastern Europe, Russia, and the former USSR were struggling hard to create viable, market economies from corrupt Communist regimes.[45] Hope was high, but progress slow. High incomes went to wheeler-dealer types (often former Communist apparatchiks), with relative poverty for many. Most Islamic states suffered economic trouble, in one form or another; there was a resurgence of anti-Western feeling also. Southeast Asia's "new tigers," especially Malaysia, Thailand, Indonesia, and the Philippines, benefited from global trade expansion for a decade and more, but recently suffered major speculative excesses, financial and stock market losses, and sharp currency declines. Japan had been the paragon of global growth and neomercantilism until a speculative bubble finally sagged in the early 1990s.[46] Japan's government thereafter attempted some liberalization measures, but became alarmed that a high yen in 1995 would cripple exports, and later kept the yen down for exports. Africa, which never fully trusted the global economy and foreign companies, remains greatly troubled. Only Latin America, for the most part, retains faith in liberalizing its own internal economies, but Latin Americans never embraced a complete opening to foreign investors. Mexico's sad experience with a massive inflow of foreign investments, the disruptive peso crisis of 1994–1995, and a 60 percent devaluation of the peso taught them sobering lessons.[47] Most of Latin America learned a good lesson from Mexico, and later from Brazil and Argentina. Overall, it seems clear that the widespread global market euphoria of 1991–1994 was waning by 1998.

Most of the world is relearning, once again, the fundamental lessons of the Great Depression: the danger of speculative manias and the need to limit excessive swings in the business cycle (boom-bust scenarios with heavy unemployment and widespread distress).[48] Interestingly, OECD countries learned in the 1940s the need for sustained, reliable economic growth (the Keynesian revolution) and the advantages of full employment. Broad OECD prosperity from the 1940s to the 1960s, and on into the 1970s was the result. The GATT 1947 charter for *gradual* trade liberalization emphasized vital safeguards and limitations to prevent serious disruptions—that is Article XII (balance of payments relief), Article VI (duties against foreign subsidies and dumping), and Article XIX (safeguard or escape clause relief). But inflation in the 1970s and structural rigidities in the 1980s brought excesses in social welfare spending, health care waste, and the entrenchment of government deficits in many countries. Partly in response, MNCs began moving offshore to avoid higher wages and fringe benefits, which made the unions in Europe, the United States, Canada, Australia, and New Zealand even more defensive. Japan avoided these difficulties until the early 1990s, because of its stronger resistance to manufactured imports (i.e., more effective safeguard relief through language, culture, marketing customs, and administrative guidance). Then GATT 1994 and the WTO agreement distorted the ground rules (at least for the United States) by weakening national access to trade law relief and by encouraging MNCs to break their national teamwork with labor, the environment, and low-middle class consumers, and move their manufacturing and processing work to low wage countries. Oddly, this opened up the industrialized OECD countries to greater import penetration, trade imbalances, and a renewed vulnerability to an "open market global capitalism" that has not really been seen since the 1920s. Greatly enlarged trade and current account deficits, of course, normally bring strong devaluation pressures to currencies.

Consumers lose again, through devaluations, higher living costs, economic slowdown, and increased unemployment. Overdependence on foreign imports and the global economy turns out to be a serious economic blunder. Many experts are worried now that many OECD countries are opening themselves up to global market imbalances and speculative disruptions, with a substantially weakened industrial employment base and a strained social safety net.[49] This situation resembles the late 1920s somewhat, although modern governments probably would print more money, increase budget deficits, and widen the safety net in the event of a broader recession and big unemployment increases.

But tragic dilemmas are built into the global economy now, because heavy Keynesian pump priming and budget deficits will aggravate the external deficits problem. Thus, a vicious cycle of devaluations and excessive deficits may be hard to break. These vulnerabilities are the natural consequence of over dependence upon foreign goods and the disruption dangers that are very large. Speculative capital flows can turn quickly against a nation through events largely out of its own control.

Monitoring and Progress: Three- to Five-Year Transition Periods

Extensive monitoring is essential for a new, reciprocity-based trade policy that achieves an overall balance in U.S. exports and imports. Reasonably accurate data must be collected and maintained on industrial output, sales, costs, imports, exports, and services (especially those involving international transactions). Most of these data have been collected by the U.S. Census Bureau, and agency of the Department of Commerce (with increasing care since the later 1930s.)[50] Statistical monitoring capabilities are greatly enhanced by computer technology. Normal tabulations on standardized definitions are easy to maintain, provided that companies are required by law to report regularly their industrial activities on this basis.[51]

Any gaps that develop for new industries or products in this information base should be promptly closed. Appropriate updating is necessary to maintain adequate, reliable data collection. In this regard, special attention must be given to MNCs and their affiliates, plants, intracompany transfers, prices, and costs. Obviously, MNCs could become a significant gap in the data, if they are not properly supervised and accounted for.

Our Department of Industry, Technology, and Trade (DITT) must have primary responsibility for maintaining a full set of current accounts for all domestic industrial and international trade-related transactions. Data from other agencies should be fed into the DITT database, so that monitoring for all aspects of international trade is as complete and up-to-date as possible. In this way, DITT can be well informed about the details of changing trade flows between the United States and its many trading partners. Obviously, normal and prompt publication of these data should be continued by DITT, so that Congress, various industries, interest groups, and the public can be informed. DITT should work with other countries on a reciprocal basis to assure adequate transparency for all international sales, shipments, services, and trading activities.[52]

Progress in the U.S. balance of payments—that is, increasing exports and (where needed) reducing imports—is a crucial priority in the new, reciprocity-based trade policy. Data are presently tabulated monthly, but published after a lag of several months. Faster and more reliable data collection will be needed for all trade involving countries (and their companies) with large and/or disproportionate trade surpluses as against the United States. Unconditional MFN treatment will be discontinued against all such countries as long as these large or disproportionate trade surpluses persist. Furthermore, 10 to 15 percent import fees could be charged for all shipments or services from these countries (or traceable to them) as long as large or disproportionate trade surpluses continue.

Collaboration in rapidly eliminating these large or disproportionate trade surpluses will be rewarded with kinder, easier treatment. A crucial dimension of collaboration will be working with U.S. companies to increase exports abroad or to relocate foreign manufacturing, assembly, or component-making back in the United States. Companies from the United States and their foreign counterparts that cooperate in the new U.S. trade policy will be welcomed into the American Partner program and given special privileges and waivers of import fees, where substantial contributions to an improved U.S. balance of payments are being made.

By contrast, foreign companies or governments that refuse to cooperate, supply inadequate data, or resist the new U.S. trade policy will be treated less favorably. Higher import fees, more extensive investigations under U.S. trade law (including antidumping, subsidy, Section 301, or Section 337 proceedings), and increased data reporting requirements will be imposed. The net result for noncollaborating countries or companies will be greater reductions in imports, substantially less trade with the United States, and penalties for nonreporting.

Reasonable transition periods of three to five years must be allowed for large and disproportionate trade surpluses to be eliminated. Careful follow-through on improved trade balances will be required, so that good performance by foreign companies and countries can be rewarded. This means that reasonably complete reporting for trade in goods and services with all countries is essential throughout, so that "good performance" (reasonably balanced trade) can be monitored. Backsliding must be promptly identified, along with desirable progress. And problems of new and growing imbalance with other countries (including possible diversion or evasive routings) must be promptly identified, too.

Another important part of DITT's trade-monitoring responsibility will be current reporting on foreign industrial policies, tariffs, industrial subsidies, and targeting efforts for all U.S. trade partners. Foreign countries that refuse to cooperate in providing adequate information may be subject to import surcharges (or other U.S. trade law sanctions), at least for the sectors suspected of substantial nonreporting.

Additional trade-monitoring expenses may be involved for DITT data gathering, surveillance, and oversight. These modest, extra, annual DITT costs should be prorated among all U.S. imports each year. A small monitoring and oversight fee will be charged each year. Discounts in these fees will be allowed for countries that actively collaborate with DITT in these efforts. Any country that resists these fees, however, or that tries to counter with penalty fees on the United States or its companies will be subjected to substantial further penalties in return.

Overall surveillance and reporting requirements for the new, reciprocity-based U.S. trade policy will be somewhat greater than present data collection requirement. But for collaborating countries and companies, these costs will be quite modest on the whole. On the other hand, for countries or companies that resist or obstruct the new data-gathering efforts, their conduct will be considered "trade hostile" to the United States. Additional investigative efforts, data-gathering charges, and U.S. trade law enforcement will be focused against countries or companies deemed "trade hostile" to the United States. Continued obstruction or resistance may lead to the imposition of special import licenses for further exports or financial dealings with the United

States. Once again, the bottom line for the new reciprocity-based U.S. trade policy is that cooperation by foreign companies and governments will be rewarded, but obstruction, resistance, and a failure to cooperate must be discouraged and made unacceptable—with reduced export access, higher import fees, oversight penalties, and, if necessary, special import licenses for continued trade and financial dealings.

Nonaction: Vulnerability and Decline

Damaging consequences follow if the United States takes no action to eliminate trade and current account deficits, restore overall balance and trade reciprocity, and rejuvenate its industries and technology. America has already lost ground in many industries; others are nearly abandoned. Recently, U.S. imports exceeded exports by more than three to two. In 2002 this meant imports of $1,200 billion and exports of $730 billion out of $10,600 billion GNP. Since 1981 the United States has accumulated –$4,000 billion in current trade deficits and –$3,500 billion in current account deficits, transforming itself from the world's largest creditor nation (+$325 billion) to become the biggest debtor country (–$3,000 billion) in these years. The United States suffered a net loss of 10 to 12 million jobs. Economic growth slowed, structural unemployment increased, poverty spread, and inequalities got worse. Morale is strained. Widespread unease exists about the economy, the reliability of social security reserves, and the future for our younger generation.

Although an upsurge in the U.S. stock market and a temporary upswing in the dollar provided a lift to the U.S. economy between 1995 and 2000, this was a fragile and, in many ways, false prosperity. Many fundamentals are unsound: (1) unsustainable, excessive U.S. imports that greatly exceed exports; (2) dependence upon large inflows of foreign capital to sustain $400 to $500 billion in annual U.S. current account deficits; (3) long-term stagnation in U.S. real wages; (4) greatly enlarged U.S. federal debt loads since 1980 (from one-third to two-thirds of GNP); (5) stock market advances in the United States between 1993 and 2000 that greatly exceeded increases in corporate earnings and profits; and (6) an overvalued dollar resulting from heavy inflows of foreign investment (in spite of large U.S. trade and current account deficits). In most countries, these numbers would undermine economic confidence, especially when prosperity depends upon foreign capital inflows and speculative momentum.[53]

In the late 1990s, Federal Reserve Chair Allan Greenspan warned that this speculative boom was peaking out. Unfortunately, the more a speculative boom gets out of hand, the larger a corrective downsurge is likely. That is what happened in 1928–1929 when a U.S. stock market boom galloped ahead to its rendezvous with destiny[54] (Table 5.1).

Failure by the United States to correct its external account deficits, restore trade reciprocity, and renew industrial vitality guarantees continued vulnerability to crises and assures relative stagnation and decline in its industries. Many other countries are expanding production and improving technology. The United States cannot afford to remain passive. Unfortunately, recent stock market euphoria and unsustainable foreign investment into the United States (largely based on speculative impulses) cannot be relied upon by Americans to maintain their industrial base. Good engineering, production operations, and marketing efforts require teamwork and continuity. In much of the American industrial scene there has been neglect. Thoughtful observers agree that there has been a short-term, speculative, stock-market-oriented mentality. Entrepreneurial talent has been devoted in the United States to takeover games (both attack and defense). Not enough effort is devoted to building first class products, maintaining low-cost production, and responding to foreign competition (often subsidized, widely sheltered, and using marginal cost discounting into open markets like the United States). The U.S. government, at least for most manufacturing industries, has been a passive bystander.

The common response by apologists to one-way free trade, which ignores U.S. industrial decline and accumulated external deficits, is that currency realignments solve any problems, effortlessly and smoothly. In other words, if world markets think U.S. external account deficits are excessive, the dollar gradually declines and the mark, yen, pound, and euro increase in value. Thus, world markets, operating skillfully and efficiently, straighten out any disequilibria without any fuss or need for serious concern by the United States or any other governments.

But if this were so, why have there been recent, severe currency crises and financial disturbances? The big Japanese downfall in the Nikkei in the 1990s, the breakdown of the European Exchange Rate Mechanism in the early 1990s, the Mexican peso crisis of 1994, and currency crises in Thailand, Malaysia, Indonesia, and the Philippines in 1997 illustrate that global financial markets are making really big miscalculations and costly blunders. Russia, Brazil, South Korea, and Argentina later joined this parade of disruptions. Speculative booms and unrealistic euphoria were very significant from the 1990s to the early twenty-first century. As Lester Thurow warned in 1996, the potential for the U.S. dollar to come down sharply in response to accumulated U.S. trade and current account deficits and resurgent doubts about the U.S. industrial economy, is very great, indeed.[55] The U.S. economy and trade situation is like living on a great fault line for earthquakes. Pressures from accumulated distortions have been building

Table 5.1

Common Stock Prices and Yields, 1957–2003[a]

Year or month	NYSE Composite Index[b] (12/31/65 = 50)	Dow Jones Industrial Average[b]	Standard & Poor's Composite Index[b]	NASDAQ Composite Index[b]	S & P common stock yield: earnings– price ratio[c]
1957	23.67	475.71	44.38	—	7.85
1958	24.56	491.66	46.24	—	6.23
1959	30.73	632.12	57.38	—	5.78
1960	30.01	618.04	55.85	—	5.90
1961	35.37	691.55	66.27	—	4.62
1962	33.49	639.76	62.38	—	5.82
1963	37.51	714.81	69.87	—	5.50
1964	43.76	834.05	81.37	—	5.32
1965	47.39	910.88	88.17	—	5.59
1966	46.15	873.60	85.26	—	6.63
1967	50.77	879.12	91.93	—	5.73
1968	55.37	906.00	98.70	—	5.67
1969	54.67	876.72	97.84	—	6.08
1970	45.72	753.19	83.22	—	6.45
1971	54.22	888.76	98.29	107.44	5.41
1972	60.29	950.71	109.20	128.52	5.50
1973	57.42	923.88	107.43	109.90	7.12
1974	43.84	759.37	82.85	76.29	11.59
1975	45.73	802.49	86.16	77.20	9.15
1976	54.46	974.92	102.01	89.90	8.90
1977	53.69	894.63	98.20	98.71	10.79
1978	53.70	820.23	96.02	117.53	12.03
1979	58.32	844.40	103.01	136.57	13.46
1980	68.10	891.41	118.78	168.61	12.66
1981	74.02	932.92	125.05	203.18	11.96
1982	68.93	884.36	119.71	188.97	11.60
1983	92.63	1,190.34	160.41	285.43	8.03
1984	92.46	1,138.48	160.46	244.88	10.02
1985	108.09	1,328.23	186.84	290.19	8.12
1986	136.00	1,792.76	236.34	366.96	6.09
1987	161.70	2,275.99	286.83	402.57	5.48
1988	149.91	2,060.82	265.79	374.43	8.01
1989	180.02	2,508.91	322.84	437.81	7.42
1990	183.46	2,678.94	334.59	409.17	6.47
1991	206.33	2,929.33	376.18	491.69	4.79
1992	229.01	3,284.29	415.74	599.26	4.22
1993	249.58	3,522.06	451.41	715.16	4.46
1994	254.12	3,793.77	460.42	751.65	5.83
1995	291.15	4,493.76	541.72	925.19	6.09
1996	358.17	5,742.89	670.50	1,164.96	5.24
1997	456.54	7,441.15	873.43	1,469.49	4.57

(continued)

1998	550.26	8,625.52	1,085.50	1,794.91	3.46
1999	619.16	10,464.88	1,327.33	2,728.15	3.17
2000	643.66	10,736.90	1,427.22	3,783.67	3.63
2001	605.07	10,189.13	1,194.18	2,035.00	2.95
2002	527.62	9,226.43	963.94	1,539.73	?
2001-Jan.	650.55	10,682.74	1,335.63	2,656.86	?
2001-Feb.	648.05	10,774.57	1,305.75	2,449.57	3.92
2002-Sept.	471.04	8,160.78	867.81	1,251.07	3.68
2003-Mar.	480.91	8,145.77	863.50	1,369.60	?
2003-June	563.14	9,072.95	981.64	1,610.75	?

Source: Economic Report of the President, Feb. 2000 and Feb. 2003, tables B93 and B95, respectively. Wall Street Journal, March 31 and June 24, 2003, respectively.

[a] Averages of daily stock prices.

[b] Includes stocks as follows: for NYSE, all stocks listed (nearly 3,000); for Dow Jones, 30 stocks; for S & P Composite 500 stocks; for NASDAQ Composite over 4,000 stocks.

[c] Annual data are averages of quarterly rates. Quarterly data are ratios of earnings (after taxes) for four quarters.

up. A really big quake could come any time soon, or, perhaps, a series of substantial, very disruptive shocks.

A big dollar devaluation could be quite damaging to the United States, like Britain's 40 percent collapse of the pound in 1949 (when the pound was cut from $4.03 to $2.80).[56] Thereafter foreign investors no longer trusted the British pound as a serious place for liquidity. The role of the British pound as a reserve currency was undermined. Britain, like the United States today, was overextended, financially and militarily. Britain's trade and current account deficits in the late 1940s were large and could not be stopped by politically acceptable policies. Britain, like the United States today, was a large net debtor. Britain, like the United States today, suffered a weakened industrial base and increasing challenge from foreign competitors.

How big a U.S. dollar downfall and correction in the U.S. stock market might occur? A 10 to 15 percent swing could be manageable. But a 25 to 30 percent downfall would be seriously disruptive—a 40–60 percent downfall even more so. Unfortunately, the bigger the downslide, the greater the potential for disruption. The growing U.S. dependence upon foreign capital makes its withdrawal, or need for much higher interest rates very troublesome. Thus, with a big U.S. devaluation, great pressure will be exerted for increased U.S. interest rates (to compensate for the risks of holding dollar financial assets). These tighter monetary pressures will be deflationary for the U.S. economy. But a sizable dollar devaluation brings inflationary pressures (increased prices for goods from abroad) to the U.S. economy. Vicious, conflicting crosscurrents will hit Americans as penalties for living beyond our means. Economic slowdown, more unemployment, higher prices, and serious demoralization will follow. Any presidential administration, whether Democratic or Republican, will be blamed for such mismanagement of the economy. Unhappiness and cynicism will increase. Frustration will be directed at foreign governments, companies, and profiteering speculators. Politicians will pass the buck to evil foreign influences.

What might trigger downfalls? Clearly the risk of downfall increases with higher dollar values and greater speculation in the stock markets. Sadly, these pressures feed each other in the final stages of a speculative bubble or euphoria. Specific triggers could come from many things: An unexpected set of corporate, financial, or other economic losses (perhaps transmitted initially from Southeast Asia, Latin America, the Middle East, or Europe). A costly military disaster (sinking U.S. carriers in the Persian Gulf or surrender of U.S. forces in Iraq). Major environmental disasters (earthquakes, hurricanes, superfloods in the Mississippi valley, or crop failures traceable to El Niño). Major riots and civil disturbances (in Los Angeles, Chicago, New York, Washington, or New York). In an overextended U.S. economy, with large and chronic external deficits, high stock market values (some say beyond justification), and an overvalued currency, bad things can happen.

Does it make sense to ignore warnings? To pretend bad things could not happen? Or not even to think of bad things, because it might trigger a correction or downfall? No! Responsible, economic policy must take stock and implement corrective action. And the sooner, the better, before things get worse and we get more vulnerable.

The United States has neglected its economic fundamentals. Countries cannot live beyond their means. Heavy foreign borrowing to sustain a speculative boom is not healthy. U.S. imports must come back into balance with exports. To continue with big, unsustainable external deficits in these circumstances would be insanity and grossly irresponsible mismanagement.

But to balance our trade accounts, the United States must remedy its underlying structural asymmetries.[57] A patient, two-pronged effort must be made: (1) A new reciprocity-oriented U.S. trade policy must be implemented. This effort should be sustained at least twenty years, a really long-term commitment. (2) U.S. industries must be renewed and brought up-to-speed with foreign competitors for the long haul. This effort should be sustained for at least twenty years. Engineering, product development, manufacturing, and international marketing take perseverance. U.S. companies, their American partners, and the government should work together in a new era of U.S. industrial teamwork. Some outsourcing can be productive, but outsourcing everything is impractical and unsustainable. How to draw the line? The key is to restore overall trade balance for the United States.

Does this mean that the United States should withdraw from the world market? No, quite the contrary. But U.S. companies can thrive and survive in tough world market competition only with strong, uncompromising government support, reciprocity-based trade policy, and a systematic renewal of America's industrial tradition, engineering, talent, and marketing success. Skillful outsourcing is needed. But complete outsourcing means mostly imports and minimal exports. To sustain continued trading there must be overall trade balance for the longer run.

Sustainable Internationalism for Americans

American internationalism comes in three dimensions: (1) liberal democratic political ideology; (2) economic practices and trade policy; and (3) military power and alliance strategies.[58] From its beginning as a nation, the United States felt the blessings of special democratic and liberal promise. But as a small, young country, it followed President Washington's advice not to get involved in foreign wars and European troubles. Instead, the United States focused upon expansion to the West. Like most developing countries today, the United States used tariffs, infrastructure investment, and extensive educational efforts to promote industrial growth and prosperity.

The United States became a world power by the mid-1890s, building a large navy and gathering colonies in the Philippines, Hawaii, Puerto Rico, and (for a while) Cuba. The nation began to compete more actively for exports. It sought an "open door" into restricted markets, although the American home market remained substantially protected. Being secure and separated by oceans from European and Asian conflicts, the United States was comfortable with an independent, neutralist policy, with no need for significant alliances.

America's first major foreign intervention was in World War I, crucial to Allied victory and Germany's defeat. President Wilson's creative idealism forged the League of Nations, but congressional unwillingness to limit U.S. sovereignty prevented U.S. membership. Between the wars, the United States receded into partial isolation, leaving world leadership mainly to Britain and France. This sufficed for the 1920s, a peaceful era, with reduced military budgets and few threats in the world.[59]

But the Great Depression changed everything. Hitler's German rearmament, the Japanese invasions of Manchuria and China, and the Italian conquest of Ethiopia undermined the peace. General rearmament followed. By the late 1930s British and French appeasement failed, and the Axis nations (Germany, Italy, and Japan) threatened further aggression. World War II followed (1939–1945).

Initially the United States tried neutrality. But when Germany's blitzkrieg occupied Czechoslavakia and Poland, France, the low countries, Den-mark and Norway, and later Yugoslavia and Greece, the Axis menace was too threatening. The United States heavily supported Britain, and later Rus-sia, with Lend Lease aid and cut off oil and other trade with Japan. Al-though Japan's attack at Pearl Harbor hurt the U.S. Navy temporarily, America's great industrial capacity allowed a massive mobilization. Within three-and-a-half years the United States created the world's biggest air force, the predominant navy and merchant marine, and more than a hundred ground divisions. By 1944–1945, at the Bretton Woods conference, the United States and Britain blocked out a postwar economic framework to promote free world prosperity.[60]

The United Nations (UN) organization was established in 1945–1946 to promote a better, lasting world peace. Although the UN failed to bridge the Cold War conflict (1946–1991) between the United States and the USSR, the multilateral institutions that complemented the UN have become very im-portant. Some are now indispensable for the world economy. Most important is the International Monetary Fund (IMF). The IMF is a financial support system for countries that are troubled with balance of payments problems and that need transitional help to ease crises. IMF support packages are linked, increasingly, to multinational banking loans, access to foreign direct invest-ment, and trade finance flows. A separate agency, the World Bank provides more liberal, long-term infrastructure and development loans, above and beyond what market risks could absorb. World Bank loans, expertise, and assistance are very important for the poorest countries and have been par-ticularly productive in improving food supplies.

Happily, these financial institutions, together with regional development banks in most parts of the world, are not tied to the policies of any particular country or regional bloc. They are multilateral, in a balanced, representative way. The IMF's Executive Board comprises twenty-four members, one for each major power, with a set of voting clusters that gives every part of the world a fair, but not excessive voice.[61] Neither the creditor countries, nor the majority debtor countries can lord it over each other. The IMF binds them as marketplace partners, with supermajority requirements for any significant changes in IMF structure or policies (see Table 5.2).

Sadly, the new World Trade Organization (WTO) was put together less carefully. EU countries have fifteen votes, EU candidates another ten votes, which together with 60 Lomé convention states (former European colo-nies) gives this grouping a voting majority. The United States has only one vote, a blatant imbalance problem. Furthermore, developing countries have a three-fourths voting majority. These imbalances combine with rigid, ex-cessive preferences for developing countries in access to tariffs, trade re-

Table 5.2

International Monetary Fund Executive Directors and Voting Power, March 6, 2003

Director *Alternate*	Casting votes of	Total votes[a]	Percent of fund total[b]
APPOINTED Nancy B. Jacklin *Meg Lundsager*	United States	371,743	17.10
Ken Yagi *Haruyuki Toyama*	Japan	133,378	6.14
Karlheinz Bishofberger *Ruediger von Kleist*	Germany	130,332	6.00
Pierre Duquesne *Sebastien Boitreaud*	France	107,635	4.95
Tom Scholar *Martin A. Bokke*	United Kingdom	107,635	4.95
ELECTED Willy Kiekens (Belgium) *Johann Prader (Austria)*	Austria, Belarus, Belgium, Czech Republic, Hungary, Kazakhstan, Luxembourg, Slovak Republic, Slovenia, Turkey	111,696	5.14
Jeroen Kremers (Netherlands) *Yuriy G. Yakusha (Ukraine)*	Armenia, Bosnia, Bulgaria, Croatia, Cyprus, Georgia, Israel, Macedonia, Moldova, Netherlands, Romania, Ukraine	105,412	4.85
Hernán Oyarzá (Venezuela) *Mario Beauregard (Mexico)*	Costa Rica, El Salvador, Guatemala, Honduras, Mexico, Nicaragua, Spain, Venezuela	92,989	4.28

(Continued)

Table 5.2 (continued)

Pier Carlo Padoan (Italy) *Harilos Vittas (Greece)*	Albania, Greece, Italy, Malta, Portugal, San Marino, Timor-Leste	90,968	4.19
Ian E. Bennett (Canada) *Nicolas A. Murchu (Ireland)*	Antigua, Barbuda, Bahamas, Barbados, Belize, Canada, Dominica, Grenada, Ireland, Jamaica, St. Kitts and Nevis, St. Lucia, St. Vincent, and Grenadines	80,636	3.71
Vilhjálmur Egilsson (Iceland) *Benny Andersen (Denmark)*	Denmark, Estonia, Finland, Iceland, Latvia, Lithuania, Norway, Sweden	76,276	3.51
Michael J. Callaghan (Australia) *Diwa Guinigundo (Philippines)*	Australia, Kiribati, Korea, Marshall Islands, Micronesia, Mongolia, New Zealand, Samoa, Seychelles, Solomon Islands, Vanuatu	72,423	3.33
Saluaiman M. Al-Turki (Saudi Arabia) *Abdallah S. Al Azzaz (Saudi Arabia)*	Saudi Arabia	70,105	3.23
Ismaila Usman (Nigeria) *Peter J. Ngumbullu (Tanzania)*	Angola, Botswana, Burundi, Eritrea, Ethiopia, the Gambia, Kenya, Lesotho, Liberia, Malawi, Mozambique, Namibia, Nigeria, Sierra Leone, South Africa, Sudan, Swaziland, Tanzania, Uganda, Zambia, Zimbabwe	69,968	3.22
ELECTED Sri Mulyani Indrawati (Indonesia) *Ismail Alowi (Malaysia)*	Brunei, Cambodia, Fiji, Indonesia, Laos, Malaysia, Myanmar, Nepal, Singapore, Thailand, Tonga, Vietnam	69,019	3.18
A. Shakour Shalaan (Egypt) *Oussama T. Kanaan (Jordan)*	Bahrain, Egypt, Iraq, Jordan, Kuwait, Lebanon, Libya, Maldives, Oman, Qatar, Syria, United Arab Emirates, Yemen	64,088	2.95
Wei Benhua (China) *Wang Xiaoyi (China)*	China	63,942	2.94

Table 5.2 (continued)

Fritz Zurbrügg (Switzerland) *Wieslaw Szczuka* (Poland)	Azerbaijan, Kyrgyz Republic, Poland, Switzerland, Tajikstan, Turkmenistan, Uzbekistan, Serbia, and Montenegro	61,827	2.84
Aleksei V. Mozhim, (Russian Federation) *Andrei Lushan* (Russian Federation)	Russia	59,704	2.75
Murilo Portugal (Brazil) *Roberto Steiner* (Colombia)	Brazil, Colombia, Dominican Republic, Ecuador, Guyana, Haiti, Panama, Suriname, Trinidad and Tobago	53,422	2.46
Abbas Mirakhor (Iran) *Mohammad Daïri* (Morocco)	Afghanistan, Algeria, Ghana, Iran, Morocco, Pakistan, Tunisia	53,247	2.45
Yaga V. Reddy (India) *R.A. Jayatissa* (Sri Lanka)	Bangladesh, Bhutan, India, Sri Lanka	52,112	2.40
Guillermo Le Fort (Chile) *A. Guillermo Zoccali* (Argentina)	Argentina, Bolivia, Chile, Paraguay, Peru, Uruguay	43,395	2.00
Damian Ondo Mañe (Equatorial Guinea) *Laurean W. Ratayisire* (Rwanda)	Benin, Burkina Faso, Cameroon, Cape Verde, Central African Republic, Chad, Comoros, Democratic Congo, Republic of (Zaire) Congo, Republic of Côte d'Ivoire, Djibouti, Equatorial Guinea, Gabon, Guinea, Guinea-Bissau, Madagascar, Mali, Mauritania, Mauritius, Niger, Rwanda, São Tomé and Príncipe, Senegal, Togo	30,749	1.41
		2,172,621[c, d]	99.98

Source: IMF Executive Directors and Voting Power, IMF, www.imf.org/external/np/sec/memdir/eds.htm.
[a]Voting power varies on certain matters pertaining to the General Department with use of the Fund's resources in that Department.
[b]Percentages of total votes 2,173, 313 in the General Department and the Special Drawing Rights Department.
[c]This total does not include the votes of Somalia, which did not participate in the 2002 Regular Election of Executive Directors. The total votes of this member is 692—0.03 percent of those in the General Department and Special Drawing Rights Department.
[d]This figure may differ from the sum of the percentages shown for individual Directors because of rounding.

strictions, subsidies, and exchange controls. The result is entrenched trade asymmetries, compounded by WTO voting imbalances that cannot be adjusted to meet the changing needs of countries like the United States (which now needs more offsets and relief against excessive imports). Thus, the United States is faced with an imminent need to withdraw from the WTO, because the new international trade regime is not sustainable for vital U.S. interests such as eliminating large trade and current account deficits and rejuvenating its industrial base. So the WTO and GATT 1994 need a major overhaul (rather unlikely), or the United States should give its six months notice for WTO withdrawal.[62]

In the world's first euphoria over the collapse of Communism and the Allied victory (of nearly all countries) after Iraq's conquest of Kuwait in 1990–1991, many concluded that a new era of consensus and multinational peacekeeping had been established. The mood in the early 1990s was like that of the mid 1920s, after Allied forces had withdrawn from the USSR and the major powers in Europe had signed the Locarno Pact.[63] No significant international conflicts among major countries were on the world's horizon. Even the intractable Arab-Israeli conflict seemed resolved in 1993, when, after negotiations between Yasir Arafat's Palestine Liberation Organization (PLO) and Israel's government, a provisional peace process was set up.

Unfortunately, the world now seems less peaceful again. U.S. economic, military, and political strength is no longer sufficient to allow this country to act unilaterally as the world's policeman or as ultimate guarantor of world peace. U.S. budget cuts (with bipartisan support in Congress) brought a 40 to 50 percent reduction in military forces by the end of Clinton's presidency. U.S. carrier task forces were cut from fifteen to ten, U.S. warships from 450 to fewer than 300, U.S. combat divisions from twenty-one to thirteen, and the U.S. Air Force was cut by nearly 50 percent in the later Clinton years. Some pressed for drastic, unilateral reductions in U.S. nuclear weapons. But, in the Moscow Treaty of 2002, President George W. Bush and President Vladimir Putin of Russia chose instead to maintain large reserve stocks of nuclear weapons, although they would gradually reduce the numbers of deployed warheads in launch vehicles over ten years to 1,700 for the United States and 2,200 for Russia by 2012. Both major powers felt less threatened by each other, but wanted ample nuclear reserves to cope with nuclear proliferation and potential dangers from rogue states. In reality, both former superpowers were reacting to a changing power balance, a more multipolar world.[64]

Meanwhile, on September 11, 2001, Arab terrorists attacked the World Trade Center in New York and the Pentagon in Washington. Hijacked airliners became suicide bombers that killed nearly 3,000 people. Americans quickly realized that they were under attack from al-Qaeda, a radical Islamic terrorist

Figure 5.1 **Major World Power Balances, 1550–2000**

In 1550

| France | Hapsburg | | | China |
| Portugal | Spain-Austria | Turkey | India | |

In 1650

| Britain | Dutch | Sweden | Russia | | China | |
| Spain | | France | Austria | Turkey | India | Japan |

In 1750

| | Britain | Prussia | Russia | China | |
| Spain | | France | Austria | Turkey | | Japan |

In 1900

| | Britain | Germany | | Russia | | Japan |
| United States | | France | Italy | Austria | China | |

In 1940

| | Britain | Germany | Russia | | Japan |
| United States | France | | Italy | China | |

In 2000

| United States | EU | | Russia | | China | |
| | | Islamic alliance (?) | | India | | Japan |

organization, supported by the Taliban government in Afghanistan. The Bush administration vowed to punish such terrorists and the nations that harbored them. Quickly the United States supported the Afghan Northern Alliance in its revolt against the Taliban, and successful air-ground collaboration overthrew the Taliban government by the spring of 2002. The United States enjoyed broad international support in its Afghan war and reconstruction efforts.

Next, the Bush administration targeted Saddam Hussein's dictatorial regime in Iraq. Sanctions against Saddam's Iraq had unraveled back in 1998, and it looked increasingly as if Saddam would benefit from increasing oil exports and profits and that his top goal would be an increased nuclear weapons program, together with more chemical and biological weapons. With many shaky, insecure Arab governments in the Middle East, subversion and pressure from Iraq could gravely weaken the moderate, Western-oriented Arab and other Muslim countries. This was a dangerous prospect. Bush tried to get UN support to reestablish inspections and counterpressure against Iraq. An ambiguous Security Council Resolution 1441 emerged with fifteen nations' (unanimous) support. The United States interpreted 1441 as giving Iraq a few more months to finally comply with outstanding UN mandates—to get rid of all weapons of mass destruction or face forcible removal. Britain and several others supported this view. But France, Germany, Russia, China, and several other countries interpreted the resolution as merely allowing additional months of inspection, after which the Security Council might decide whether any enforcement action was appropriate.

Bush and the United States felt that Saddam already had been given twelve years to comply with the UN's weapons of mass destruction disarmament mandate. Some 250,000 U.S. soldiers, sailors, and air force personnel were already staging into attack positions in the Middle East. Bush decided to attack promptly, in mid-March 2003, before the hot summer season, in order to force the removal of Saddam and his sons, Uday and Qusay, and get a regime change in Iraq. Bush had obtained in October 2002 a strong authorization to use force against Iraq from the U.S. Congress (by 3 to 1 majorities in both houses). Bush advisers wanted to act promptly in the spring of 2003 rather than wait until fall, when the 2004 election campaigns would be under way. Unfortunately, France, Germany, Russia, and China, refusing to support the prompt use of force, sought to delay any UN action until summer or fall. In this situation, the Bush administration went ahead with a limited Coalition of the Willing (thirty nations publicly supporting war against Iraq and another fifteen not publicly disclosed). The UN Security Council could not take consensus action in these circumstances.

The renewed war in Iraq was controversial. While few around the world really supported Saddam's dictatorship, the U.S. action caused widespread misgivings and opposition in many countries. If the coalition's operation succeeded and a more moderate regime could be established, this intervention would have benefits and might not long be resented. But U.S. and international politics set significant limits on the scope and duration of the coalition's intervention in any event. Critics complained of too much unilateralism by President Bush. His supporters responded that he had sought more international support, but many nations chose to stand aside as neutrals. But the ultimate consequences will depend on military and political success. Saddam had a significant weakness—no safe sanctuary like North Vietnam enjoyed and no open, continuing supply from outside sources. Much depended on the will and cohesion of contestants—the coalition against Saddam's forces. Reconstruction of a healthy Iraq is proving difficult.

Many are concerned that the renewed war in Iraq could aggravate alienation in Arab nations, although "successful" removal or limitation of Saddam's regime might help in this regard. Some feared that Islamic or Arab alienation could trigger a growing anti-Western Islamic alliance. Accordingly, both coalition and Saddamite forces emphasized the political, moral, and economic legitimacy of their conflict. The propaganda front was a crucial battleground— well understood by each side. Rebuilding Iraq is a crucial challenge.

In the longer run, however, the war on terrorism and the coalition's intervention in Iraq could have significant benefits for the global economy. To the extent that a dominant alliance of responsible states could act to limit and punish disruptive international misconduct, the security essential for healthy global investments, trade, and finance could be maintained. On the other hand, a multipolar power balance is hard to coordinate and it seems unlikely that U.S. hegemony can be restored, if it ever really existed.[65] All this means that a more nuanced "concert" of major powers and regional states is really the governing security system of the world. The UN Security Council could be helpful, but effective consensus can not be relied upon in all situations. Traditional diplomacy and international relations will have to fill the gaps in the multipolar realities of the twenty-first century.[66]

Meanwhile, however, the United States faces various challenges in its relationships with other countries. U.S. and NATO relations with Russia under Putin have improved. Putin seems to be a rational nation builder. But Russian military officer cadres remain somewhat alienated; many seek a Greater Russia policy that renews military, industrial, and economic power. Gradually Russia is recovering economically, which may increase global stability. Yet Russians are worried about U.S. strength, NATO expansion, and the menace of China, and they want stronger influence in Europe and the Middle East. Russian arms sales, including missiles and nuclear technology, are a tool of Russian policy; leakage occurs through black market or nongovernmental transactions. Russia's government could produce anti–U.S. policies. Russia, which clearly sees itself as independent and a major nuclear power, insists upon serious respect, and this desire should not be ignored.

China feels some tension with the United States and Asian neighbors. Although China still needs U.S. and Western markets, technology, and capital, it resents human rights criticism and other pressures from abroad. China wants Taiwan isolated and militarily weakened. Meanwhile, China has been willing to sell significant weapons technology to Middle Eastern countries. But China's trade with the United States is so large and unbalanced now that the United States enjoys substantial import leverage. Another complication for China is growing unease among its Asian neighbors about the Chinese giant. Yet China also seeks more respect and considers itself a major power now.

Relations between Japan and the United States are a little strained and need improvement. The Japan–U.S. trade deficit is the biggest and longest U.S. trading imbalance problem (lasting more than fifteen years). Frictions over U.S. military bases in Japan are a problem. Many Japanese want a stronger military now to offset China's growing strength, although whether Japan needs its own nuclear deterrent is an awkward question. If the current Middle East conflicts are not resolved and nuclear proliferation continues, Japan is likely to want a broader security policy (with nuclear weapons). But Japan's industrial and economic power makes it a useful ally and trading partner, not only to the United States but perhaps to others as well.

India has become a major power in recent years as well. With an enlarging nuclear weapons program, and other military and naval strength, India is the leading power of South Asia. It feels threatened by Pakistan and China and reaches out to Russia, the United States, the Arab states, and the EU for friendly relations. India has increasing exports and trade, but is less dependent on export relationships than China.

Although the United States regards the current EU countries as allies, growing frictions in U.S.–EU relations are a serious problem. The EU naturally seeks consensus and cohesion within its expanding federation. Ten additional countries (Poland, Hungary, the Czech Republic, Slovakia, Slovenia, Lithuania, Latvia, Estonia, Malta, and Cyprus) are scheduled for EU admission in 2004–2005, and a few more later. These additions will enhance EU influence in the world, although EU internal governance becomes more complicated. Many expect the EU to become more mercantilist (above and beyond its restrictive Common Agricultural Policy). Current trade conflicts with the United States include agriculture, airlines, commercial aircraft, banking and finance, fisheries, steel, shipbuilding, shipping, telecommunications, subsidies, safeguards, dumping, antitrust and competition policy, corporate governance and mergers, tax havens and avoidance, and WTO panel proceedings. Most EU countries want more active diplomacy for Europe beyond trading relations, but consensus among the United Kingdom, France, Germany, and other states is often difficult (as in the recent Iraq–Middle East crises). The UK wants to maintain a close relationship between the United States, UK, and Europe. Many other nations in the EU, especially the incoming Eastern European states agree. France and Germany, on the other hand, want more independence from the United States, and see themselves as partial rivals to the United States in foreign and defense policies.

With most other countries in the world—the rest of Asia, Australia and New Zealand, the Americas, and Africa—U.S. relations have been relatively comfortable. South Korea, Taiwan, and Southeast Asia have been good trading partners for the United States, except that the United States allowed them to accumulate excessive trade surpluses, which need to be corrected. Australia and New Zealand are friendly democracies and good trading partners. In Latin America and the Caribbean, after a decade of economic slump from the debt overload crisis, market-oriented reforms are unleashing substantial economic growth. But Latin America is not ready for completely open trade with the United States. Africa has been widely troubled in recent years, although the new South African Republic shows promise as a multiracial society. The biggest problem in Africa has been weak, irresponsible military governments. Reliable property rights and incentives need to be established in many areas, but most of Africa can be more successful with internal reforms that create stable, productive teamwork.

In this world scene, three conclusions should be drawn. First, the United States lacks the economic, military, and political strength to enforce American-style institutions, marching orders, or policy prescriptions. This means that the United States cannot dictate what other countries should do in trade and industrial policy. Most countries want to decide these things themselves, using selectively the best lessons from British, U.S., French, German, Swiss, Scandinavian, Japanese, Korean, Taiwanese, or Singaporean success. Each country tries to learn from the most productive, rapidly growing nations, how that experience can be adapted most productively in its own culture. To be sure, experts and scholars from the United States and other nations are welcome in this work, along with teams from the IMF and the World Bank. Certainly world market forces, access to capital, loans, and investment affect what countries and governments can afford. Countries that default on loans, confiscate investments, or become unreliable trade partners pay penalties in the global marketplace. Access to trade, financing, and capital is valuable and should not lightly be sacrificed. But the mix of responsible compromises, for good or ill, is a challenge for the relevant local authorities, national governments, and regional decision makers (for trading areas like the EU, NAFTA, ASEAN, CIS, Mercosur, Andean Pact, Central American Common Market, Caribbean Basin Association, and Organization of African States).[67]

Second, the United States must rely mainly upon its own efforts to eliminate excessive trade and current account deficits, renew industries, and strengthen technology. Other countries cannot assume responsibility for past U.S. self-neglect, and they will not volunteer concessions to rebalance U.S. trade flows. Other countries (and groupings like the EU, NAFTA, ASEAN, a revitalized CIS, or an Islamic bloc) naturally focus on their own needs, and internal political constituencies, and they will try to cut the best deal they can with the global marketplace. The United States must do likewise by switching to a new, reciprocity-based trade policy. No longer can the country afford to be the global banker, creditor, importer, and concessionaire of last resort. The United States suffers from a generation of stagnant real wages. Inequalities, poverty, and structural unemployment have increased. Americans must first take care of their own people. U.S. domestic politics must enforce this priority. For many purposes, the global economy, international bankers, IMF, MNCs, and the World Bank can take care of themselves. But the United States can, should, and must concentrate on getting a better, fair share of global industry, technology, trade, work, and profits. Other countries and regional blocs watch out for themselves. The United States should do no less. A strong, new Department of Industry, Technology, and Trade (DITT) must be established immediately by the United States to implement the new American trade policy.

Unfortunately, the GATT 1994 and WTO agreement were deeply flawed from the standpoint of U.S. interests.[68] The WTO voting regime is badly unbalanced and should be replaced with an IMF-like executive board, GDP weighted voting, and better balanced representation (Table 5.2). The WTO's excessive, rigid, and unsustainable preference for developing countries needs correction. And the GATT 1994, with its weakening of national safeguard, unfair trade practice, and balance of payments relief measures cannot cope with major asymmetries in trade flows.

Third, the United States must implement a realistic, overall foreign policy for the twenty-first century. A naive faith in U.S. hegemony, U.S. predominance as the world's policeman, and the U.S. role as beneficent law giver to the world is unworkable. Reality is more subtle, nuanced, and complex. The twenty-first century world is multipolar, with at least six or seven major power blocs (in economic, military, nuclear, and political terms). The U.S. and NAFTA, the European Union, Russia, China, Japan, India, and possibly an Islamic alliance, are the world's major powers in 2004 (see Figure 5.1). An expanded ASEAN or some South American grouping might also be added to the list of major powers.[69]

Clearly, none of these big six or seven regional powers (or blocs) is strong enough to dominate the others. But all the major powers are strong enough to enforce substantial deference and independence for themselves. Fortunately, most of the major world powers today understand their interdependence in a global economy and on the fragile ecosphere of our planet Earth. This means that regular IMF meetings, economic summit conferences among the major powers, and a broader UN Security Council will be the principal forums for accommodation in the world economy. In this multipolar system, strong incentives will operate for the smaller, isolated states to affiliate with one or another of the major power blocs. This inner logic is evident already in political competition for memberships in the EU, NAFTA, and ASEAN expansion. This momentum could be influential in shaping possible economic and political blocs among Islamic states and in South America. In a global economy of powerful regional blocs, smaller nations can be isolated, lonely, and marginalized in competition for export markets, fair treatment, and economic well-being.

We should not be alarmed at these regional developments. They do not mean that the world is drifting toward increasing conflict, rivalry, or war. They do mean, however, that the twenty-first century world is more complex than the bipolar world that existed from the late 1940s to 1991. The blocs that are successful in getting along with others will accept realistically the logic of mutual self-restraint and avoid excessive claims or interventions in other parts of the world. If the United States does not promptly adjust to this new reality but rather tries to assert hegemonic priority over other nations, the reactions of other blocs will be unfriendly, hostile, and involve likely countermeasures. But collaboration among blocs for their joint advantage will be encouraged. And each major power—the United States, the EU, Russia, China, Japan, India, and any others—must assure its own vital interests. Each major power will nurture and safeguard its industries, technology, prosperity, and military strength.

Recent Trade Bargaining—Multilateral, Regional, and Bilateral

Realism is crucial to U.S. trade policy in the early twenty-first century. Negotiations are proceeding on three tracks: multilateral, regional, and bilateral. The current WTO Doha Round is logjammed so far—on agricultural trade restrictions; pharmaceutical patents, prices, and licensing; safeguards and dumping relief; mitigating dislocations from increasing openness; and disagreement on the extent that "freer" trade should be trusted in the coming years. Increasing worry over the WTO dispute settlement process is a problem, too. This reflects unresolved tensions and conflicts among nations over allocating trade, economic growth, and resulting prosperity.[70]

Interestingly, the earlier 1947 vision of GATT "freer" trade that preserved more safeguard relief, remedies for balance of payments deficits, antidumping duties, and offsets to foreign subsidies turns out to be more realistic in the present situation. GATT 1947 resonates better with the fundamental needs of most nations and peoples for fuller employment, secure businesses, and prospects for industrial growth. GATT 1947 is a better framework to limit disruptive and speculative capital flows. Finally, GATT 1947 provides a more realistic understanding of the social productivity of accumulated capital, engineering talents, and workplace skills. Countries need substantial industrial continuity, longer-run family incomes, and reliable business and farming activities. MNCs should be woven into these matrices as productive partners for the longer haul, but not as short-term opportunists, transitory deal makers, and cut-and-run profit artists.

In contrast, the vision of GATT 1994 and the WTO was dominated by MNCs, whose interests and freedoms have priority. "Rules-based" WTO panels were designed by MNC enthusiasts among the OECD industrial nations to protect MNC interests—not workers, family incomes, local communities, national employment, or the environment. Because most MNC stockholders and higher-level managers would presumably gain, this was thought sufficient, for a while, to make general globalization seem attractive. But in most OECD nations now, there is less confidence in general benefits from "total free trade."

For some years many believed that developing countries (NICs and LDCs) would gain widely, because large numbers of jobs would be shifted to lower-wage markets in the outsourcing process. General benefits would thus flow to the developing world, although they had to protect foreign investors, intellectual property holders, and MNCs under Uruguay Round agreements and Bilateral Investment Treaties. Only modest numbers of inefficient local businesses and farmers in developing countries might suffer. But as things turned out, the boom-bubble-crisis-devaluation-slump parade produced many more losers and wider insecurities than expected for developing nations. Therefore, the anticipated "rapid completion" of freer trade, and the elimination of all remaining tariffs, safeguards, antidumping, and countersubsidy remedies are not trusted any more in most NICs and LDCs.[71]

The developing world now wants stronger limitations on globalization, especially since giant China, Russia, and other transitional economies refuse complete openness and unrestricted freedom for foreign MNCs in their territories. So most developing countries and transitional nations no longer accept full openness. Developing states now insist upon substantial limits, while demanding more access to and preferences in the advanced (OECD bloc) markets. In other words, structural asymmetry and unequal openness are being entrenched. Sadly, there is no way that the greatly excessive U.S. trade and current account deficits can be eliminated in the Doha WTO Round in progress.

Meanwhile, most EU countries, Japan, South Korea, and Taiwan now want to limit the completion of "total" openness to foreign competition. The EU's Common Agricultural Policy, together with Japanese and Korean agricultural restrictions, have strongly protectionist, small farmer, food "safety," and food "security" themes. Antidumping and safeguard relief is faster and more effective through prompt settlements in these countries. These other OECD countries also enforce overall trade balances (and often very large trading surpluses). In contrast to U.S. foreign economic policies, most "allies" and rivals of the United States do not feel they can afford significant current account deficits or disruptive devaluations. Through more effective policy coordination and industrial responsibility and teamwork, most OECD countries learned after World War II that overall trade balance discipline is an essential complement to sound macroeconomic policies. Thus, they understand that fiscal, monetary, and wage-price discipline must be joined by trade balance discipline, too.

Naive hopes in the United States from the Uruguay Round and the new Doha Round are proving unsound. Americans were persuaded in 1993 to 1994 that a major opening of world agriculture markets, together with a rapid completion of free trade abroad, with all countries using only minimal restrictions, was under way. This would quickly universalize total free trade around the world. Thus, an integrated global economy, led by the United States and MNCs, would bring great benefits overall to Americans, in spite of occasional job losses by union members in a limited number of U.S. industries. Unfortunately, the U.S. boom-bubble expansion from 1995 to 2000 failed to sustain itself. Moreover, in the following global recession and slowdown of 2001 and beyond, U.S. outsourcing has continued at a brisk pace. Net U.S. job losses are increasing (as in 1978–1994). In response, the Bush administration used fairly strong steel safeguard relief (for three years) from 2001 to 2003 in order to survive the elections of 2002 and 2004. This was shrewd politics, but it shows the limits on U.S. "give" in the Doha Round to the EU, Japan, NICs, and LDCs. Ironically, similar toughness took over trade bargaining in the EU, Japan, most developing economies, and the transitional countries (former Communist states). All this strongly limits additional trade opening in the WTO Doha Round.

In this situation, many MNC interests and WTO officials urge that the Doha Round be delayed and continued. Their prime goal is to maintain their system—that is, a framework within which MNCs relocate plants, processing, R & D, service, and headquarters activities at their convenience. Perhaps this is what is left of the "bicycle theory" to "protect" MNCs around the world. Can the United States get improved awareness and recognition of its special balance of payments and current account needs?—that is, can it enlarge export earnings while cutting back on imports? Not likely, and certainly not by multilateral agreements and concessions in the Doha Round.

Therefore, many trade observers emphasize bilateral and regional trade bargaining as better vehicles for improving trade balance.[72] The EU, Japan, and many NICs already have been aggressive in seeking a broad range of bilateral free trade agreements with many active and potential trading partners. The Bush administration in the last three and a half years has been aggressively seeking more bilateral trade agreements, too. Jordan, Chile, Singapore, Central America, Morocco, Australia, and five southern African countries have been early, special, and promising candidates for these purposes. The Bush administration also pushed for a thirty-four-nation Free Trade Area of the Americas, although key countries (most notably Brazil) are resisting the wider arrangement. It is becoming apparent that bilateral bargaining is a fast-track, mutually productive, and a better framework within which the United States can press for improved and meaningful reciprocity. The increasingly close relationship among the EU's own membership, and its favoritism to former European colonies, illustrate the increasing scope for their bilateral regional trade bargaining. Japan, China, ASEAN, and India are actively pursuing bilateral deals as well. This trend is logical and desirable for most nations; few countries can afford to be left out of bilateral trade and investment security arrangements. Bilateral networks (widely reciprocated) could become dominant, especially if GATT 1994 and the WTO collapse.

In this regard, growing discontent with the overly rigid, "negative consensus" panels, WTO's Dispute Settlement system must be emphasized.[73] Under GATT 1947, the dispute resolution process was basically mediation, and yet panel reports were taken seriously and scholars now realize that settlements occurred in something like 85 percent of the cases. But the WTO's success rate is not nearly as good; many countries are becoming more rigidly contentious, especially EU countries with their neomercantilism. American experts are noticing a bias against the United States in important recent cases, particularly in overruling the United States's use of its own trade laws to achieve reasonable safeguarding and relief against dumping or subsidies and in defending intellectual property and investment interests.

The whole concept of automatic, rigid enforcement of complete free trade rules by WTO panels was unrealistic. It seemed desirable only from a strongly MNC-oriented viewpoint. What the world really needed in 1993–1994, and needs even more urgently in the early twenty-first century, is a trading system with more "flex." Excessive trading unbalances, unsustainable trade deficits, disruptive capital flows (in and/or out), and needless destruction and relocation of industries, companies, plants, and workers are not sound trade policy or economic development. The political backlash against an unbalanced trading system of *unrestricted globalization* is overwhelming. Most countries want instead a more humane, realistically constrained global economy. Yes, the world's technologies must be shared out more equally. "Freer" trading, cross-investment, and risk pooling are desirable. But blind, unlimited laissez-faire, MNC favoritism, and lack of respect for accumulated talent, industrial capital, communities, and engineering know-how, are unsound. The earlier GATT 1947 framework with mediation-oriented dispute resolution was wiser, more resilient, and more humane. In the GATT 1947 framework, the vital role for appropriate safeguarding, antidumping relief, limitations on disruptions, offsets to foreign subsidies, reasonable reciprocity, and defense of national interests was properly understood.

When the present GATT 1994 and WTO trading system breaks down over its lack of flexibility and an inability to cope with massive U.S. trade and current account deficits, the "A, B, C, D" system of tiered tariffs makes better sense.[74] "A-class" countries with minimal tariffs and open capital markets would enjoy minimal U.S. tariffs and restrictions. Most OECD, NAFTA, and recent U.S. bilateral FTA partners fit this framework already. "B-class" countries would face 6 to 10 percent U.S. tariffs. This category would apply to countries using 12 to 25 percent average tariffs and somewhat restricted capital markets. "C-class" countries would face 15 to 20 percent U.S. tariffs. This class includes nations with 30 to 50 percent tariffs and substantial capital and intellectual property restrictions. "D-class" countries, which would face greatly restricted access to U.S. markets, would include nations offering little access to their own markets and little or no access for capital flows and/or intellectual property protection. With this reciprocity-based ladder of conditional access to U.S. markets, countries choose the degree of access they prefer in trading with the United States, and vice versa. The "A, B, C, D' class system of graduated access would solve the free rider and asymmetry problems left uncorrected by the Uruguay Round (1985–1994). This graduated class system would better balance trade flows and provide for the elimination of the U.S. structural and current account deficits after a few years.

Finally, we must recognize that the United States faces an overriding danger and urgency in greatly enlarged trade and current account deficits. The WTO and multilateral bargaining cannot solve these problems. Only direct action by the United States itself, combined with skillful bilateral and/or regional bargaining, can make much progress. The "A, B, C, D" tiered system of graduated access could be the best solution. Clearly, this external imbalance problem for the United States was easier to deal with 10 to 15 years ago. But MNC lobbies, international banks, and U.S. diplomats were reluctant to get into complications. Free market enthusiasts preferred simply to let global currency markets solve these imbalance problems. Lack of imagination also inhibited questions about the dollar's value and exchange rate adjustments. The U.S. dollar was king of the global currency markets from 1919 (or at least from 1945) until the recent euro challenge. Not only the Americans, but also Europeans, Asians, Africans, and Latin Americans relied upon the permanence of a dollar-based international finance and trading system. But a major structural realignment in currencies, trading flows, and investment activity will be working itself out in the next few years. Serious adjustment strains are unavoidable. The world will not long tolerate continued U.S. trade and current account deficits of $500–600 billion annually (or

to 6 percent of U.S. GNP). The United States would be extremely unwise to simply let these imbalances build up until the dollar crashes with a major, highly disruptive devaluation and a spreading global breakdown in exports and prosperity.[75] Entrenched structural U.S. trade and current account deficits must be eliminated by the United States and its significant trade partners for the sake of a sustainable global economy. This architectural reform is a high priority for the international marketplace.

Notes and References

References to Chapters 1 and 5 follow the notes to Chapter 5. References also follow the notes to Chapters 3 and 4. Sources for Chapter 2 are contained in the notes to Chapter 2.

Notes to Chapter 1

1. Lovett (1987) provides many sources on British economic development, industrial, and trade policies. But special emphasis should be given to Kitson and Solomou (1990) (for about the 1920s–30s) and Middlemas and Barnes (1969), (for about the 1920s–30s). See also Feis (1930) and Bougkin (1991). And see Aldcroft 1970, Amery 1969, Brittan 1971, 1995, Bairoch 1993, Caves and Krause 1980, Cairncross and Eichengreen 1983, Crouzet 1982, and Shonfield 1958. Finally, Kindleberger (1993), is helpful for general background.

2. See Kindleberger 1993, generally, along with deVries 1986, Cairncross and Eichengreen 1983, James 1996, Kenen 1994, Funabashi 1989, Bergsten 1991, Dobson 1991, Volcker and Gyohten 1992, Root 1994, Bergsten 1996, Blecker 1996, and Lowenfeld 2002.

3. For the significance of safeguard and unfair trade practice relief under GATT 1947, see Lovett (1994a, 1994b); Jerome (1992); and Mastel (1996). See also Schott 1996, Jackson 1989, Hufbauer and Erb 1984, and Jackson 1997.

4. See, for example, Stein (1990); and standard texts like Peterson and Estenson 1992, Kidwell 2003, and Lovett 2001.

5. See Thurow 1996, Blecker 1992, Godley 1995, McKinnon 1996, James 1996, Erdman 1996, Eichengreen 1994, Dornbusch 1988, Kenen 1995, and Krugman 1989.

In this connection, we should remember the fundamental importance of the overall "balance of produce and consumption" in Adam Smith's *Wealth of Nations*. Smith explains that this overall balance determines whether a nation prospers or decays (Smith 1776, 81, 464).

6. See this text, Tables 1.1A, 1.1B, and 1.2. Also, Blecker 1992, Thurow 1996, Godley 1995, and Beinart 1997. Some foreign policy writers recognize the U.S. "twin deficits" as a problem. See Brzezinski (1993, 109); Paul Kennedy's thesis of imperial overstretch is nicely illustrated by U.S. deficits in the 1980s and 1990s. See Kennedy (1987).

7. A rough estimate of the shifting capital position for the United States can be suggested from its accumulated current account deficits. Thus, because the net creditor position of the United States was estimated in 1980 to be +$141 billion and the

accumulated current deficits between 1981 and 1997 totaled some $1,650 billion as of the end of 1997, the United States stood roughly –$1,500 billion in debt as of the end of 1997. Between the years 1981 and 1988, the U.S. net position went from +$141 billion to –$532 billion—a swing of –$671 billion in a period with about –$700 billion in current account deficits (*Survey of Current Business*, June issues). If the same valuation estimates were extended (based largely on historical costs), the net U.S. debtor position would have reached around –$1,500 billion by the end of 1997. Since June 1990, however, a different valuation procedure, based more upon contrasting stock market indexes, has been utilized by the *Survey of Current Business* (June issues, for most years, except Oct. 1997). This new procedure yields a creditor position for the United States of +$374 billion in 1981 versus –$870 billion at the end of 1996. Either way, the U.S. net international investment position suffered a major deterioration between 1981 and 1997, anywhere from –$1,250 to –$1,500 billion, depending upon the valuation procedure.

Recently, Michael R. Sesit, writing the Foreign Exchange column for the *Wall Street Journal*, estimated that "America's net external debt—that Americans owe foreigners—of $1.2 trillion is roughly 15% of its total output. By contrast, the rest of the world owes Switzerland 130% of its gross national product, Japan about 23% and Germany 9%" (Nov. 4, 1997).

William Burke, a former Federal Reserve economist, estimated in mid-1995 that the U.S. net external debt was then $1,048 billion (Burke 1995). We estimate that the net U.S. investment position at the end of 1997 was at least –$1,250 billion, and it could have been somewhat worse.

Unfortunately for the *Survey of Current Business*, contrasting stock market indexes are complicated by major declines in Asian stock market values for 1997. According to Muriel Seibert & Co., Inc. (*Behind the Numbers*, April 1997, 2), foreign ownership of the U.S. federal government's debt had risen to –27.61 percent in 1997. Thus, the willingness of foreign investors and governments to continue investing in U.S. debt (or not) has become a major factor in U.S. interest rates, economic growth prospects, and prosperity.

By the end of 2003 (i.e., from 1998 through 2003), the United States had accumulated another –$2,300 billion in current account deficits. These current account deficits had to be made up or "covered" by net capital imports. Accordingly, a conservative net capital position for the United States at the end of 2003 was at least –$3,000 to –$3,200. (See also Lovett 2002, note 75.)

8. See Bergsten 1997, Lovett 1996a, Eichengreen 1997, Pitchford 1997, Feldstein 1997, Temperton 1993, Kenen 1992, and Cecco 1989.

9. A very large literature has developed since the early 1980s on the U.S. economic slowdown, job losses, industrial competitiveness problems, wage and earnings squeeze, growing inequality, and weakness in U.S. trade policies. See Choate and Garfield 1980, Bluestone and Harrison 1982, Peterson 1982, Hofheinz and Calder 1982, Reich and Magaziner 1982, Kuttner 1982, Zysman and Tysen 1983, Eckstein 1984, Murray 1984, Lovett 1984, Culbertson 1985, Priore and Sabel 1984, Adams and Klein 1983, Phillips 1984, Johnson 1984, Shepard 1983, Reich and Donahue 1985, National Commission on Competitiveness 1985, Nelson 1984, Shutt 1985, Lamont 1986, Lodge and Vogel 1987, Cohen and Zysman 1987, Lovett 1987, Porter 1986, Prestowitz 1988, Kaden and Smith 1988, Mishel and Simon 1988, Starr 1988, Kuttner 1989, Culbertson 1989, Fallows 1989, Van Wolferen 1989, McCraw 1989, Krugman 1990, Dertouzos 1990, Chandler 1990, Fligstein 1990, Lincoln 1990, Frieden

and Lake 1991, Ohmae 1990, Florida and Kenney 1990, Porter 1990, Derian 1990, Lodge 1990, Holbrooke 1991, Mishel and Frankel 1991, Reich 1991, Kuttner 1991, Graham 1992, Thurow 1992, Jerome 1992, Vargish 1992, Marshall and Tucker 1992, Kaden and Smith 1992, Kearns 1992, Wood 1992, Coote 1992, Lovett 1993, Newman 1993, Batra 1993, Perot and Choate 1993, Bergsten 1996, Tolchin 1993, Adler and Bernstein 1994, Goldsmith 1994, Fallows 1994, Layard 1994, Lovett 1994, Phillips 1984, Korten 1995, Godley 1995, Dryden 1995, Eckes 1995, Madrick 1995, Mishel and Bernstein 1995, Faux 1997, Pozo 1996, Thurow 1996, Beinert 1997, Bernstein and Munro 1997, Greider 1997, Hirst and Thompson 1997, Faux 1997, Mastel 1997, Wallach 1997b, and Wolman and Colamosca 1997.

10. Most of the media-highlighted trade debate focused upon NAFTA. See, for example, Hufbauer and Schott (1993) versus Perot and Choate (1993). Later, of course, after the Mexican peso collapsed in value by 60 percent in 1994–1995, most of the U.S. export gains slumped, and a large U.S. trade deficit developed with Mexico. See Lovett (1996c). Also, see Table 1.2 in this text.

But the Uruguay Round GATT deal of 1985 to 1994 led to controversy as well. See, for example, Jerome 1992, Lawrence and Schultze 1990, Kuttner 1989, Blecker 1992, Schott 1990, Rubin and Jones 1989, Prestowitz 1988, Lovett 1987, Culbertson 1989, Lovett 1993, Lovett 1994, Schott 1994, Godley 1995, Schott 1996, Jackson 1997, Thurow 1996, Lovett 1996, Blecker 1996.

Unfortunately, the only open government debate on the final Uruguay Round GATT deal was held in a half-day hearing before the House Ways and Means Committee on June 10, 1994. Favoring the GATT were Mickey Kantor (USTR), Jeff Lang, Julius Katz, Bill Frenzel, and Willard Workman (U.S. Chamber of Commerce). Opposing were Pat Choate, Bruce Fein, and William Lovett (Lovett 1994b). Hardly any media coverage was devoted to GATT and WTO issues in 1994. (It seemed too complicated for most of the media and their reporters to cover.)

11. The GATT 1994–WTO deal needs careful review of its lengthy text to fully understand it.

Most of the text is set forth in the documentary supplements to two international trade law casebooks: Jackson et al. (1995) and Bhala (2002). Limited selections of material relating to these issues are provided in the Jackson and Bhala casebooks. Remarkably, most U.S. economists and lawyers remain poorly informed on the Uruguay Round—that is, GATT 1994 and the WTO. Favorable reviews are given by Schott (1994), Schott (1996), and Jackson (1997). Critical evaluations and emphasis on the shortcomings are provided by Jerome (1992), Lovett (1994 and 2002), and Mastel (1996).

12. The extent of job losses (or gains) from expanding world trade is an emotional issue.

Divergent claims are offered by free trade enthusiasts versus labor-oriented and other critics. Unfortunately, the data have not been properly tabulated or disclosed, so that only rough estimates can be offered. An estimate of U.S. job flows and turnover between 1972 and 1988 was offered recently, but major ambiguities remain about its underlying data (Davis et al. 1996).

We must be clear about the crucial questions in estimating trade-related job losses and creation. The real problem for trade policy is to decide by how much U.S. manufacturing jobs (and collateral employment in communities) would have grown without such a decline, if a stronger, reciprocity-based U.S. trade policy had been enforced. Experts should agree that the U.S. opened up industrial markets substantially more than most of its trade partners, so that industrial growth, exports, and net jobs expansion were greater (in varying degree) elsewhere. We concede that improved productivity and "fair trade" expansion probably required some U.S. downsizing and job relocation. But a stronger U.S. trade policy that enforced effective reciprocity, greatly limited asymmetries, and used rationalization measures to keep more manufacturing in the United States would have saved a substantial number of U.S. jobs from the late 1960s through 1997. This author estimates that 8 to 9 million U.S. industrial jobs (and another 2 to 3 million collateral jobs in the affected communities) would have been saved by a stronger policy that used more systematic rationalization measures. This means that more U.S. economic growth, exports, and employment would have resulted on a cumulative, mutually reinforcing basis. Why were not such measures taken? Overly partisan politics, lack of interest by MNCs, rigid job-saving attitudes by unions, and a lack of concern and imagination by top U.S. leaders responsible for trade-industrial policies.

This is how the job losses played out in recent presidential administrations. Truman-Eisenhower: 300,000 to 500,000 job losses; U.S. economy growing substantially, still competitive, and only limited asymmetries. Kennedy-Johnson: 200,000 to 400,000 job losses; U.S. economy growing well, largely competitive, and only somewhat greater asymmetries. Nixon-Ford: 400,000 to 800,000 job losses; U.S. growth slowing, foreign competition increasing, and asymmetries accumulating (especially in NICs). Carter: 800,000 to 1 million job losses; increased foreign competition, more asymmetries, and U.S. trade policy encouraging more job relocation abroad. Reagan: 2 to 3 million job losses; greater foreign competition pressures, major recession, and increased job relocation. G.H.W. Bush: 2 to 3 million job losses; more explicit U.S. job relocation policies with slowed domestic growth. Clinton: 2 to 3 million job losses; somewhat better growth, but continued U.S. job relocation policies. G.W. Bush: 2 to 3 million job losses; slowdown and slump after the bubble, with continued outsourcing to low-wage countries. NAFTA 1993 and GATT 1994 trade deals entrenched MNC influence and sustained job relocation trends. NOTE: Until recent years, no adequate U.S. government data were provided on jobs displacement. But some effort at disclosing these job losses was made in the *Statistical Abstract of the United States* (1996, Table 635: Displaced Workers, by Selected Characteristics). These data reveal 10 million displaced workers between 1987 and 1993 (about half were involved in plant closings). These job loss estimates are consistent with the foregoing analysis, except that not all displaced workers between 1987 and 1993 were trade-related (and the jobs growth forgone by weakened U.S. manufacturing was not counted as displaced workers). A special problem, widely neglected, is rural workers (Podgursky 1989).

U.S. trade and current account deficits have grown increasingly large and chronic since the mid-1970s, with imports exceeding exports. This should have been prevented by stronger U.S. trade and rationalization measures. Imports should have been capped each year at export levels. U.S. manufacturing, exports, and balanced trade would have been somewhat larger since the mid-1970s, when serious asymmetries began to bite into the country's industrial growth prospects. At each stage no drastic net increase in jobs, manufactures, and exports would have resulted, but the cumulative benefits for employment, economic growth, and industrial progress would have been substantial. These data are consistent with estimates provided in Chapter 2 that the U.S. economy probably lost around 1 percent per annum in real economic growth in recent years as a result of U.S. trade policy. See note 96, Chapter 2, below.

13. In other words, the U.S. must reemphasize its overall balance of production and consumption (Smith 1776, 464).

References to Chapter 1

All references to Chapters 1 and 5 follow the Notes to Chapter 5. References are provided after the Notes for Chapters 3 and 4 also, but sources for Chapter 2 are contained in the Notes for that chapter.

Notes to Chapter 2

1. John J. McCusker and Russell R. Menard, *The Economy of British North America, 1607–1789* (Chapel Hill: University of North Carolina Press, 1985), p. 86.

2. On cotton diplomacy, see Frank L. Owsley, *King Cotton Diplomacy: Foreign Relations of the Confederate States of America* (Chicago: University of Chicago Press, 1931).

3. On oil, see Daniel Yergin, *The Prize* (New York: Simon & Schuster, 1991), pp. 178, 183; Alfred E. Eckes, *The United States and the Global Struggle for Minerals* (Austin: University of Texas Press, 1979), pp. 15, 51.

4. U.S. Bureau of the Census, *Historical Statistics of the United States*, Bicentennial Edition (Washington, DC: Government Printing Office, 1975), 2:903–907; *Statistical Abstract of the United States* (various issues); and *Survey of Current Business* (June 1992, July 1997, April 2002).

5. McCusker and Menard, *Economy of British America*, p. 357; Gerald Stourzh, *Benjamin Franklin and American Foreign Policy,* 2nd ed. (Chicago: University of Chicago Press, 1969).

6. Alfred E. Eckes Jr., *Opening America's Market: U.S. Foreign Trade Policy since 1776* (Chapel Hill: University of North Carolina Press, 1995), pp. 2–3; John Adams to John Jay, Feb. 26, 1786, in Mary A. Giunta, ed., *The Emerging Nation: A Documentary History of the Foreign Relations of the United States under the Articles of Confederation, 1780–1789* (National Historical Records Commission) (Washington, DC: Government Printing Office, 1996), 3:108–109. On Franklin's free trade vision, see Drew R. McCoy, "Benjamin Franklin's Vision of a Republican Political Economy for America," *William and Mary Quarterly* 35:4 (October 1978): 605.

7. Eckes, *Opening America's Market*, pp. 5–6.

8. On problems implementing the Franco-American commercial treaty, see Giunta, *Emerging Nation*, 2:261–268, 844–846, 883, 917, 954, 958.

9. Samuel Shaw to John Jay, May 19, 1785, in Giunta, *Emerging Nation*, 2:637–641; Foster Rhea Dulles, *The Old China Trade* (New York: AMS, 1970, reprint of 1930 ed.), p. 26; Elizabeth M. Nuzoll and Mary A. Gallagher, *The Papers of Robert Morris* (Pittsburgh: University of Pittsburgh Press, 1995), 8:857–865.

10. John Adams to John Jay, Aug. 30, 1785, in Giunta, *Emerging Nation*, 2:785.

11. *Brown v. Maryland*, 25 U.S. 420 (1827).

12. Eckes, *Opening America's Market*, pp. 13–14.

13. Harold C. Syrett, ed., *The Papers of Alexander Hamilton* (New York: Columbia University Press, 1961), 10:262, 285–286, 297.

14. Arthur H. Vandenberg, *The Greatest American: Alexander Hamilton* (New York: G.P. Putnam's Sons, 1921), p. 200; James D. Richardson, comp., *A Compilation of the Messages and Papers of the Presidents* (New York: Bureau of National Literature, 1917), 1:470.

15. Emory R. Johnson, T.W. Van Metre, G.G. Huebner, and D.S. Hanchett, *History of Domestic and Foreign Commerce of the United States* (Washington, DC: Carnegie Institute, 1915), 2:35. Jefferson also favored bilateral free-trade agreements, but he insisted on strict reciprocity and enforcement. See Eckes, *Opening America's Market*, pp. 12–13.

16. Tariff data from Bureau of the Census, *Historical Statistics of the United States*, 2:888. On Clay's system, see Robert V. Remini, *Henry Clay: Statesman for the Union* (New York: W.W. Norton, 1991), pp. 225–233.

17. Hong Kong and Singapore may have relied more on free trade, but they are small city trading states. Hong Kong prospered on account of proximity and access to the large, but restricted, Chinese market. A strategic location and a development-minded government benefited Singapore. Of course, not every nation that practiced protectionism pursued successful development policies. David Landes, *The Wealth and Poverty of Nations* (New York: W.W. Norton, 1998), pp. 265–268; Paul Bairoch, *Economics and World History* (Chicago: University of Chicago Press, 1993), pp. 44–55.

18. Kirk H. Porter and Donald Bruce Johnson, *National Party Platforms* (Urbana: University of Illinois Press, 1956), pp. 107, 123.

19. Elizabeth Feaster Baker, *Henry Wheaton, 1785–1848* (1937; reprint, New York: Da Capo Press, 1971), pp. 235–253.

20. Naomi C. Miller, ed., *The Political Writings of Richard Cobden* (1903; reprint, New York: Garland, 1973), 1:36; *Economist*, August 1843, pp. 14–15.

21. Edward Stanwood, *American Tariff Controversies in the 19th Century* (New York: Russell & Russell, 1903), 2:41–45.

22. William Belmont Parker, *Life and Public Services of Justin Smith Morrill* (Boston: Houghton Mifflin, 1924), p. 320; *Congressional Globe*, Feb. 5, 1857 (appendix, p. 226), April 23, 1860 (p. 1832).

23. Charles W. Calhoun, "Political Economy in the Gilded Age: The Republican Party's Industrial Policy," *Journal of Policy History* 8, no. 3 (1996): 304.

24. In 1932, cotton and tobacco amounted to 26 percent. U.S. Bureau of the Census, *Historical Statistics of the United States*, Bicentennial Edition, 2:889–898.

25. Ida M. Tarbell, *The Tariff in Our Times* (New York: Macmillan, 1911); Arthur Link, ed., *The Papers of Woodrow Wilson* (Princeton, NJ: Princeton University Press, 1982), 40:343, 372, 384.

26. Eckes, *Opening America's Market*, pp. 37–42.

27. National Association of Manufacturers, "Chronological Documents of NAM Positions on the Tariff and Reciprocity Agreements since 1895," April 1947, NAM Papers, Hagley Library, Box 196, Wilmington, DE. See generally William H. Becker, *The Dynamics of Business-Government Relations: Industry and Exports, 1893–1921* (Chicago: University of Chicago Press, 1982).

28. Eckes, *Opening America's Market*, pp. 82–84.

29. Richardson, *Compilation of the Messages and Pages of the Presidents*, 18:8939.

30. U.S. Tariff Commission, *Information Concerning Dumping and Other Unfair Foreign Competition in the United States and Canada's Anti-Dumping Law* (Washington, DC: Government Printing Office, 1919), pp. 22–23.

31. U.S. Census Bureau, *Statistical Abstract of the United States, 1929* (Washington, DC: Government Printing Office, 1930), p. 469.

32. U.S. Census Bureau, *Statistical Abstract of the United States, 1929*, p. 469.

33. U.S. Bureau of the Census, *Historical Statistics*, 2:888.

34. Ibid.

35. Eckes, *Opening America's Market*, pp. 44–45.

36. U.S. Senate, Committee on Finance, *Hearings on H.R. 8687*, 73rd Cong., 2nd scss., April–May 1934, pp. 1, 7; Edgar B. Nixon, ed., *Franklin D. Roosevelt and Foreign Affairs* (Cambridge, MA: Harvard University Press, 1969), 2:1–3.

37. Fowler and Hawkins memo, Feb. 13, 1935, Committee on Trade Agreements, RG 353, National Archives.

38. Eckes, *Opening America's Market*, pp. 145–146. On Roosevelt's views, see William Phillips Papers, Feb. 14, 16, 1935, Houghton Library, Harvard University.

39. Emphasis added. U.S. House of Representatives, Committee on Ways and Means, *Report to Accompany H. J. Res. 96*, 75th Cong., 1st sess., H. Rept. 166, pp. 1–2.

40. William Diebold, Jr., *The End of the I.T.O.: Essays in International Finance*, No. 16, (Princeton, NJ: Princeton University, Department of Economics, 1952), p. 4.

41. See generally David Broscious, "One World Into Two Worlds: The Evolution of U.S. Grand Strategy, 1947–1950," doctoral dissertation, Ohio University, 1997, pp. 196–202.

42. Philip Cortney, "Havana ITO Charter: A Dishonest Document," *Vital Speeches*, June 1, 1949, pp. 490–493.

43. American Tariff League, *The Story Behind GATT* (New York: American Tariff League, 1955), p. 19; Diebold, *End of the I.T.O.*

44. George Bronz, "An International Trade Organization: The Second Attempt," *Harvard Law Review* 69, no. 3 (1956): 440–482.

45. U.S. House of Representatives, Ways and Means Committee, *The Agreement on the Organization for Trade Cooperation*, H.R. 5550, 84th Cong., 2nd sess., House Report 2007, 1956, p. 47.

46. U.S. Tariff Commission, *Operation of the Trade Agreements Program* (OTAP) (19 Report, 1967), (Washington, DC: U.S. Tariff Commission, 1969), 240–241; Reginald Maudling to Prime Minister Macmillan, October 27, 1959, BT 11/5771, Public Record Office, Kew, England. See also Alan S. Milward and George Brennan, *Britain's Place in the World: A Historical Enquiry into Import Controls 1945–1960* (London: Routledge, 1996).

47. Unpublished pages from "memoirs," Truman Library, Independence, Missouri.

48. Robert Ferrell, *Eisenhower Diaries Dwight D. Eisenhower,* (New York: W.W. Norton, 1981), p. 242; *Public Papers of the Presidents of the United States 1957*, (Washington, DC: Government Printing Office), pp. 460–462.

49. *Public Papers of the Presidents: Harry S. Truman, 1947*, pp. 167–172.

50. *Public Papers of the Presidents: Eisenhower, 1954*, pp. 585–590.

51. Minutes of meetings, March 27 and April 18, 1955, International Trade File, box 234, RG 43, National Archives.

52. Meeting, March 26, 1955, International Trade Files, RG 43, National Archives.

53. Quote from various meetings, Feb. 22 to April 18, 1955, International Trade Files, box 234, RG 43, National Archives.

54. *Public Papers of the Presidents: Lyndon B. Johnson, 1968*, p. 199; *1967*, pp. 1073, 1148; U.S. Tariff Commission, OTAP, 19th Report, 1967, TC Pub. 287, pp. 170–174.

55. Gilbert to Nixon, June 15, 1969, WHCF, RMN; Public Law 93–618, 93rd Cong., H.R. 10710, January 3, 1975.

56. U.S. Tariff Commission, *Trade Barriers* (Invs. 332–66 and 332–67) (TC Pub. 665) (Washington, DC: U.S. Tariff Commission, 1974), 8:113.

57. Data from John W. Evans, *The Kennedy Round in American Trade Policy: The Twilight of the GATT?* (Cambridge, MA: Harvard University Press, 1971), p. 253; U.S. Tariff Commission, OTAP, 19th Report, 1967 (Washington, DC: U.S. Tariff Commission, 1967), p. 172.

58. Steve Dryden, *Trade Warriors: USTR and the American Crusade for Free Trade* (New York: Oxford University Press, 1995), pp. 107–109.

59. U.S. Department of State, *Bulletin*, July 31, 1967, pp. 127–129.

60. Alfred E. Eckes Jr., and Thomas W. Zeiler, *Globalization and the American Century* (New York: Cambridge University Press, 2003), pp. 157–160; Theodore Levitt, "The Globalization of Markets," *Harvard Business Review* 61, no. 3 (May–June 1983): 92–102.

61. Tun Razak quote from Mohd, Ariffin, "A Fantasy Theme Analysis of Selected Speeches of Tun Abdul Razak Hussein on the Issues of New Economic Policy in Malaysia 1971–1975." MA thesis, Ohio University, 1989; Rajah Rasiah, "Free Trade Zones and Industrial Development in Malaysia," in Jomo Kwame Sundaram, ed. *Jomo Industrializing Malaysia*, (New York: Routledge, 1993), pp. 118–146.

62. "Taiwan's 'Export Processing Zone': Foreign Concessions in Disguise," Xinhua News Service, June 19, 1977; Rupert Pennant-Rea, "Free Trading EPZs," *Economist*, June 23, 1979, p. 10; Peter Drucker, *Managing in Turbulent Times* (New York: Harper & Row, 1980), pp. 173–175.

63. Eckes and Zeiler, *Globalization and the American Century*, p. 268; U.S. International Trade Commission, *Year in Trade 1995: Operations of the Trade Agreements Program* (Washington, DC: Government Printing Office, 1996), p. 79; USTR, *Annual Report on National Trade Estimates Report on Foreign Trade Barriers* (Washington, DC: Government Printing Office 1985–2003).

64. U.S. Senate, Committee on Finance, *Trade Reform Act of 1974*, 93rd Cong, 2nd sess, Nov. 26, 1974, report no. 93–1298, pp. 11, 94.

65. I.M. Destler, *Making Foreign Economic Policy* (Washington, DC: Brookings Institution, 1980), pp. 151–190.

66. Committee on Finance, *Trade Reform Act of 1974*, pp. 94–95; Public Law 93–618, secs. 103–104.

67. U.S. International Trade Commission, *Operation of the Trade Agreements Program*, 31 Report, 1979, pp. 29–56.

68. Thomas R. Graham, "Results of the Tokyo Round," *Georgia Journal of International and Comparative Law* 9 (1979): 153–179; Strauss to Carter, June 5, 1979, Jimmy Carter Library, Atlanta, GA; Andreas F. Lowenfeld, *International Economic Law* (New York: Oxford University Press, 2002), pp. 54–60.

69. Susan C. Schwab, *Trade Offs: Negotiating the Omnibus Trade and Competitiveness Act* (Boston: Harvard Business School Press, 1994), p. 45; U.S. House of Representatives, Committee on Ways and Means, *Multilateral Trade Negotiations*, 96th Cong., 1st sess., April 27, 1979, pp. 498–502; *Public Papers of the Presidents: Jimmy Carter, 1979*, 1:944.

70. U.S. Senate, Committee on Finance, *Trade Agreements Act of 1979*, 96th Cong., 1st sess, Report No. 96–249, July 17, 1979, pp. 234–236. But see Jagdish Bhagwati, "Departures from Multilateralism: Regionalism and Aggressive Unilateralism," *Economic Journal* 100 (Dec. 1990): 1304–1317; Thomas O. Bayard and Kimberly Ann Elliott, *Reciprocity and Retaliation in U.S. Trade Policy* (Washington, DC: Institute for International Economics, 1994), pp. 26–27.

71. U.S. Senate, Committee on Finance, *MTN and the Legal Institutions of Inter-*

national Trade, 96th Cong., 1st sess., 1979, CP 96–14, p. 14; Leslie Alan Glick, *Multilateral Trade Negotiations: World Trade after the Tokyo Round* (Totowa, NJ: Rowman & Allanheld, 1984), p. 174.

72. U.S. International Trade Commission, *OTAP,* 42nd Report, 1990, (USITC Pub. 2403, July 1991), pp. 53–54.

73. U.S. House of Representatives, Committee on Government Operations, *Buy America Act of 1987*, Hearings on HR 1750, 100th Cong., 1st sess, March 25, 1987, pp. 2, 15; AFL-CIO, "States Should Keep Their 'Buy America' Laws Intact," 1990.

74. Alfred E. Eckes Jr., ed., *Revisiting U.S. Trade Policy: Decisions in Perspective* (Athens: Ohio University Press, 2000), pp. 164, 169.

75. U.S. Senate, Finance Committee, *Trade Agreements Act of 1979*, pp. 162–165; U.S. Census Bureau, *Statistical Abstract of the United States, 1986*, pp. 809–817; *1990*, pp. 804–815; *Survey of Current Business*, June 1992, pp. 90–92; July 1997, pp. 64–65.

76. U.S. House of Representatives, Committee on Energy and Commerce, Subcommittee on Oversight and Investigations, *Unfair Foreign Trade Practices: Barriers to U.S. Exports*, 99th Cong., 2nd sess., May 1986, Committee Print 99-BB, p. 2; U.S. Senate, Committee on Finance, *Omnibus Trade Act of 1987, Report* on S. 490, 100th Cong., 1st sess., June 12, 1987, Report 100–171, pp. 2–3.

77. Trade data from *Survey of Current Business*, June 1992, pp. 90–91; exchange rate from *Economic Report of the President, 1997*, p. 422; data on debt from U.S. Treasury *Bulletin*, various issues, and *Survey of Current Business* (July 1997 and April 2003).

78. Congressional Research Service, *Protectionist Policies of Major U.S. Trading Partners* (April 30, 1986), in House Commerce Subcommittee, Unfair Trade Practices, pp. 33–34; President's Export Council, *Coping with the Dynamics of World Trade in the 1980's* (Washington, DC: Government Printing Office, December 1984), pp. 165–173.

79. William A. Niskanen, *Reaganomics: An Insider's Account of the Policies and the People* (New York: Oxford University Press, 1988), p. 137.

80. *Public Papers of the Presidents: Ronald Reagan, 1987*, pp. 476–478.

81. U.S. International Trade Commission, OTAP 36th Report, 1984 (USITC Pub. 1725, June 1986), pp. 26–33; B.R. Mitchell, *International Historical Statistics: Africa, Asia & Oceania, 1750–1988* (New York: Stockton Press, 1995); *Washington Post*, April 23, 1985, p. C-4; Israel, Central Bureau of Statistics, www.cbs.gov.il/shnaton/st08–05.gif; www.cbs.gov.il/yarhon/h5_e.htm; U.S. Trade Representative, *Foreign Trade Barriers*, 1997, pp. 178–180.

82. U.S. International Trade Commission, OTAP, 39th Report, 1987, pp. 1–5 to 1–12.

83. *Survey of Current Business*, July 1997 and April 2003; USTR, *Foreign Trade Barriers,* 2003, pp. 31–38, www.ustr.gov.

84. For a summary of the NAFTA agreement, see U.S. International Trade Commission, *The Year in Trade, 1992* (USITC Pub. 2640, July 1993), pp. 1–13.

85. U.S. International Trade Commission, *The Year in Trade 1993: Operation of the Trade Agreements Program*, 45 report (USITC Pub. 2769, June 1994), pp. 55–63.

86. U.S. Senate, Committee on Finance, *NAFTA and Related Side Agreements, Hearing*, 103rd Cong., 1st sess., Sept. 15, 1993, pp. 25–33; Henry Kissinger, "The Trade Route: NAFTA a Step Toward a Prosperous World Order," *Cleveland Plain Dealer,* July 18, 1993.

87. C.W. McMillion data on NAFTA, www.mbginfosvcs.com, April 15, 2003.

88. Joel Millman and David Luhnow, "A Decade After NAFTA, Prospects for Mexico Seem to Be Dimming," *Wall Street Journal*, April 21, 2003, online edition. See generally Edward J. Chambers and Peter H. Smith, eds., *NAFTA in the New Millennium* (Edmonton, Alberta: University of Alberta Press; La Jolla, CA: Center for U.S.-Mexican Studies, University of California–San Diego, 2002).

89. Paul Volcker and Toyoo Gyohten, *Changing Fortunes: The World's Money and the Threat to American Leadership* (New York: Times Books, 1992), p. 189.

90. U.S. Senate, *Uruguay Round Agreements Act*, Joint Report of the Committee on Finance, Committee on Agriculture, Nutrition and Forestry, and Committee on Governmental Affairs, 103rd Cong., 2nd sess., Report 103–412, pp. 3–12.

91. Supachai Panitchpakdi and Mark L. Clifford, *China and the WTO: Changing China, Changing World Trade* (New York: John Wiley, 2002), pp. 55–56.

92. Mickey Kantor, "Review and Outlook" of the President's Trade Policy Agenda, 1994, www.ustr.gov/html/1995_review-outlook.html.

93. Testimony of Jerry R. Junkins, chair of Texas Instruments, to House Ways and Means Committee, February 22, 1994, web.lexis-nexis.com/congcomp/document.

94. "WTO's Would-Be Chief Vows to Support Developing Countries," *Xinhua*, March 6, 2002. See generally, Supachai and Clifford, *China and the WTO*, pp. 185–219.

95. Alan William Wolff, "America's Trade Policy," presentation at the Tuck School of Business, Dartmouth College, November 1, 2002; Christopher S. Rugaber, "Administration Outlines Strategy on WTO Dispute Settlement Panels," *International Trade Reporter* 20, no. 2 (January 9, 2003), p. 56. For problems with NAFTA dispute panels, see Anthony DePalma, "NAFTA's Powerful Little Secret; Obscure Tribunals Settle Disputes, but Go Too Far, Critics Say," *New York Times*, March 11, 2001.

96. Business Roundtable press release, January 26, 2000 www.brtable.org/press.cfm/374; Andrew Hill, "Greed and Fear Fuel Pro-China Deal Campaign," *Financial Times*, May 24, 2000, p. 16.

97. General Electric, *Annual Report 2002* (Fairfield, CT: General Electric, 2003), p. 13; Michael Skapinker, "Different Games, but the Same Winners," *Financial Times* (January 20, 2003), p. 2. Lisa Biank Fasig, "Honeywell to Shut Rhode Island Plant, Send 374 Jobs to Mexico, China," *Providence Journal*, April 3, 2003, online via Lexis-Nexis Academic; "Multinationals Locate More R&D Centers in China," *Asia Pulse*, March 20, 2003, online via Lexis-Nexis Academic; Robert F. Kelley, Mashpee, Rhode Island, letter to editor, *Providence Journal-Bulletin*, April 6, 2003, p. 9.

98. Coalition for a Sound Dollar, "The Overvalued Dollar: Six Years Later," www.sounddollar.org.

99. "Foreign Trade Barriers Continue to Interfere with U.S. Telcos," *Communications Daily*, April 2, 2003; Jeffrey Sparshott, "U.S. Lists Countries as Trade Obstacles," *Washington Times,* April 2, 2003; Stetson Sanders, "The Good, the Bad, and the Ugly; Report Cards on TRIPS," *Legal Times,* March 24, 2003; U.S. Trade Representative, "USTR Releases 2003 Inventory of Trade Barriers," press release, April 1, 2003, www.ustr.gov.

100. UNCTAD, *International Investment Report 2002* (New York: United Nations, 2002), p. xv.

101. Jagdish Bhagwati, "The Capital Myth: The Difference between Trade in Widgets and Dollars," *Foreign Affairs* 77, no. 3 (May–June 1998): 6; Joseph E. Stiglitz, *Globalization and Its Discontents* (New York: W.W. Norton, 2002), pp. 53–54, 86–88; Robert C. Shelburne, "Improving the Economic Performance of the Global

Economy: The Challenge Ahead," presidential address to the 12th international conference of the International Trade and Finance Association, Bangkok, Thailand. May 31, 2002.

102. CEO's letter to Ambassador Zoellick, March 22, 2002, www.uscib.org/index.asp?documentID'1984.

103. Edward Alden, "US Backs Curbs on Capital Controls," *Financial Times*, April 2, 2003; Christopher S. Rugaber and Rossella Brevetti, "USTR Releases Text of Singapore FTA, Summary of Chile Free Trade Pact Chapters," *International Trade Reporter*, March 13, 2003, pp. 459–460.

104. Sharon Gaudin, "Deloitte Says Two Million Jobs Moving Offshore," (April 24, 2003 www.Itmanagement.earthweb.com/career/article.php/2196601; Peter Engardio et al. "New Global Job Shift," *Business Week*, February 3, 2003, p. 50; Diane E. Lewis, "Shift of Tech Jobs Abroad Speeding Up, Report Says," *Boston Globe*, December 25, 2002.

105. Paul Craig Roberts, "Globalism's Offshore Undercurrents," *Washington Times*, January 9, 2003.

106. Adam Smith, *The Wealth of Nations* (New York: Modern Library, 1937), p. 431.

107. Conference Board, "War and Terrorism Put Globalization at Risk," www.conference-board.org/utilities/pressDetail.cfm?press; Stephen E. Flynn, "America the Vulnerable," *Foreign Affairs* 81, no. 1 (January–February 2002): 60–74; Jessica Stern, "Dreaded Risks and the Control of Biological Weapons," *International Security* 89 (Winter 2002–2003). See also Eckes and Zeiler, *Globalization and the American Century*, pp. 238–259.

108. Rosie Mestel, "The World: SARS May Be Just the Start," *Washington Post,* May 3, 2003; Chris Taylor, "In China It Seems the 'Big One' Is Yet to Come," *South China Morning Post*, May 11, 2003.

Notes to Chapter 3

1. A spectrum of theories and ideologies appears in the literature exemplified by the neoliberal view of Yergin and Stanislaw (1998), the Keynesian view of Stiglitz (2002), the heterodox views of Korten (2001), Greider (1997), and Barber (1995), and the Marxist views of Hardt and Negri (2000).

2. A staunch classical economist, Lionel Robbins, as well as Gunnar Myrdal, has conceded that Adam Smith was more concerned with the nation, in particular Britain, than with a cosmopolitan perspective of global welfare (Robbins 1978, 9; Myrdal 1957, 148). Smith urged three exceptions to freer trade internationally: national defense and merchant marine; retaliation against foreign restrictions or dislocations; and easing displacement costs. Smith also stressed the productivity of manufacturing and public works. See Chapter 5 below and the citations therein.

3. Some argue that "Ricardo never made use of the comparative cost idea in his criticism of the Corn Laws but relied on absolute cost differences" (Gomes 1990, 5); for the argument that the free trade battle was based upon science, see Cunningham (1904), or on politics, see Condliffe (1950, 203–236).

4. For a sampling of a large literature addressing the view of long-term American economic decline and the need to change policy and economic structure, see Bernstein and Adler 1994; Blecker 1996; Cuomo Commission 1992; Dertouzos, Lester and Solow 1989; Madrick 1995; Mishel, Bernstein and Schmitt 1997; Peterson 1994; and

Schafer and Faux 1996. Certainly not everyone agreed: see Nau 1990. The issue of long-term decline is still with us and is discussed more thoroughly and updated in Chapter 5 of this study.

5. Although there were predecessors, the origin of free trade theory is credited to Adam Smith (Viner 1965, 91–96); for the history, see Bhagwati 1964, Chipman 1965, Gomes 1990, and Irwin 1991, 1996.

6. Wheras Viner (1965, 437–526); and Gomes (1990, 8–9); referred to Ricardo's matrix of comparative costs as a "doctrine," the usual reference in the literature relates to the "law" (Dear Jorff 1980). "This is one of the most important and still unchallenged laws of economics with many practical applications" (Salvatore 1998, 30); see also Paul Samuelson (in Levinsohn, Deardorff and Stern (1995, 22).

7. "[A]lmost a quarter of the *Wealth of Nations* is devoted to an exposition or scathing criticism of that which Adam Smith conceived mercantilism to be" (Heckscher 1955, 1: 29). On mercantilism, see Heckscher 1955 and Viner 1968.

8. Myrdal (1957, 46, 39–49), draws a distinction between an "oppressor state" characteristic of mercantilism and a "welfare state" characterizing the twentieth century.

9. Marshall apparently conceded that mercantilism was "consistent with a national organization of external trade" and the advent of industrialism (1927, 41–51).

10. Kindleberger's work (1973) has resulted in many discussions concerning the relevancy of global hegemony, be it British or American, to the successsessful operation of the global economy; note also Blecker (1996, 12–19).

11. Viner, in dealing with "The Emergence of Free-Trade and Laissez-Faire Doctrine," states that "The history of the free-trade doctrine is largely a history of a phase of laissez-faire doctrine" (Irwin 1991, 54–62, 85–113, 200–225; Condliffe 1950, 135–168; Polanyi 1944, 132). Viner (1927) also has noted that Adam Smith was not that doctrinaire in his conception of laissez- faire.

12. Yergin and Stanislaw raised the question as to whether the East Asia Economic Miracle was a function of the government or the market: "The unambiguous answer is both" (1998, 159). Chalmers Johnson states: "There was no question that Japan's development was 'plan-rational,' that it was guided by the state in directions that the state wanted to go. It was not purely 'market-rational' as American ideology maintained that it should be" (1995, 10). Consequently, if Johnson's hypothesis is correct, the conception of a developmental state along with the conception of acquired absolute advantage would serve to reintroduce the "industrial policy" debate once again. But of course, the Washington consensus would argue in converse that "industrial policies, in which governments try to shape the future direction of the economy, are a mistake." However, East Asian nations by comparison took such policies "as one of their central responsibilities" (Stiglitz 2002, 92).

13. Kindleberger 1996, 134. "Moreover, in this supposedly laissez-faire period, India, far from being evacuated, was subjected to intensive development as an economic colony along the best mercantilist lines" (Gallagher and Robinson 1953, 4; Semmel 1970). On the new colonialism, see Korten (1995), and on IMF policies constituting a "new form of colonialism" (Stiglitz 2002, 30, 41).

14. Bhagwati 1964. If two countries trade, "it is assumed that they are not under any obligations to make foreign payments excepting those arising from trade, so that in equilibrium the exports of each country exchange for her imports" (Marshall 1949, 1). Wow! A minor assumption—this eliminates capital flows, private direct foreign investment (DFI) and, consequently, the MNCs as well, let alone denying the existence of balance of payments problems.

15. Meier 1968, 22, 216. Also "[S]uch development has to be pictured as an outward movement in the production possibility curve" (Haberler 1968, 107).

16. Free trade served as an "engine of development" for Great Britain but as an "engine of growth" for the LDC world. This important distinction between growth and development will be dealt with in the next chapter.

17. Flam and Flanders 1991, 1, 25, 30. Fixed quantities of factors fit neatly into the Edgeworth-Bowley box diagram but do not portray the evolutionary reality of a dynamic economic process. Resources, others might argue, are a function of knowledge and technological advance and therefore are not to be assumed as fixed or given (Peach and Constantin 1972).

18. "Now it is true that the theory of comparative costs is static" (Haberler 1968, 106); "The trade theory discussed thus far is completely static in nature" (Salvatore 1998, 185). Heckscher also draws attention to the static nature of the classical laissez-faire worldview, but adds that the mercantilists were equally guilty (1955, 1: 23–26). Meier says that "traditional theory still remains an analysis of full *static* equilibrium" (Meier 1968, 1; italics added).

19. Knight 1921, xix; Klein 1977, 13–14. The conception of a dynamic economics offered by Kuznets is noteworthy (1930). For general discussions of the static versus dynamic issue, see Baumol 1951 and 1968, Blatt 1983, Klein 1977, and Machlup 1963.

References to Chapter 3

Barber, Benjamin R. 1995. *Jihad vs. McWorld.* New York: Ballantine Books.

Baumol, William J. 1951. *Economic Dynamics.* New York: Macmillan.

————. 1968. "Statics and Dynamics in Economics." In D.L. Sills, ed., *International Encyclopedia of the Social Sciences,* 15:169–177. New York: Free Press.

Bernstein, Michael, and David E. Adler, eds. 1994. *Understanding American Economic Decline.* New York: Cambridge University Press.

Bhagwati, J.N. 1964. "The Pure Theory of Trade." *Economic Journal* 74 (March): 1–84

Blatt, John M. 1983. *Dynamic Economic Systems: A Post-Keynesian Approach.* Armonk, NY: M.E. Sharpe.

Blecker, Robert A. 1996. *U.S. Trade Policy and Global Growth.* Armonk, NY: M.E. Sharpe.

Bloomfield, Arthur I. 1975. "Adam Smith and the Theory of International Trade." In Andrew S. Skinner and Thomas Wilson, eds., *Essays on Adam Smith,* pp. 455–481. London: Oxford University Press.

————. 1994. *Essays in the History of International Trade Theory.* Brookfield, VT: Edward Elgar.

Brandis, Royall. 1967. "The Myth of Absolute Advantage." *American Economic Review* 57 (March): 169–175.

Brinkman, Richard L. 1995. "Growth versus Economic Development: Toward a Conceptual Clarification." *Journal of Economic Issues* 29 (December): 1171–1188.

Chipman, John. 1965. "A Survey of the Theory of International Trade: Part 2, The Neo-Classical Theory." *Econometrica* 33 (October): 685–761.

Condliffe, John B. 1950. *The Commerce of Nations.* New York: W.W. Norton.

Cunningham, William. 1904. *The Rise and Decline of the Free Trade Movement.* London: C.J. Clay.

Cuomo Commission on Competitiveness. 1992. *America's Agenda: Rebuilding America's Strength.* Armonk, NY: M.E. Sharpe.

Deane, Phyllis. 1965. *The First Industrial Revolution.* New York: Cambridge University Press.

Deardorff, Alan V. 1980. "The General Validity of the Law of Comparative Advantage." *Journal of Political Economy* 88 (October): 941–957.

Dertouzos, Michael L., Richard K. Lester, and Robert M. Solow. 1989. *Made in America.* Cambridge, MA: MIT Press.

Dosi, Giovanni, Keith Pavitt, and Luc Soete, eds. 1990. *Economics of Technical Change and International Trade.* New York: New York University Press.

Dosi, Giovanni, Laura D'Andrea Tyson, and John Zysman. 1989. "Trade Technologies and Development: A Framework for Discussing Japan." In Chalmers Johnson, Laura D'Andrea Tyson, and John Zysman, eds., *Politics and Productivity,* pp. 3–38. New York: Harper Business.

Dowd, Douglas. 1993. *U.S. Capitalist Development Since 1776.* Armonk, NY: M.E. Sharpe.

Dugger, William M., and Howard J. Sherman. 2000. *Reclaiming Evolution.* New York: Routledge.

Ellsworth, P.T. 1969. *The International Economy.* New York: Macmillan.

Flam, Harry, and M. June Flanders, eds. 1991. *Heckscher-Ohlin Trade Theory.* Cambridge, MA: MIT Press.

Gallagher, John, and Ronald Robinson. 1953. "The Imperialism of Free Trade." *Economic History Review,* 2nd series, 6:1–15.

Gomes, Leonard. 1990. *Neoclassical International Economics: An Historical Survey.* New York: St. Martin's.

Greider, William. 1997. *One World Ready or No: The Manic Logic of Global Capitalism.* New York: Simon & Schuster.

Haberler, Gottfried. 1968. "International Trade and Economic Development." In James D. Theberge, ed., *Economics of Trade and Development,* pp. 103–112. New York: John Wiley.

———. 1979. "The Present Economic Malaise." In William Fellner, ed., *Contemporary Economic Problems.* Washington, DC: American Enterprise Institute.

Hardt, Michael, and Antonio Negri. 2000. *Empire.* Cambridge, MA: Harvard University Press.

Heaton, Herbert. 1948. *Economic History of Europe.* New York: Harper & Row.

Heckscher, Eli. 1955. *Mercantilism.* 2 vols. New York: Macmillan.

Heckscher, Eli, and Bertil Ohlin. 1991. *Heckscher-Ohlin Trade Theory.* Cambridge, MA: MIT Press.

Irwin, Douglas A., ed. 1991. *Jacob Viner: Essays on the Intellectual History of Economics.* Princeton, NJ: Princeton University Press.

———. 1996. *Against the Tide.* Princeton, NJ: Princeton University Press.

———. 2002. *Free Trade Under Fire.* Princeton, NJ: Princeton University Press.

Johnson, Chalmers. 1995. *Japan, Who Governs? The Rise of the Developmental State.* New York: W.W. Norton.

Jones, Ronald W., and Peter B. Kenen, eds. 1984. *Handbook of International Economics,* vol. 1. Amsterdam: Elsevier.

Kindleberger, Charles P. 1973. *The World in Depression.* Berkeley: University of California Press.

———. 1996. *World Economic Primacy: 1500–1990.* Oxford: Oxford University Press.

Klein, Burton. 1977. *Dynamic Economics.* Cambridge, MA: Harvard University Press.

Knight, Frank H. 1921. *Risk Uncertainty and Profit.* Boston: Houghton Mifflin.

———. 1951. "Statics and Dynamics." In *The Ethics of Competition and Other Essays,* pp. 161–186. New York: Augustus M. Kelley.

Korten, David C. 1995. *When Corporations Rule the World.* West Hardford, CT: Kumarian Press.

Krugman, Paul. 1997. "What Should Trade Negotiators Negotiate About?" *Journal of Economic Literature* 35 (March): 113–120.

Kuznets, Simon. 1930. "Static and Dynamic Economics." *American Economic Review* 20 (September): 426–441.

———. 1973. "Modern Economic Growth: Findings and Reflections." *American Economic Review* 63 (June): 247–258.

Levinsohn, Jim, Alan V. Deardorff, and Robert M. Stern, eds. 1995. *New Directions in Trade Theory.* Ann Arbor: University of Michigan Press.

Lovett, William A. 2000. "The WTO: A Train Wreck in Progress." *Fordham Law Journal* 24 (November/December): 410–426.

MacDonald, Glenn M., and James R. Markussen. 1985. "A Rehabilitation of Absolute Advantage." *Journal of Political Economy* 93 (April): 277–297.

Machlup, Fritz. 1963. "Static and Dynamics: Kaleidoscopic Words." In *Essays on Economic Semantics,* pp. 9–41. Englewood Cliffs, NJ: Prentice-Hall.

Madrick, Jeffrey. 1995. *The End of Affluence.* New York: Random House.

Marshall, Alfred. 1927. *Industry and Trade.* London: Macmillan.

———. 1949. *The Pure Theory of Foreign Trade: The Pure Theory of Domestic Values.* London: London School of Economics and Political Science.

Meier, Gerald M. 1968. *The International Economics of Development.* New York: Harper & Row.

Mendell, Marguerite, and Daniel Salee. 1991. *The Legacy of Karl Polanyi.* New York: St. Martin's.

Mill, John S. 1911. *The Principles of Political Economy.* London: Longmans.

Mishel, Lawrence, Jared Bernstein, and John Schmitt. 1997. *The State of Working America, 1996–1997.* Armonk, NY: M.E. Sharpe.

Mitchell, Broadus, and Louise Pearson Mitchell. 1947. *American Economic History.* Boston: Houghton Mifflin.

Myint, H. 1958. "The 'Classical Theory' of International Trade and Underdeveloped Countries." *Economic Journal* 68 (June): 317–337.

Myrdal, Gunnar. 1957. *Rich Lands and Poor.* New York: Harper.

———. 1974. "What Is Development?" *Journal of Economic Issues* 8 (December): 729–736.

Nau, Henry R. 1990. *The Myth of America's Decline.* New York: Oxford University Press.

Packard, Laurence B. 1948. *The Commercial Revolution: 1400–1776.* New York: H. Holt.

Peach, W.N., and James A. Constantin, eds. 1972. *Zimmermann's World Resources and Industries.* New York: Harper & Row.

Peterson, Wallace C. 1994. *The Silent Depression.* New York: W.W. Norton.

Polanyi, Karl. 1944. *The Great Transformation.* New York: Rinehart.

Robbins, Lord. 1978. *The Theory of Economic Policy in English Classical Political Economy.* Philadelphia: Porcupine Press.

Robinson, Joan. 1980. "Reflections on the Theory of International Trade." In *Collected Economic Papers*, 5: 130–145. Cambridge, MA: MIT Press.

Rostow, Walt W. 1968. *The Stages of Economic Growth.* Cambridge, MA: Cambridge University Press.

Salvatore, Dominick. 1998. *International Economics.* New York: Macmillan.

Samuelson, Paul. 1939. "The Gains from International Trade." *Canadian Journal of Economics and Political Science* 5 (May): 195–205.

———. 1970. *Economics.* New York: McGraw-Hill.

Schafer, Todd, and Jeff Faux, eds. 1996. *Reclaiming Prosperity.* Armonk, NY: M.E. Sharpe.

Schumpeter, Joseph A. 1954. *History of Economic Analysis.* New York: Oxford University Press.

Semmel, Bernard. 1970. *The Rise of Free Trade Imperialism.* Cambridge, UK: Cambridge University Press.

———. 1983. *The Theory of Economic Development.* New Brunswick, NJ: Transaction Books.

Smith, Adam. 1937. *The Wealth of Nations.* New York: Random House.

Stanfield, Ron. 1986. *The Economic Thought of Karl Polanyi.* New York: St. Martin's.

Stiglitz, Joseph E. 2002. *Globalization and Its Discontents.* New York: W.W. Norton.

Theberge, James D., ed., *Economics of Trade and Development,* pp. 103–112. New York: John Wiley.

———. 1979. "The Present Economic Malaise." In William Fellner, ed., *Contemporary Economic Problems,* pp. 261–290. Washington, DC: American Enterprise Institute.

Thurow, Lester. 1992. *Head to Head.* New York: William Morrow.

———. 1996. *The Future of Capitalism.* New York: William Morrow.

Viner, Jacob. 1927. "Adam Smith and Laissez Faire," *Journal of Political Economy* 35 (April): 198–232.

———. 1952. *International Trade and Economic Development.* Glencoe, IL: Free Press.

———. 1965. *Studies in the Theory of International Trade.* New York: Augustus M. Kelley.

———. 1968. "Mercantilism." *International Encyclopedia of the Social Sciences,* 4:435–443. New York: Free Press.

Yergin, Daniel, and Joseph Stanislaw. 1998. *The Commanding Heights.* New York: Simon & Schuster.

Notes to Chapter 4

1. The problem addressed by Ricardo was not absolute costs, but the "ratios between costs" and that "imports could be profitable even though the commodity imported could be produced at less cost at home than abroad" (Viner 1965, 338–341).

2. Again, the point was made by Smith: "The most opulent nations, indeed, generally excel all their neighbours in agriculture as well as in manufactures" (Smith 1937, 6)—that is, absolute advantage for *both* agricultural and industrial production.

3. Such specialization also explains vicious circles of cumulative causation and why rich lands are rich and why poor lands are poor (Myrdal 1957). The key for the LDCs rests not with agricultural specialization in terms of static economic growth but rather how to engage the dynamics of modern economic growth and industrialization.

4. Soros 1998, v. "The applicability of Polanyi's analysis to our own age of glo-

balization seems obvious" (Steger 2002, 140–142) and though not explicit is implied in the whole of Stiglitz's analysis (Stiglitz 2002).

5. For the sequential pattern of "logistic surges" relevant to transportation technology and general culture evolution, see Brinkman (1995, 1181).

6. The "principle of similitude" (Bell 1973, 163–174), provides a framework from which to combine Hornell Hart's "logistic surges" and Schumpeter's creative destruction.

7. Mill 1911, 351; "Mill's hypothetical history of development through international trade strikes us as roseate, naive" (Hughes 1970, 6–7).

8. In his Nobel address, Kuznets (1973) drew attention to the basic characteristics of modern economic growth and the dynamic function of the institution known as science.

9. On the conception of social technology, see Kuznets (1968, 2, 17, and, 35); "The social sciences are becoming increasingly called upon to develop a new social technology" (Myrdal 1957, 14; Brinkman 1997).

10. Given the "dichotomy of useful knowledge," to change technology is to change culture (civilization), in that culture is made up of the technics of technology, not all of culture, but rather the "core of culture" (Brinkman 1995, 1183).

11. "The new growth theory, while advertising its break from traditions, in fact has stayed very close to the status quo ante," but there is a need to pioneer into the domain of "cultural and institutional factors" (Nelson 1997, 35, 39); see also Bernstein and Adler (1994, 379, 383).

12. In numerous instances, Grossman and Helpman endorse traditional trade theory and the Heckscher-Ohlin model (1991, 187, 191, and 204), and they are further supported by Baldwin (1992).

13. Once having achieved a level of acquired absolute advantage, a transformed LDC can then apply Schumpeterian innovation, taking advantage of machines of manufacturing, such as the "fire engine" (steam engine) (Smith 1937, 9, 1–12), and engaging the advantages of a larger market size and the "productivity doctrine"; see also Young (1928).

14. On the Japanese model, even Yergin and Stanislaw state that "all nations shared a reference to a common model. That model was Japan" (1998, 160). See Stiglitz on the "Asian model" (2002, 10).

15. Chalmers Johnson might be considered the father of the developmental state model. The path for Japan appears circuitous, having run from the German Historical School to the Meiji restoration (circa 1868) and on to the post–World War II era. "Japan's development was 'plan rational.' . . . It was not purely 'market rational,' as American ideology maintained that it should be" (Johnson 1995, 10).

16. Certainly, enough has been written on the paradigmatic blinders and lack of relevancy of orthodox economic analysis: on a "beam in our eyes" (Myrdal 1968, 1:5–35; Kindleberger 1982; Bernstein and Adler 1994, 361–393; Whalen 1996).

17. On a central issue, jobs and wages, Bhagwati and Kosters express the orthodox view: "This volume offers strong skepticism concerning the evidence in support of the fear that freer trade has been pushing down the wages of the unskilled" (1994, xii); see also Levy and Murnane (1992). This view is challenged by Mishel, Bernstein, and Schmitt 1997, Belman and Lee 1996, and Wood 1994.

18. And while many nations give lip service to free trade, which nations really practice or want it (Batra 1993; Shutt 1985)?

19. While Adam Smith (1937, 31) felt that wealth is translated into economic, but not political, power, many would argue the converse, especially in relation to the

multinational corporations: Bowman 1996, Dugger 1989, Elliott 2000, Greider 1997, Harrison 1994, especially, Korten 1995. To be expected, given their neoliberal bias, Yergin and Stanislaw, in a rather large book (464 pages), were able to squeeze in two pages on MNCs, treating them of course in a favorable light: "Instead of being seen as predators, they are now courted as investors, who bring capital, technology, skills, and access to global markets. They are seen as less threatening for other reasons" (1998, 391–392).

20. Lovett, Eckes, and Brinkman 1999, 103 and "Corporate Sovereignty" by Brent Foster in Dudley and Goddin (2003, 69, 32–36).

21. Madrick 1995; Bernstein and Adler 1994; Peterson 1994; Cuomo Commission 1992. "I think the changes are in favor of sclerosis and decline" (Kindleberger 1996, 190). It appears that the declinist dialogue and analysis have once again become relevant.

22. In mainstream textbooks dealing with international economics, the Swan diagram (Salvatore 1998, 576) offers a static model devoid of structural transformation and comprised of three static macroeconomic options: exchange rate manipulations plus monetary and fiscal options. Dertouzos, Lester, and Solow (1989, 38), among others, argue that such standard macroeconomic policies are not enough. This analytical perspective is also presented in Chapter 5 of this study, which suggests innovative policies to include the dynamics of technological advance and institutional adjustment under the rubric of DITT (Department of Industry, Technology, and Trade).

References to Chapter 4

Abramowitz, Moses. 1993. "The Search for Sources of Growth: Areas of Ignorance, Old and New." *Journal of Economic History* 53 (June): 217–243.
Aghion, Phillipe, and Peter Hewitt. 1998. *Endogenous Growth Theory.* Cambridge, MA: MIT Press.
Arndt, H.W. 1981. "Economic Development: A Semantic History." *Economic Development and Cultural Change* 29 (April): 457–466.
Atlantic Institute. 1970. *The Technology Gap: U.S. and Europe.* New York: Praeger.
Baldwin, Robert E. 1992. "Are Economists' Trade Policy Views Still Valid?" *Journal of Economic Literature* 30 (June): 804–809.
Barber, Benjamin R. 1995. *Jihad vs. McWorld.* New York: Ballantine Books.
Batra, Ravi. 1993. *The Myth of Free Trade.* New York: Charles Scribner's Sons.
Baum, Gregory. 1996. *Karl Polanyi on Ethics and Economics.* Montreal and Kingston: McGill-Queen's University Press.
Baumol, William J. 1951. *Economic Dynamics.* New York: Macmillan.
Bell, Daniel. 1973. *The Coming Post-Industrial Society.* New York: Basic Books.
Belman, Dale, and Thea M. Lee. 1996. "International Trade and the Performance of U.S. Labor Markets." In R.A. Blecker, ed., *U.S. Trade Policy and Global Growth*, pp. 61–107. Armonk, NY: M.E. Sharpe.
Bernstein, Michael A., and David E. Adler, eds. 1994. *Understanding American Economic Decline.* New York: Cambridge University Press.
Bhagwati, Jagdish, and Marvin H. Kosters, eds. 1994. *Trade and Wages: Leveling Wages Down?* Washington, DC: AEI Press.
Blecker, Robert A. ed. 1996. *U.S. Trade Policy and Global Growth.* Armonk, NY: M.E. Sharpe.

Bloomfield, Arthur I. 1994. *Essays in the History of International Trade Theory.* Brookfield, VT: Edward Elgar.

Bowman, Scott R. 1996. *The American Corporation and American Political Thought: Law Power and Ideology.* University Park: Pennsylvania State University Press.

Brinkman, June E., and Richard L. Brinkman. 1997. "Cultural Lag: Conception and Theory." *International Journal of Social Economics* 26:609–627.

———. 2001. "The New Growth Theories: A Social and Cultural Addendum." *International Journal of Social Economics* 28:506–525.

———. 2002. "CEO Profits: The Berle and Means Thesis Revisited." *International Journal of Social Economics* 29:385–410.

Brinkman, Richard L. 1992. "Culture Evolution and the Process of Economic Evolution." *International Journal of Social Economics* 19:248–267.

———. 1995. "Economic Growth versus Economic Development: Toward a Conceptual Clarification." *Journal of Economic Issues* 29 (December): 1171–1188.

———. 1997. "Toward a Culture-Conception of Technology." *Journal of Economic Issues* 31 (December): 1027–1038.

Burtless, Gary, Robert Z. Lawrence, Robert E. Litan, and Robert J. Shapiro. 1998. *Globaphobia: Confronting Fears About Open Trade.* Washington, DC: Brookings Institution Press.

Clower, Robert, George Dalton, Mitchell Hawitz, and A.A. Walters. 1966. *Growth Without Development: An Economic Survey of Liberia.* Evanston, IL: Northwestern University Press.

Crystal, Graef S. 1991. *In Search of Excess: The Overcompensation of American Executives.* New York: W.W. Norton.

Cuomo Commission on Competitiveness. 1992. *America's Agenda: Rebuilding America's Strength.* Armonk, NY: M.E. Sharpe.

Davis, John B. 1999. "Is Trade Liberalization An Important Cause of Increasing U.S. Wage Inequality?" *Review of Social Economy* 57:488–506.

Dertouzos, Michael L., Richard L. Lester, and Robert M. Solow. 1989. *Made in America.* Cambridge, MA: MIT Press.

Dosi, Giovanni, Keith Pavitt, and Luc Soete. 1990. *The Economics of Technological Change and International Trade.* New York: New York University Press.

Dosi, Giovanni, Laura D'Andrea Tyson, and John Zysman. 1989. "Trade Technologies and Development: A Framework for Discussing Japan." In Chalmers Johnson, L. Tyson, and J. Zysman, eds., *Politics and Productivity,* pp. 3–38. New York: Harper Business.

Dudley, Barbara, and Karen Wilde Goddin, eds. 2003. "International Trade." *Oregon's Future* 4 (Spring): 3–71.

Dugger, William M. 1989. *Corporate Hegemony.* Westport, CT: Greenwood Press.

Easterlin, Richard A. 1996. *A Growth Triumphant: The Twenty-first Century in Historical Perspective.* Ann Arbor: University of Michigan Press.

Elliott, John. 2000. "Adam Smith's Conception of Power, Markets and Politics." *Review of Social Economics* 58 (December): 429–454.

Findlay, Ronald. 1984. "Growth and Development in Trade Models." In Ronald W. Jones and Peter Kenen, eds., *Handbook of International Economics*, 1:185–236. Amsterdam: Elsevier.

Friedman, Milton, and Rose D. Friedman. 1980. *Free to Choose.* New York: Harcourt Brace Jovanovich.

Galbraith, John Kenneth. 1973. "Power and the Useful Economist." *American Economic Review* 63:1–11.

———. 1983. *The Anatomy of Power.* Boston: Houghton Mifflin.

———. 1994. *A Journey Through Economic Time.* Boston: Houghton Mifflin.

Gillis, Malcolm, Dwight H. Perkins, Michael Roemer, and Donald R. Snodgrass. 1992. *Economics of Development.* New York: W.W. Norton.

Greider, William. 1997. *One World, Ready or Not: The Manic Logic of Global Capitalism.* New York: Simon & Schuster.

Griffin, Keith, and Terry McKinley. 1994. *Implementing a Human Development Strategy.* New York: St. Martin's.

Grossman, Gene M., and Elhanen Helpman. 1991. *Innovation and Growth in the Global Economy.* Cambridge, MA: MIT Press.

Hammonds, Keith H. 1997. "Freer Trade Gets an Unfriendly Reception." *Business Week* (September 22): 34.

Harrison, Bennet. 1994. *Lean and Mean.* New York: Basic Books.

Hart, Hornell. 1946. "Technological Acceleration and the Atomic Bomb." *American Sociological Review* 11 (June): 277–293.

Hughes, Jonathan. 1970. *Industrialization and Economic History.* New York: McGraw-Hill.

Irwin, Douglas A. 1996. *Against the Tide.* Princeton, NJ: Princeton University Press.

———. 2002. *Free Trade Under Fire.* Princeton, NJ: Princeton University Press.

Johnson, Chalmers. 1995. *Japan: Who Governs? The Rise of the Developmental State.* New York: W.W. Norton.

Johnson, Chalmers, Laura D'Andrea Tyson, and John Zysman, eds. 1989. *Politics and Productivity.* New York: Harper Business.

Kindleberger, Charles P. 1982. "Assets and Liabilities of International Economics: The Postwar Bankruptcy of Theory and Policy." In F. Caffe, ed., *Experiences and Problems of the International Monetary System,* pp. 47–64. Siena, Italy: Monte Dei Paschi Di Siena.

———. 1996. *World Economic Primacy: 1500–1990.* New York: Oxford University Press.

Korten, David C. 1995. *When Corporations Rule the World.* West Hartford, CT: Kumarian Press.

Kreinen, Mordechai E. 1998. *International Trade: A Policy Approach.* Fort Worth, TX: Dryden Press.

Kroeber, Alfred A., and Clyde Kluckholm. 1952. *Culture: A Critical Review of Concepts and Definitions.* Cambridge, MA: Peabody Museum.

Krugman, Paul. 1986. *Strategic Trade Policy and the New International Economics.* Cambridge, MA: MIT Press.

Kuznets, Simon. 1959. *Six Lectures on Economic Growth.* New York: Macmillan.

———. 1966. *Modern Economic Growth.* New Haven: Yale University Press.

———. 1968. *Toward a Theory of Economic Growth: With Reflections on the Economic Growth of Modern Nations.* New York: W.W. Norton.

———. 1973. "Modern Economic Growth: Findings and Reflections" [Nobel laureate address]. *American Economics Review* 63 (June): 247–258.

———. 1989. *Economic Development, the Family, and Income Distribution.* New York: Cambridge University Press.

Lee, James R. 2000. *Exploring the Gaps: Vital Links between Trade, Environment and Culture.* West Hartford, CT: Kumarian Press.

Levinsohn, Jim, Alan V. Deardorff, and Robert M. Stern, eds. 1995. *New Directions in Trade Theory.* Ann Arbor: University of Michigan Press.

Levy, Frank, and Richard J. Murnane. 1992. "U.S. Earnings Levels and Earnings Inequality: A Review of Recent Trends and Proposed Explanations." *Journal of Economic Literature* 30 (September): 1333–1381.

Lovett, William A., Alfred E. Eckes, Jr., and Richard L. Brinkman. 1999. *U.S. Trade Policy: History, Theory, and the WTO.* Armonk, NY: M.E. Sharpe.

Lucas, Robert E. 1988. "On the Mechanisms of Economic Development." *Journal of Monetary Economics* 22 (July): 3–42.

Madrick, Jeffrey. 1995. *The End of Affluence.* New York: Random House.

Marshall, Alfred. 1927. *Industry and Trade.* London: Macmillan.

McClintock, Brent. 1996. "International Trade and the Governance of Global Markets." pp. 225–255. In C.J. Whalen, ed. *Beyond Neoclassical Thought: Political Economy for the Twenty-first Century.* Armonk, NY: M.E. Sharpe.

McCord, Norman. 1970. *Free Trade: Theory and Practice from Adam Smith to Keynes.* Newton Abbot, UK: David and Charles.

Meier, Gerald M. 1968. *The International Economics of Development.* New York: Harper and Row.

Meier, Gerald M., and Robert E. Baldwin. 1959. *Economic Development.* New York: John Wiley.

Mendell, Marguerite, and Daniel Salée. 1991. *The Legacy of Karl Polanyi.* New York: St. Martin's.

Mill, John S. 1911. *The Principles of Political Economy.* London: Longmans.

Mishel, Lawrence, Jared Bernstein, and John Schmitt. 1997. *The State of Working America 1996–97.* Armonk, NY: M.E. Sharpe.

Mittelman, James H. 2000. *The Globalization Syndrome: Transformation and Resistance.* Princeton, NJ: Princeton University Press.

Myrdal, Gunnar. 1957. *Rich Lands and Poor.* New York: Harper.

———. 1968. *Asian Drama: An Inquiry into the Poverty of Nations.* 3 vols. New York: Twentieth Century Fund.

———. 1974. "What Is Development?" *Journal of Economic Issues* 8 (December): 729–736.

Nelson, Richard. 1997. "How New Is New Growth Theory?" *Challenge* 40 (September–October): 29–58.

New York Times. 1996. *The Downsizing of America.* New York: Times Books.

North, Douglas C. 1961. *The Economic Growth of the United States 1790–1860.* Englewood Cliffs, NJ: Prentice-Hall.

———. 1990. *Institutions, Institutional Change and Economic Performance.* New York: Cambridge University Press.

Peterson, Wallace C. 1994. *Silent Depression.* New York: W.W. Norton.

Polanyi, Karl. 1944. *The Great Transformation.* New York: Farrar & Reinhart.

Porter, Michael E. 1990. *The Competitive Advantage of Nations.* New York: Free Press.

President's Commission on Industrial Competitiveness. 1985. *Global Competition: The New Reality*, vol. 1. Washington, DC: Government Printing Office.

Ricardo, David. 1912. *The Principles of Political Economy and Taxation.* London: J.M. Dent.

Robbins, Lord. 1978. *The Theory of Economic Policy in English Classical Political Economy.* Philadelphia: Porcupine Press.

Rostow, Walt Whitman. 1960. *The Stages of Economic Growth, a non-Communist Manifesto.* New York: Cambridge University Press.

Schafer, Todd, and Jeff Faux, eds. 1996. *Reclaiming Prosperity.* Armonk, NY: M.E. Sharpe.

Schumpeter, Joseph A. 1947. *Capitalism, Socialism and Democracy.* New York: Harper and Brothers.

———. 1983. *The Theory of Economic Development.* New Brunswick, NJ: Transaction Books.

Scott, Maurice Fitzgerald. 1989. *A New View of Economic Growth.* New York: Oxford University Press.

Shutt, Harry. 1985. *The Myth of Free Trade.* Oxford: Oxford University Press.

Smith, Adam. 1937. *The Wealth of Nations.* New York: Random House.

Solow, Robert F. 1957. "Technological Change and Aggregate Production Function." *Review of Economics and Statistics* 39 (August): 312–320.

Soros, George. 1997. "The Capitalist Threat." *Atlantic Monthly* 329 (February): 45–70.

———. 1998. *The Crisis of Global Capitalism: Open Society Endangered.* New York: Public Affairs.

Steger, Manfred B. 2002. *Globalism: The New Market Ideology.* Boston: Roman & Littlefield.

Stiglitz, Joseph E. 2002. *Globalization and Its Discontents.* New York: W.W. Norton.

Thurow, Lester. 1992. *Head to Head.* New York: William Morrow.

———. 1996. *The Future of Capitalism.* New York: William Morrow.

Todaro, Michael P. 1989. *Economic Development in the Third World.* New York: Longman.

Tonelson, Alan. 2000. *The Race to the Bottom: Why a World-Wide Worker Surplus and Uncontrolled Free Trade Are Sinking American Living Standards.* Boulder, CO: Westview Press.

Useem, Michael. 1996. *Investor Capitalism.* New York: Basic Books, 1996.

Viner, Jacob. 1952. *International Trade and Economic Development.* Glencoe, IL: Free Press.

———. 1965. *Studies in the Theory of International Trade.* New York: Augustus M. Kelley.

Whalen, Charles J., ed. 1996. *Political Economy for the 21st Century.* Armonk, NY: M.E. Sharpe.

Wood, Adrian. 1994. *North-South Trade, Employment and Inequality.* Oxford: Clarendon Press.

Yergin, Daniel, and Joseph Stanislaw. 1998. *Commanding Heights.* New York: Simon & Schuster.

Young, Allyn A. 1928. "Increasing Returns and Economic Progress." *Economic Journal* 38 (December): 527–542.

Notes to Chapter 5

1. In note 12 of Chapter 1 we considered the net job losses from a weaker U.S. trade-industrial policy that failed to enforce reciprocity and overall balance in U.S. trading activities. Since the mid-1970s the United States lost 10 to 12 million jobs from "weaker" trade policy, and perhaps another 1.5 million jobs were lost between 1945 and 1975. But if the United States had retained these jobs and nurtured more export manufacturing (without allowing trade deficits since the mid-1970s), the cumulative U.S. economic growth would have been stronger. In the end, U.S. GNP

by 2003 would have been at least 10 percent larger and perhaps even 20 percent higher. Obviously, these estimates assume that U.S. industry, manufacturing, and economic growth would have benefited from a more level playing field, stronger export nurturing, industrial rationalization measures, and the elimination of significant U.S. trade deficits.

2. In the debates over expanded fast-track authority to allow more trade deals like NAFTA, critics emphasized the dangers of weakened environmental standards, reduced food, drug, and other consumer protection and safety standards, and an erosion of import surveillance that would bring even larger volumes of illegal drug trafficking.

3. See Table 1.1.

4. Only a few allies (e.g., De Gaulle's France) grumped about U.S. profits from "seigneurage," but it was clear that no other U.S. ally could afford to maintain a reserve currency comparable to the dollar. After the British pound was heavily devalued in 1949 and 1967, no other currency but the dollar was strong enough to assume major reserve currency responsibilities. In September 1997, the dollar constituted almost 60 percent of currency reserves ($423 billion out of a global total of $762 billion in government currency reserves were held in dollars), while 14 percent were in German marks and 6 percent in Japanese yen. (David Wessel, "Dollar's Share of World Reserves Grow," *Wall Street Journal*, Sept. 10, 1997).

5. Obviously, U.S. labor, many local communities, and environmental interests lost influence over U.S. trade policy. But why did the United States neglect the accumulating trade and current account deficits? Simply because the U.S. dollar remained the dominant reserve currency between the early 1980s and 2002. Only in 2003 did the EU's euro mount a serious challenge to U.S. dollar dominance.

6. Macroeconomic adjustment cannot be avoided. Sooner or later, and for most countries sooner, current account deficits must be eliminated. See Cairncross and Eichengreen 1983, deVries 1986, Dornbusch 1988, Kenen 1994, Helleiner 1994, Godley 1995, McKinnon 1996, James 1996, Lovett 1996a, b, c, Erdman 1996, and Murphy 1997. Of special importance was Adam Smith's emphasis upon the *overall balance* of "produce and consumption" in the *Wealth of Nations* (1776, 464). Although Smith urged that less attention be paid to some bilateral trading imbalances, as part of his overall case for laissez-faire internally, he recognized three exceptions to freer trade internationally: (i) national defense and the maritime industry (429–431), (ii) retaliation against restrictions or distortions by other nations (434–435), and (iii) easing displacement costs (435–436). But Smith also stressed the special productivity of manufactures and public works (410–414 and 651–716). Only a modest extension of Smith's reasoning explains the protective tariff and national development policies of Alexander Hamilton, Friedrich List, and Henry Clay, especially for countries like the United States and Germany that needed to catch up with British industrial progress.

7. The unique, long-sustained boom in U.S. stock prices from the early 1980s to 2000 also helps explain continuing capital inflows into the United States. But most argue that U.S. increases of stock prices, recently at least, constituted a speculative bubble. Accordingly, many fear a substantial downward correction, as bad as, or worse than the October 1987 correction or downslide in U.S. stock prices. Experts differ, however, on how much, if any, correction is "required" for the next several years (Table 5.1.) Recovery of the U.S. and global economy were uncertain in 2003–2004.

8. See Table 1.2 for bilateral trade balances. And see Lovett 1996c, Witt and Trossman 1997, Faux 1997.

9. See "Rescuing Asia," *Business Week*, Nov. 27, 1997, pp. 116–132. South Korea and Japan also suffered financial stresses. Fortunately, the Fifty-second Annual Meetings of the IMF (Hong Kong, 1997) concluded with an agreement to increase quotas (IMF capitalization) by 45 percent and to double of SDR allocations. This will greatly increase IMF liquidity resources at a crisis period for global financial markets (with strains in Asia and another emerging markets and a stressful challenge from the euro against the dollar). See IMF Survey (26:18; 289–292, October 6, 1997). See also Kenen 2001, Blustein 2001, Blecker 1999, Eichengreen 1999 and 2003, Stiglitz 2002, and Mussa 2002.

10. See Cohen and Zysman 1987, Prestowitz 1988, Vargish 1988, Fallows 1989, Culbertson 1989, Kuttner 1989, Lodge 1990, Dertouzos et al. 1990, Kearns 1992, Thurow 1992, Jerome 1992, Blecker 1992, Graham, 1992, Perot and Choate 1993, Lovett 1994a, b, Phillips 1984, Godley 1995, Thurow 1996, Blecker 1996, and Beinert 1997.

11. The OECD's volume *New World Trading System, Readings*, Paris: OECD (1994, Tables 1 and 4, pp. 47, 50) summarizes the trade-weighted tariff averages pre-Uruguay (and post-Uruguay) for many countries. Trade-weighted average tariffs were for the United States 5.4 (3.5) percent, E.C. 5.7 (3.6), Japan 3.9 (1.7), Canada 9.0 (4.8), Australia 20.1 (12.2), New Zealand 23.8 (11.9), South Africa 24.6 (17.3), Argentina 38.2 (30.9), Brazil 40.7 (27.0), Chile 34.9 (24.9), Colombia 44.3 (35.3), Costa Rica 54.9 (44.1), India 71.4 (32.4), Indonesia 20.4 (36.9), South Korea 18.0 (8.3), Malaysia 10.0 (9.1), Romania 11.7 (33.9), Senegal 13.7 (13.8), Sri Lanka 28.6 (28.1), Thailand 35.8 (28.1), Tunisia 28.3 (40.3), Turkey 25.1 (22.3), Uruguay 20.9 (30.9), and Venezuela 50.0 (31.1). Thus, net tariff reductions for most NICs are not drastic, which leaves significantly protective tariffs in place.

12. See Kennedy 1987. And see Huntington 1996, Brzezinski 1997, Mahbubani 1994, Bodanski 1993, Miller 1995, Kohout 1995, Lehman 1988, Myers 1997, and Bernstein and Munro 1997. In "America's Defense Policy" *Economist*, Nov. 15, 1997, we see that U.S. defense spending has come down from $400 billion to $250 billion (in 1998 dollars) between 1991 and 1998, a 40 percent reduction. See also, IISS (1997, 2002) for a breakdown in U.S. force reductions.

13. See Peterson 1994. Also, see Mishel et al., *The State of Working America* (1988, 1991, 1993, 1995, and 1997). And see Adler and Bernstein 1994, Kuttner 1989, 1991, and 1997; Newman 1993, Layard 1994, Phillips 1984, Madrick 1995, and Wolman and Colamosca 1997. (See Tables 1.1A and B, 1.2, 1.3, 1.4, 1.5, and 1.6 in this volume.)

14. Most countries do not have large or disproportionate trade surpluses with the United States.

15. A few EU countries have developed fairly large trade surpluses with the United States, most notably Germany ($37 billion), Italy ($15 billion), France ($26 billion), and Ireland ($15 billion) in 2002. But the rest of Western Europe has only a moderate trade surplus—that is, $10 billion on exports to the United States of $100 billion and imports from the United States of $90 billion in 2002.

16. Some historical perspective is interesting. In 1980 only Japan had a "serious" trade imbalance problem (exports to the United States of $33 billion and imports from the United States of $21 billion). By 1987 Western Europe had a $24 billion trade surplus (on exports to the United States of $85 billion and imports from the United States of $61 billion), and West Germany accounted for $16 billion of Europe's trade surplus. But in 1987 Japan had a $60 billion trade surplus with the United States (on

exports to the United States of $88 billion and imports from United States of $28 billion), Taiwan had a $21 billion trade surplus, and South Korea a $10 billion trade surplus. By 1996 the European imbalance was not that disproportionate, but large Mexican, Chinese, and other Asian country trade surpluses had developed—except that South Korea had a modest trade *deficit* with the United States of –$3 billion.

17. Some might say a tougher U.S. trade policy could provoke a "trade war." The best response is—"Hah, get real. Everybody knows there has been a trade war going on for twenty years. But the United States has been losing badly. Americans can no longer afford neglect, industrial erosion, and national decline. We must put our house in order and rejuvenate the American economy."

18. The United States should be impartial, of course, in enforcing reciprocity-based trade policy.

Corrective import fees should be imposed against any country (in any part of the world) with large, disproportionate trade surpluses in manufactured goods that is not equally open to U.S. manufactures and exports. However, a few large raw materials suppliers (e.g., Saudi Arabia or Venezuela) do not fit this characterization although the United States imports a lot from them. Trade imbalances with raw materials suppliers result merely from disproportionate natural resource endowments among countries.

19. For comparative industrial policy appraisals, see Reich and Magaziner 1982, Zysman 1983, Adams and Klein 1983, Shepherd 1983, Johnson 1984, Lovett 1984, Eckstein et al. 1984, Phillips 1984, Nelson 1984, Shutt 1985, Reich and Donahue 1985, Culbertson 1985, President's Commission 1985, Porter 1986, Cohen and Zysman 1987, Lodge and Vogel 1987, Lovett 1987, Rubner 1987, Kaden and Smith 1988, Prestowitz 1988, Kuttner 1989, Porter 1990, Lodge 1990, Derian 1990, Dertouzos et al. 1990, Kaden and Smith 1992, Thurow 1992, Graham 1992, Hart 1994, OECD 1994, Faux and Schafer 1996, Forrant 1997, Japan Commission on Industrial Performance 1998.

20. For macroeconomic policy that incorporates industrial trade concerns, see Peterson 1982, Lovett 1987, Kaden and Smith 1988, Kaden and Smith 1992, Peterson and Estenson 1992, Thurow 1992, Adler and Bernstein 1994, Faux and Schafer 1996, and Thurow 1996.

21. For the growing economic stress on U.S. politics, see Phillips 1984, Lodge and Vogel 1987, Prestowitz 1988, Friedman 1988, Fallows 1989, Stabile and Cantor 1991, Kuttner 1991, Thurow 1992, Calleo 1992, Peterson 1993, Phillips 1984, Drew 1994, Woodward 1994, Lind 1995, Fukayama 1995, Greenberg 1995, Walker 1996, Thurow 1996, Darman 1996, Johnson and Broder 1996, and Beinart 1997. See Smith 1776, 81.

22. See, particularly, with respect to deficits, Lovett 1987, Friedman 1988, Stein 1990, Stabile and Cantor 1991, Peterson 1993, Woodward 1994, Drew 1994, Phillips 1984, Greenburg 1995, and Darman 1996. For trade policy concerns, see Bluestone and Bennett 1982, Kuttner 1982, Phillips 1984, Johnson 1984, Culbertson 1985, President's Commission 1985, Lodge and Vogel 1987, Lovett 1987, Kaden and Smith 1988, Prestowitz 1988, Culbertson 1989, Kuttner 1989, Fallows 1989, Dertouzos et al. 1990, Lodge 1990, Kuttner 1991, Kearns 1992, Graham 1992, Thurow 1992, Blecker 1992, Lovett 1987, Adler and Bernstein 1994, Peterson 1994, Faux and Schafer 1996, and Thurow 1996.

23. See Johnson and Broder 1996.

24. Both the Dunkel draft Uruguay Round GATT agreement and the final Uruguay Round GATT WTO agreement had many hundreds of text pages. The legal language was highly technical, for the most part, and required extensive background

understanding of the seven previous GATT rounds (1947–1979) and familiarity with the massive accumulation of prior national trade concessions, reservations, and tariff rates.

25. The best books by far on post–World War II trade history were Alfred Eckes's *Opening America's Market* (1995) and Steve Dryden's *Trade Warriors* (1995). Both were published *after* Congress accepted GATT 1994 and the WTO agreement.

26. For the House and Senate votes, see *Congressionary Quarterly Weekly* (Dec. 3, 1994, 3469–3471). Clearly, the NAFTA opposition would have been more successful in challenging GATT 1994 and the WTO agreement. The Uruguay Round deal was full of asymmetries and nonreciprocity and vulnerable to challenge on many details. If seriously attacked, GATT 1994 and the WTO would have been a much harder sell with Congress, and a solid majority could have been mobilized against it.

27. See, for example, Zysman and Tyson 1983, Nelson 1984, Eckstein et al. 1984, Johnson 1984, Porter 1986, Lodge and Vogel 1987, Prestowitz 1988, Porter 1990, Derian 1990, Lodge 1990, Dertouzos et al. 1990, Graham 1992, Thurow 1992, Thurow 1996, and Forrant 1997.

28. See Eckes 1995 and Dryden 1995.

29. For the mission and style of the new agency, see Lodge (1987, 1990). The newly established DITT should take over the functions of the Office of the U.S. Trade Representative, together with most of the Commerce Department, including the Office of the Secretary, Economics and Statistics Administration, Bureau of Economic Analysis, Census Bureau, Bureau of Export Administration, and Technology Administration. The domestic Economic Development Administration, Minority Business Development Agency, and Small Business Administration might be consolidated into a Domestic Business Promotion Agency. The National Oceanic and Atmospheric Administration (Weather Bureau) should become an independent scientific agency.

30. Among the most dramatic areas of U.S. industrial decline are the shipping and shipbuilding industries. The United States came out of World War II with the biggest shipbuilding effort in history and nearly 60 percent of oceangoing tonnage. But through neglect, kindness to allies (who needed balance of payments revenues), and favors to flag-of-convenience vessels, the U.S. maritime sector became marginalized. By 2002 the United States accounted for less than 4 percent of world merchant tonnage (ranking fifth behind the EU, Japan, China, and Norway), and only 1.3 percent of world merchant shipbuilding. Japan, South Korea, China, and Taiwan now make nearly 75 percent of the world's merchant shipbuilding tonnage. And three fourths of U.S. tonnage does not fly the U.S. flag; it sails under convenience registry. An emergency U.S. maritime revival effort is needed now. Only a cabinet-level Maritime Department can give the heft and visibility required. Its mandate must be to greatly enlarge the U.S. merchant marine, its share of world commerce, and U.S. shipbuilding. The Maritime Department must work hand in hand with DITT to expand U.S. exports, enlarge U.S. balance of payments earnings, and, where appropriate, reduce U.S. imports and dependence upon foreign suppliers. For background, see Lovett (1996b).

31. On tax haven complications, see Tanzi 1995, Jorgenson and Landau 1993, Hufbauer 1992, and Richards 1996. For these reasons it is easier, relatively speaking, to get adequate data on merchandise trade, real products, raw materials, components, and finished manufactured products, than on financial flows and services.

This is especially so if a nominal import fee (say 1 percent) is imposed upon all merchandise imports. (See the section on monitoring and targets below.)

32. See President's Commission on Industrial Competitiveness (1985, 41–42). Also, see Lovett (1987, 89–90).

33. See Jackson et al. 1995, Bhala 2002, Lovett 1994a, b, 1996a, b, c.

34. In Section 102 of the Uruguay Round Agreements Act of 1994 (codified as Title 19, § 3512 of the U.S. Code), Congress provided that: "(1) U.S. LAW TO PREVAIL IN CONFLICT. No provision of any of the Uruguay Round Agreements, nor the application of any such provision to any person or circumstance, that is inconsistent with any law of the United States shall have effect. (2) CONSTRUC-TION.—Nothing in this Act shall be construed—(A) to amend or modify any law of the United States, including any law relating to—(i) the protection of human, animal, or plant life or health, (ii) the protection of the environment, or (iii) worker safety, or (B) to limit any authority conferred under any law of the United States, including section 301 of the Trade Act of 1974, unless specifically provided for in this Act."

Yet the agreement establishing the World Trade Organization, Article 16, Miscellaneous Provisions, provided that: "4. Each member shall ensure the conformity of its laws, regulations and administrative procedures with its obligations as provided in the annexed agreements." Under U.S. implementing law, therefore, Congress clearly intended that U.S. law prevails over GATT 1994 and the WTO agreement.

35. Withdrawal from the WTO is allowed for any member after six months notice to the director general. See Agreement Establishing the World Organization, Article 15 (1994).

36. Extensive use by the U.S. of "trade sanctions," often to please splinter groups in politics, has become a problem for U.S. export competitiveness. See, for example, Haass 1997, Bernstein and Munro 1997, and Carter 1988. Sanctions by one or only a few countries tend to be ineffectual. On the other hand, when a broad consensus among many nations supports sanctions, they can be effective politically and economically.

37. During the mid-1980s, increasing disharmony developed over U.S. trade policy, and it continues in the early twenty-first century. Most of the AFL-CIO, its congressional supporters, most environmental organizations, and the country's leading consumer advocate, Ralph Nader, strongly criticized U.S. negotiators. This contrasts greatly with the general harmony and agreement over U.S. trade policy that prevailed from the late 1890s–1913, an era of major growth and prosperity in the roaring 1920s, and even from 1940 to the early 1970s, a strong growth period, before heavy job losses and displacement affected Americans. The current era, from the mid 1970s to 2003, illustrates a breakdown in effective teamwork and industrial collaboration in America. See the sources cited in notes 13, 19, 21, and 22, above.

38. See the sources cited in notes 13, 19, 21, and 22, above.

39. See Eckes 1995, Dryden 1995, Lovett 1987 and 1994a, b, and many unfair trade practice cases and safeguard proceedings brought under the U.S. trade laws (cited by Jackson et al. 1995 and Bhala 2002). In 2001–2002 President Bush approved safeguard relief for U.S. steelmakers, too.

40. See Jerome 1992, Lovett 1994a, b, and Mastel 1996.

41. There is some evidence, however, that a further acceleration of the U.S. stock market boom from 1996 to 2000 combined with a transitory surge in the dollar's

value, between the summer of 1995 into 2000, to lift real U.S. incomes for the late 1990s. Clearly, more foreign investment shifted medium-term into U.S. dollar investments as the yen and mark sagged and as euphoria in emerging markets ebbed. Thus, a special short-term inflow of foreign liquidity added strength to the "final" stages of a U.S. stock market bubble or speculative boom. This spilled over into a temporary upsurge in "United States, Inc." consumer incomes as against other countries. But, rather ominously, U.S. current account deficits grew even larger, U.S. export expansion stalled, and signs of dollar overvaluation were noticeable. The dollar sagged in 2002–2003.

For good analysis of speculative mania and slumps, see Minsky 1982 and Minsky 1986, Kindleberger 1993 and 1997, Balder 1997, and Miller 1997. See also note 9 above, and especially Kenen 2001.

42. See Peterson 1994, Phillips 1984, Marshall and Tucker 1992, Batra 1993, Vargish 1992, Newman 1993, Layard 1994, Madrick 1995, Korten 1995, Kuttner 1997, Galbraith 1997, Briggs 1992, Wolman and Colamosca 1997, Coote 1992, Greider 1997, Hirst and Thompson 1997, and Beinert 1997. Special attention has been focused upon these issues by Mishel et al. (*The State of Working America*, 1988, 1991, 1993, 1995, and 1997). Worth emphasizing is the substantial understatement of real unemployment (and underemployment) in the U.S. official unemployment statistics, which, broadly speaking, require unemployment compensation recipients to be actively seeking employment. Many of the unemployed are no longer eligible, are lost track of, drift into marginal unreported work, or become discouraged. Mishel and his coauthors consistently report a large understatement of real unemployment. This affects rural workers, urban workers, and especially blacks in the labor force. Many believe that real U.S. unemployment rates have been more like 9 or 10 percent (or more) in recent years, which helps explain the limited inflation pressure in recent years. These *real* U.S. unemployment rates are more like Western and Northern European structural unemployment rates.

43. In the fall of 1997, when Clinton failed to get expanded "fast-track" trade negotiation authority approved by the House of Representatives, polls were showing a public majority opposed. Too many families experienced wage stagnation and feared job losses. With a growing slump and heavy outsourcing of jobs, unease about nonreciprocal freer trade was increasing in 2002–2003. This should be significant in the 2004 elections.

44. Many European countries would have rejected Maastricht 1992 and the EMU if popular referenda had been held in every country. High structural unemployment and worries about job prospects for younger workers were widespread. And as financial strains, stock market slumps, and devaluations spread in Asia and other emerging markets, confidence in the global marketplace was eroding.

45. The public in Russia and Eastern Europe strongly felt that market progress, increased incomes, and broad prosperity were needed. The older Communist ways were discredited, but until solid improvements became entrenched there was widespread dissatisfaction.

46. See Wood 1992, McKinnon and Ohno 1997, Cargill et al. 1997, Murphy 1997, and Japan Commission on Industrial Performance 1998. Also, see Burke 1995, Mikuni and Murphy 2002, Mikitani and Posen 2000.

47. See Lovett 1996a.

48. See sources cited in notes 6, 9, 41. And see Table 5.1.

49. See, for example, Culbertson 1989, Kuttner 1991 and 1997, Goldsmith 1994,

Mishel et al. 1988, 1991, 1993, 1995, 1997, Godley 1995, Thurow 1992 and 1996, Faux and Schafer 1996, Phillips 1984, Choate and McMillion 1997, Thomas 1997, Beinart 1997, Lovett 1996a, b, c, Wolman and Colamosca 1997, Greider 1997, Aaronsen 2001, Stiglitz 2002, James 2001, and Mishel 2003.

50. Other industrial data have been collected by the Department of Interior, Maritime Administration, Department of Agriculture, Treasury Department (Internal Revenue Service), the Federal Reserve System, U.S. International Trade Commission (formerly the U.S. Tariff Commission), and the U.S. Federal Trade Commission. This database has spread internationally through more or less comparable information in the standardized industrial classification (the SITC) system.

51. The confidentiality of industrial reports by particular companies is safeguarded by government statistics-gathering agencies.

52. Transparency has been a legitimate goal of the IMF for many years, and this principle should be extended into trade activities (at least for summary data) as well.

53. In Mexico, Thailand, Malaysia, Indonesia, and the Philippines, it only took several years for this kind of speculative boom to collapse with a major, costly, and inevitable correction. How much longer can the U.S. import, high dollar, and speculative boom sustain itself? Another fundamental problem with the U.S. economy has been low productivity growth since 1973. Annual U.S. productivity growth (nonfarm) was only 1.3 percent between 1973 and 1980, 1.1 percent between 1981 and 1990, and 1.1 percent between 1990 and 1997 (*Business Week*, Nov. 17, 1997, 40). See also Krugman (1990, 12–13).

54. See Galbraith 1979a, Kindleberger 1993, and James 2001. Also, see sources cited in note 41 above. Why had the U.S. boom surged so far from 1995 to 1997? It was the conjunction of recent slowdowns and worries in the European and Japanese economies combined with a rather surprising turnabout in U.S. fiscal deficits. From 1995 to 1997 Europe was troubled about meeting EMU convergence criteria, trying to cut budget deficits, and suffering the blues. Japan's yen went too far up in 1994–1995, with the Japanese economy not recovered fully from the big downslide of the early 1990s. Accordingly, Japanese and German interest rates were reduced. Meanwhile, in the United States there was bitter partisan conflict over how to cut excessive budget deficits in 1994–1996. But then in 1996–1997 U.S. budget discipline actually improved, and the U.S. economy recovered somewhat. Meanwhile, the mood was sour in most of Europe and Japan. The 1996 U.S. election, in an odd way, provided reassurance. Because Clinton was reelected with a Republican Congress, U.S. spending was constrained, moderate tax cuts were enacted, and reasonable ease could continue in monetary policy. In these circumstances, a further surge in the U.S. stock market occurred in 1997. Interestingly, financial crises in Southeast Asia (Thailand, Malaysia, Indonesia, and the Philippines) in the summer and fall of 1997 cooled enthusiasm for many emerging markets, so that investment favor for the United States was actually accentuated, at least for the short term. The U.S. boom surged into a bubble that peaked in early 2001.

55. Thurow 1996. This book deserves much more professional and public attention than it has received so far. And see Tables 1.1A and B, 1.2, 1.3, 1.4, 1.5, 1.6, 5.1, and 5.2 of this text.

56. See Cairncross and Eichengreen 1983.

57. See Lovett 1987, Peterson 1994, Goldsmith 1994, Thurow 1996, and Beinart 1997, among many other works cited thus far. Also, for the urgency of industrial rejuvenation, see Choate and Schwartz 1980, Choate and McMillion 1997, Eckstein

et al. 1984, Cohen and Zysman 1987, Culbertson 1989, Dertouzos et al. 1990, Prestowitz 1988, Kuttner 1991, and Graham 1992.

58. See the following: Kennedy 1987, Huntington 1996, Crankshaw 1981, Morganthau 1954, Kissinger 1994, Crockatt 1996, Lehman 1988, Lovett 1996b, Perry 1989, Kohout et al. 1995, Miller 1995, Sheehan 1995, Brzezinski 1993, Allison and Treverton 1992, Johnson 1996, Ruggie 1996, Kennedy 1993, Mandelbaum 1996, Kennan 1996, "America's Defense Policy" 1997, Myers 1997, IISS, *Military Balance*, 1996-97 and 1997-98, Joffee 1997, Huntington 1997, Beinert 1997, Mahbubani 1994, Lewis and Xue 1994, Bernstein and Munro 1997, Dunlop 1997, Brzezinski 1997, Nye 1992, Bodansky 1993, Darwish 1993, Esposito 1992 and 1996, Viorst 1997.

See also Gaddis 2002, Mead 2001, Halberstam 2001, Nabulsi 1999, Howard 1994, and 2000, Gray 2000, Bobbit 2002, and Becket 1999.

59. The Washington Naval Treaty of 1921 was a major British–U.S. arms control initiative to prevent a postwar naval arms race. Britain and the United States were limited to fifteen battleships each, Japan could have ten battleships, and soon after France and Italy each could have six battleships.

60. See Mikesell 1994. And see deVries 1986, Kindleberger 1993, Bordo and Eichengreen 1993, James 1996, Helleiner 1994, Bretton Woods Commission 1994. But see Solomon 1995, Dominguez and Frankel 1993, Shelton 1994, Cavanaugh et al. 1994, Bandow and Vasquez 1994, George and Sabelli 1994, and Lowenfeld 2002.

61. See Table 5.2.

62. This is a pity, because an IMF-style voting regime combined with stronger WTO safeguards, unfair trade practice remedies, and balance of payments relief (the original GATT 1947) would have allowed the United States to remain within the WTO. Note: Some WTO supporters (e.g., John Jackson) claim that WTO dispute settlement proceedings are a blessing of the new system. By 2003 hundreds of trade disputes had been filed. But most disputes involve only relatively narrow, minor issues. Hardly any impact on U.S. trade deficits, asymmetries, and unequal access is likely to result from these proceedings. Unfortunately, the major U.S. trade imbalance problems result from the country's accumulated neglect of its industrial and trade interests over the past twenty to twenty-five years, its failure to assert its rights under GATT and U.S. trade laws, and its prior trade concessions. In fact, WTO dispute settlement panels have their greatest impact in inhibiting the vigorous assertion of U.S. interests under U.S. trade laws. For recent analyses of these dispute settlement proceedings, see Lovett 2002 and Barfield 2001.

63. See Kagan 1997; Middlemas and Barnes 1969.

64. See IISS 1997; "America's Defense Policy" 1997; James Schlesinger, "Nukes: Test Them or Lose Them" (*Wall Street Journal*, Nov. 19, 1997, 22); and National Academy of Sciences, "The Future of U.S. Nuclear Weapons Policy" (*Arms Control Today*, May, 1997, 14–18). And see Myers 1997, Bodansky 1993, Darwish 1993, Esposito 1992 and 1996, Viorst 1997. See also Jehl Douglas, "Gulf Alliance: A Falling Out" (*New York Times*, Nov. 13, 1997). Michael Gordon, "Russia and Iraq Draft Plan for Ending Gulf Crisis" (*New Orleans Times-Picayune*, Nov. 19, 1997).

Also, see more recently, IISS 2002, the Moscow Treaty (text and congressional debates, 2002–2003). "Middle East Countdown" (*Foreign Affairs* Jan./Feb. 2003); "Palestine," "Iraq," "Force," "Re-alignments," and "Grand Strategy for the West" (*Survival*, Winter 2002–2003); Herzog 1984, Mottale 2001, Enderlin 2002, Zakaria 2003.

65. Multipolar power balances have been the dominant experience in Medieval, Renaissance, early modern, and modern history. See Figure 5.1. And see Israel 1995, Ergang 1954, Feuchtwanger 2002, and Bobbit 2002. The predominance of only two superpowers, the United States and the USSR, in the Cold War was really a short-lived historical anomaly (1946–1991). It was based upon unusual concentrations of nuclear weapons and other power that proved unsustainable for the long term. See Kennedy 1987, Gaddis 1997, Crockatt 1996, Brzezinski 1996, Huntington 1996, Matlock 1995, and Thurow 1992.

66. See Kissinger 1994, Bobbit 2002, IISS, *Military Balance* 2002, Barnett 1974 and 1999, Becket 1999, Gaddis 2002, Halbertstam 2001, Kennedy and Hitchcock 2000, and Mearsheimer 2001.

67. Many states find it helpful to secure markets and supplies by bilateral, regional, and multilateral arrangements. In a multipolar, more fluid situation, all three avenues will be employed by many nations, depending on their needs and aspirations. Widening alternatives, reasonable reciprocity, and mutual advantage will be prevailing themes.

68. John Jackson (1990) strongly argued for weighted voting in any new, restructured, multilateral trade organization. But this advice was not followed in the WTO. Many quarters now are expressing increasing dissatisfaction about the WTO and its decision making. See Lovett 2001a and 2002, Wolff 2001, Ragosta 2000, and Barfield 2001. If the current WTO founders cannot be restructured, and fails to relieve major trade imbalances, it will be bypassed and perhaps collapse in disagreements.

69. Conceivably, Taiwan, Korea, Austria, New Zealand, Sri Lanka, or Burma could join ASEAN. Islamic states could form one or several groupings—Arab countries, Turkish countries, the Persian Gulf nations, and/or Iran and Pakistan. In the Americas the Caribbean basin, Central America, Mercosur, and Andean states could affiliate more strongly or join in some measure with NAFTA (the United States, Canada, and Mexico). The EU and NAFTA bloc could be rivals or allies in these regional arrangements.

70. See notes 69 and 68 (along with sources cited in note 68).

71. Because many nations, including Mexico, Brazil, Ecuador, Venezuela, Argentina, Russia, Thailand, Indonesia, South Korea, the Philippines, and Malaysia, are suffering disruptive crises and devaluations, most NICs are moving away from complete openness to imports of goods and complete openness for capital flows. Thus, freer trade is not being completed; instead we see asymmetrical, one-sided, and partial openness among most developing nations now.

72. An unfortunate feature of multilateral trade bargaining is the need for total consensus, which is very difficult to achieve. The United States provided more concessions and openness than most other nations in previous GATT rounds. This facilitated resolution, but left a trade system with increasingly unequal access, entrenched asymmetries, and increased U.S. structural trade and current account deficits.

73. See Barfield 2001, Lovett 2002, Wolff 2001, and Ragosta 2000.

74. See Lovett 2002, 987–989. This "A, B, C, D," tiered access system would greatly improve the U.S. trade regime. More flexibility, reasonable reciprocity, and the elimination of burdensome free-riding would follow. It is a logical alternative to a GATT-WTO breakdown that threatens the present world trade networks.

75. See Thurow 1992 and 1996, Bergsten 1997, Lovett 2001 and 2002, and James 2001.

References to Chapters 1 and 5

Aaron, Henry, et al. 1990. *Setting National Priorities: Policy for the 1990s*. Washington, DC: Brookings Institution.

Aaronsen, Susan Ariel, 2001. *Taking Trade to the Streets: The Lost History of Public Efforts to Shape Globalization*. Ann Arbor: University of Michigan Press.

Adami, Fuad, Michael Doran, Richard Betts, Jahanghir Amuzegar, and John Waterbury. 2003. "Middle East Countdown." *Foreign Affairs* 82 (1).

Adams, F. Gerard, and Lawrence R. Klein. 1983. *Industrial Policies for Growth and Competitiveness*. Lexington, MA: Lexington Books.

Adler, David E., and Michael A. Bernstein. 1994. *Understanding American Economic Decline*. New York: Cambridge University Press.

Akyüz, Yilmaz. 2002. *Reforming the Global Financial Architecture: Issues and Proposals*. Geneva: UNCTAD; Peang: Third World Network; and London: Zed.

Aldcroft, Derek M. 1970. *The Inter-War Economy: Britain, 1919–1939*. New York: Columbia University Press.

Aliber, Robert Z. 1997. "The U.S. Trade Deficits Revisited." *Jobs and Capital* 6 (2): 7–13.

Allison, Graham, and Gregory F. Treverton. 1992. *Rethinking America's Security: Beyond Cold War to New World Order*. American Assembly and Council on Foreign Relations. New York: W.W. Norton.

"America's Defence Policy: Absence of 2020 Vision." *Economist*, Nov. 15, 1997, 26–27.

Amery, Julian. 1969. *Joseph Chamberlain and the Tariff Reform Campaign*. New York: St. Martin's.

Amsden, Alice. 1989. *Asia's Next Giant: South Korea and Late Industrialization*. New York: Oxford University Press.

Åslund, Anders. 1995. *How Russia Became a Market Economy*. Washington, DC: Brookings Institution.

Bairoch, Paul. 1993. *Economics and World History: Myths and Paradoxes*. Chicago: University of Chicago Press.

Balder, John M., Jr. 1997. "Financial Market Volatility and Monetary Policy." *Challenge* 40 (6): 32–52.

Bandow, Doug, and Ian Vasquez. 1994. *Perpetuating Poverty: The World Bank, the IMF, and the Developing World*. Washington, DC: Cato Institute.

Barfield, Claude E. 2001. *Free Trade, Sovereignty, Democracy: The Future of the World Trade Organization*. Washington, DC: American Enterprise Institute.

Barnett, Corelli. 1999. *Marlborough*. London: Methuen.

Batra, Ravi. 1993. *The Pooring of America: Competition and the Myth of Free Trade*. New York: Collier Books.

Bayard, Thomas, et al. 1994. *Reciprocity and Retaliation in U.S. Trade Policy*. Washington, DC: Institute for International Economics.

Beales, Derek. 1969. *From Castlereagh to Gladstone*. New York: W.W. Norton.

Beck, Roy. 1996. *The Case Against Immigration: The Moral, Economic, Social and Environmental Reasons for Reducing U.S. Immigration Back to Traditional Levels*. New York: W.W. Norton.

Becket, Ian F.W. 1999. *Encyclopedia of Guerilla Warfare*. Santa Barbara, CA: ABC CLIO.

Beinert, Peter. 1997. "An Illusion for Our Time: The False Promise of Globalization." *New Republic*, Oct. 20, 1997, 20–24.

Bergsten, C. Fred. 1997. "The Dollar and the Euro." *Foreign Affairs* 76 (4): 83–95.

———. 1996. *Dilemmas of the Dollar: The Economics and Politics of United States Economic Policy.* 2nd ed. New York: Council on Foreign Relations.

———. ed. 1991. *International Adjustment Financing: The Lessons of 1985–1991.* Washington, DC: Institute for International Economics.

Bernstein, Richard, and Ross Munro. 1997. *The Coming Conflict with China.* New York: Alfred A. Knopf.

Bhala, Raj. 2002. *International Trade Law.* Charlottesville, VA: Michie.

Blecker, Robert A. 1999. *Taming Global Finance: A Better Architecture for Growth and Equity.* Washington, DC: Economic Policy Institute.

———. ed. 1996. *U.S. Trade Policy and Global Growth: New Directions in the International Economy.* Washington, DC: Economic Policy Institute; Armonk, NY: M.E. Sharpe.

———. 1992. *Beyond the Twin Deficits: A Trade Strategy for the 1990s.* Washington, DC: Economic Policy Institute; Armonk, NY: M.E. Sharpe.

Bluestone, Barry, and Bennett Harrison. 1982. *The Deindustrialization of America: Plant Closings, Community Abandonment, and the Dismantling of Basic Industry.* New York: Basic Books.

Blustein, Paul. 2001. *The Chastening: Inside the Crisis That Rocked the Global Financial System and Humbled the IMF.* New York: Public Affairs.

Bobbit, Philip. 2002. *The Shield of Achilles: War, Peace and the Course of History.* London: Allen Lane.

Bodanski, Yossef. 1993. "The Grand Strategy of Iran." *Global Affairs: American Journal of Geopolitics*, Fall 1993: 19–36.

Bordo, Michael, with Barry Eichengreen. 1993. *A Retrospective on the Bretton Woods System: Lessons for International Monetary Reform.* Chicago: University of Chicago Press.

Bosworth, Barry P., and Gur Ofer. 1995. *Reforming Planned Economies in an Integrating World Economy.* Washington, DC: Brookings Institution.

Bretton Woods Commission. 1994. *Bretton Woods: Looking to the Future.* Washington, DC: Bretton Woods Committee.

Briggs, Vernon M., Jr. 1992. *Mass Immigration and the National Interest.* Armonk, NY: M.E. Sharpe.

Brittan, Samuel. 1995. *Capitalism With a Human Face.* Cambridge, MA: Harvard University Press.

———. 1971. *Steering the Economy: The British Experiment.* New York: Library Press.

Brzezinski, Zbigniew. 1997. "A Geostrategy for Eurasia." *Foreign Affairs* 76 (5): 50–64.

———. 1993. *Out of Control: Global Turmoil on the Eve of the 21st Century.* New York: Charles Scribner's.

Burke, William M. 1995. "Rising Sun . . . Falling Dollar." *Challenge* 38 (4): 46–51.

Cairncross, Alec, and Barry Eichengreen. 1983. *Sterling in Decline: The Devaluations of 1931, 1949 and 1967.* Oxford: Basil Blackwell.

Calleo, David P. 1992. *The Bankrupting of America: How the Federal Budget Is Impoverishing the Nation.* New York: William Morrow.

Cameron, Rondo, and V.I. Bovykin, eds. 1991. *International Banking, 1870–1914.* New York: Oxford University Press.

Cargill, Thomas F., et al. 1997. *The Political Economy of Japanese Monetary Policy.* Cambridge, MA: MIT Press.

Carter, Barry. 1988. *International Economic Sanctions: Improving the Haphazard U.S. Legal Regime.* Cambridge, MA: Cambridge University Press.

Cass, Ronald A., and John R. Haring. 1997. *International Trade in Telecommunications: Monopoly, Competition and Trade Strategy.* Cambridge MA; MIT Press; Washington, DC: American Enterprise Institute.

Cavanaugh, John, et al. 1994. *Beyond Bretton Woods: Alternatives to the Global Economic Order.* London: Institute for Policy Studies and Transnational Institute, Pluto Press.

Caves, Richard, and Lawrence Krause. 1980. *Britain's Economic Performance.* Washington, DC: Brookings Institution.

Chandler, Alfred D., Jr. 1990. *Scale and Scope: The Dynamics of Industrial Capitalism.* Cambridge, MA: Harvard University Press.

Choate, Pat, and Charles McMillion. 1997. *The Mysterious U.S. Trade Deficit.* Occasional Paper. Washington, DC: Manufacturing Policy Project.

Choate, Pat, and Gail Garfield Schwartz. 1980. *Being Number One: Rebuilding the U.S. Economy.* Lexington, MA: Lexington Books.

Cline, William R. 1984. *Exports of Manufactures from Developing Countries.* Washington, DC: Brookings Institution.

Cohen, Stephen, and John Zysman. 1987. *Manufacturing Matters: The Myth of the Post-Industrial Economy.* Council on Foreign Relations. New York: Basic Books.

Coote, Belinda. 1992. *The Trade Trap: Poverty and the Global Commodity Markets.* Oxford: Oxfam.

Crandall, Robert W. 1993. *Manufacturing on the Move.* Washington, DC: Brookings Institution.

Crankshaw, Edward. 1981. *Bismarck.* New York: Viking Press.

Crockatt, Richard. 1996. *The Fifty Years War: The U.S. and the Soviet Union in World Politics, 1941–1991.* London: Routledge.

Crouzet, Francois. 1982. *The Victorian Economy.* New York: Columbia University Press.

Culbertson, John M. 1989. *The Trade Threat and U.S. Trade Policy.* Madison, WI: 21st Century Press.

———. 1985. *The Trade Threat.* Madison, WI: 21st Century Press.

Darman, Richard. 1996. *Who's In Control: Polar Politics and the Sensible Center.* New York: Simon & Schuster.

Darwish, Abel. 1993. "Iran's Internal Struggle: Fanatic vs. Pragmatist." *Global Affairs: The American Journal of GeoPolitics,* Fall 1993; 37–54.

Davis, Steven J., et al. 1996. *Job Creation and Destruction.* Cambridge, MA: MIT Press.

DeCecco, Marcello, and Alberto Giovannini. 1989. *A European Central Bank? Perspectives on Monetary Unification After Ten Years of the EMS.* Centre for Economic Policy Research. Cambridge, MA: Cambridge University Press.

Derian, Jean-Claude. 1990. *America's Struggle for Leadership in Technology.* Cambridge, MA: MIT Press.

Dertouzos, Michael L., et al. 1990. *Made in America: Regaining the Productive Edge.* The MIT Commission on Industrial Productivity. Cambridge, MA: MIT Press.

deVries, Margaret Garritsen. 1986. *The IMF in a Changing World, 1945–85.* Washington, DC: International Monetary Fund.

Dobson, John M. 1976. *Two Centuries of Tariffs: The Background and Emergence of the United States International Trade Commission.* Washington, DC: U.S. International Trade Commission.

Dobson, Wendy. 1991. *Economic Policy Coordination: Requiem or Prologue.* Washington, DC: Institute for International Economics.

Dominguez, Kathryn M. and Jeffrey A. Frankel. 1993. *Does Foreign Exchange Intervention Work?* Washington, DC: Institute for International Economics.

Dornbusch, Rudiger. 1988. *Exchange Rates and Inflation.* Cambridge, MA: MIT Press.

Drew, Elizabeth, 1994. *On the Edge: The Clinton Presidency.* New York: Simon & Schuster.

Dryden, Steve. 1995. *Trade Warriors: USTR and the American Crusade for Free Trade.* New York: Oxford University Press.

Dunlop, John B. 1997. "Aleksandr Lebed and Russian Foreign Policy." *SAIS Review* 17 (1): xx.

Easterly, William, 2001. *The Elusive Quest for Growth: Economists' Adventures and Misadventures in the Tropics.* Cambridge, MA: MIT Press.

Eckes, Alfred E., Jr. 1997. "Evaluating the Fast-Track Debate." *Speech,* Miller Center, Charlottesville: University of Virginia, Oct. 28, 1997.

———. 1995. *Opening America's Market: U.S. Foreign Trade Policy Since 1776.* Chapel Hill: University of North Carolina Press.

Eckley, Robert S. 1991. *Global Competition in Capital Goods: An American Prospective.* Westport, CT: Quorum Books.

Eckstein, Otto, et al. 1984. *The DRI Report on U.S. Manufacturing Industries.* Data Resources, Inc. New York: McGraw Hill.

Edwards, Richard, and Paolo Garonna. 1991. *The Forgotten Link: Labor's Stake in International Economic Cooperation.* Savage, MD: Rowman and Littlefield.

Eichengreen, Barry. 2003. *Capital Flows and Crises.* Cambridge, MA: MIT Press.

———. 1999. *Toward A New International Financial Architecture.* Washington, DC: Institute for International Economics.

———. 1997. *European Monetary Unification.* Cambridge, MA: MIT Press.

———. 1994. *International Monetary Arrangements for the 21st Century.* Washington, DC: Brookings Institution.

Enderlin, Charles. 2002. *Shattered Dreams: The Failure of the Peace Process in the Middle East, 1993–2002.* New York: Other Press.

Erdman, Paul. 1996. *Tug of War: Today's Global Currency Crisis.* New York: St. Martin's.

Ergang, Robert. 1954. *Europe Since Waterloo.* Boston: D.C. Heath.

Esposito, John L. 1992. *The Islamic Threat: Myth or Reality?* New York: Oxford University Press.

Esposito, John L., and John O. Voll. 1996. *Islam and Democracy.* New York: Oxford University Press.

Esty, Daniel C., 1994. *Greening the GATT: Trade, Environment and the Future.* Washington, DC: Institute for International Economics.

Evans, John W. 1971. *The Kennedy Round in American Trade Policy: The Twilight of the GATT?* Cambridge, MA: Harvard University Press.

Fallows, James. 1994. *Looking at the Sun: The Rise of New East Asian Economic and Political System.* New York: Pantheon Books.

———. 1989a. *More Like Us: Making American Great Again.* Boston: Houghton Mifflin.

———. 1989b. "Containing Japan." *Atlantic Monthly,* May 1989.

Faux, Jeff. 1997. "NAFTA's Rules Don't Work: So Why Rush Down a Track to Extend Them to All of Latin America?" *EPI Journal,* Fall 1997: 1, 6.

Faux, Jeff, and Todd Schafer, eds. 1996. *Reclaiming Prosperity: A Blueprint for Progressive Economic Reform.* Washington, DC: Economic Policy Institute; Armonk, NY: M.E. Sharpe.

Feis, Herbert. 1930. *Europe: The World's Banker, 1870–1914.* Council on Foreign Relations. New Haven: Yale University Press.

Feldstein, Martin. 1997. "EMU and International Conflict." *Foreign Affairs* 76 (6): 60–64.

———. 1992. "Europe's Monetary Union: The Case Against EMU." *Economist,* June 13, 1992.

Feuchtwanger, Edgar. 2002. *Bismarck.* London: Routledge.

Flamm, Kenneth. 1996. *Mismanaged Trade? Strategic Policy and the Semiconductor Industry.* Washington, DC: Brookings Institution.

Fligstein, Neil. 1990. *The Transformation of Corporate Control.* Cambridge, MA: Harvard University Press.

Florida, Richard, and Martin Kenney. 1990. *The Breakthrough Illusion: Corporate America's Failure to Move From Innovation to Mass Production.* New York: Basic Books.

Forrant, Robert. 1997. *Good Jobs and the Cutting Edge: The U.S. Machine Tool Industry and Sustainable Prosperity.* Working Paper No. 199. Annandale-on-Hudson, NY: Jerome Levy Institute of Bard College.

Frieden, Jeffrey A., and David A. Lake. 1991. *International Political Economy: Perspectives on Global Power and Wealth.* 2nd ed. New York: St. Martin's.

Friedman, Benjamin. 1988. *Day of Reckoning: The Consequences of American Economic Policy Under Reagan and After.* New York: Random House.

Fukao, Mitsuhiro. 1995. *Financial Integration, Corporate Governance, and the Performance of Multinational Companies.* Washington, DC: Brookings Institution.

Fukuyama, Francis. 1995. *Trust: The Social Virtues and the Creation of Prosperity.* New York: Free Press.

Funabashi, Yoichi. 1994. *Japan's International Agenda.* Japan Center for International Exchange. New York: New York University Press.

———. 1989. *Managing the Dollar: From the Plaza to the Louvre.* 2nd ed. Washington, DC: Institute for International Economics.

Gaddis, John Lewis. 2002. "A Grand Strategy of Transformation." *Foreign Policy,* Nov./Dec.

———. 1997. *We Now Know: Rethinking Cold War History.* Council on Foreign Relations. Oxford: Clarendon Press.

Galbraith, James K. 1997. *Dangerous Metaphor: The Fiction of the Labor Market: Unemployment, Inflation, and the Job Structure.* Public Policy Brief No. 3G. Annandale-on-Hudson, NY: Jerome Levy Institute of Bard College.

Galbraith, John Kenneth. 1979a. *The Great Crash.* 50th anniversary ed. New York: Avon (with Houghton Mifflin).

———. 1979b. "The Founding Faith: Adam Smith's *Wealth of Nations.*" Chapter 7 in *Annals of An Abiding Liberal.* Boston: Houghton Mifflin.

George, Susan, and Fabrizio Sabelli. 1994. *Faith and Credit: The World Bank's Secular Empire.* Boulder, CO: Westview Press.

Giersch, Herbert, et al. 1992. *The Fading Miracle: Four Decades of Market Economy in Germany.* Cambridge, MA: Cambridge University Press.

Godley, Wynne. 1995. *A Critical Imbalance in U.S. Trade*, Public Policy Brief, No. 23. Annandale-on-Hudson, NY: Jerome Levy Institute of Bard College.

Goldsmith, Sir James. 1994. *The Trap*. New York: Carroll & Graf.

Graham, Edward M. 1996. *Global Corporations and National Governments*. Washington, DC: Institute for International Economics.

Graham, Otis L., Jr. 1992. *Losing Time: The Industrial Policy Debate*. Cambridge, MA: Harvard University Press.

Gray, Christine. 2000. *International Law and the Use of Force*. Oxford: Oxford University Press.

Greenberg, Stanley B. 1995. *Middle Class Dreams: The Politics and Power of the New American Majority*. New York: Times Books.

Greider, William. 1997. *One World, Ready or Not: The Manic Logic of Global Capitalism*. New York: Simon & Schuster.

Grunwald, Joseph, and Kenneth Flamm. 1985. *The Global Factory: Foreign Assembly in International Trade*. Washington, DC: Brookings Institution.

Gutman, Amy. 1987. *Democratic Education*. Princeton, NJ: Princeton University Press.

Haass, Richard N. 1997. "Sanctioning Madness." *Foreign Affairs* 76 (6): 74–85.

Halberstam, David. 2001. *War in a Time of Peace: Bush, Clinton, and the Generals*. New York: Scribner.

Hamilton, Alexander. 1791. *Report on the Subject of Manufactures*. Philadelphia: William Brown, 1827.

Hart, Jeffrey A. 1994. "A Comparative Analysis of the Sources of America's Relative Economic Decline." Chapter 6 in Michael Bernstein and David Adler, eds. *Understanding American Economic Decline*. New York: Cambridge University Press.

———. 1992. *Rival Capitalists: International Competitiveness in the United States*. Ithaca, NY: Cornell University Press.

Helleiner, Eric. 1994. *States and the Reemergence of Global Finance: From Bretton Woods to the 1990's*. Ithaca, NY: Cornell University Press.

Henderson, W.O. 1983. *Friedrich List: Economist and Visionary, 1789–1846*. London: Frank Cass.

Highashi, Chikara. 1983. *Japanese Trade Policy Formulation*. New York: Praeger.

Hirst, Paul, and Grahame Thompson. 1997. *Globalization in Question: The International Economy and the Possibilities of Governance*. Cambridge, MA: Polity Press.

Hofheinz, Roy, Jr., and Kent E. Calder. 1982. *The Eastasia Edge*. New York: Basic Books.

Holbrooke, Richard. 1991. "Japan and the U.S.: The Unequal Partnership." *Foreign Affairs* 70 (5): 41–57.

Hossein-Zadeh, Esmail. 1995. "Rethinking the Trade-Currency Relationship." *Challenge*. 38 (4): 55–56.

Howard, John. 2000. *The Invention of Peace*. New Haven: Yale University Press.

———. 1994. *The Laws of War*. New Haven: Yale University Press.

Hufbauer, Gary Clyde. 1992. *U.S. Taxation of International Income*. Washington, DC: Institute for International Economics.

Hufbauer, Gary Clyde, and Joana Shelton Erb. 1984. *Subsidies in International Trade*. Institute for International Economics. Cambridge, MA: MIT Press.

Hufbauer, Gary Clyde, and Jeffrey J. Schott. 1993. *NAFTA: An Assessment*. Rev. ed. Washington, DC: Institute for International Economics.

Huntington, Samuel P. 1997. "The Erosion of American National Interests." *Foreign Affairs* 76 (5): 28–49.

———. 1996. *The Clash of Civilizations and the Remaking of World Order.* New York: Simon & Schuster.

Hwang, Y. Dolly. 1991. *The Rise of a New World Economic Power: Postwar Taiwan.* Westport, CT: Greenwood Press.

International Institute for Strategic Studies. 2003. *Strategic Survey 2002–2003.* Washington, DC: IISS.

———. 2002. *The Military Balance 2002–2003.* Oxford: Oxford University Press.

———. 1997. *The Military Balance 1997–1998.* Oxford: Oxford University Press.

Israel, Jonathan. 1995. *The Dutch Republic.* Oxford: Clarendon.

Jackson, John H. 1997. *The World Trading System: Law and Policy of International Economic Relations.* 2nd ed. Cambridge, MA: MIT Press.

———. 1990. *Restructuring the GATT System.* London: Chatham House.

———. 1989. *Antidumping Law and Practice: A Comparative Study.* Ann Arbor: University of Michigan Press.

Jackson, John et al. 1995. *International Economic Relations.* St. Paul, MN: West Publishing.

James, Harold. 2001. *The End of Globalization: Lessons from the Great Depression.* Cambridge, MA: Harvard University Press.

———. 1996. *International Monetary Cooperation Since Bretton Woods.* Washington, DC: International Monetary Fund; Oxford: Oxford University Press.

Japan Commission on Industrial Performance. 1998. *Made in Japan: A Guide to Restructuring Japanese Manufacturing.* Cambridge, MA: MIT Press.

Jerome, Robert W. 1992. *World Trade at the Crossroads: The Uruguay Round, GATT, and Beyond.* Washington, DC: Economic Strategy Institute, University Press of America.

Joffee, Josef. 1997. "How America Does It." *Foreign Affairs* 76 (5): 13–27.

Johnson, Chalmers, ed. 1984. *The Industrial Policy Debate.* San Francisco: Institute for Contemporary Studies.

Johnson, Haynes, and David Broder. 1996. *The System: The American Way of Politics at the Breaking Point.* Boston, MA: Little, Brown.

Johnston, Douglas, ed. 1996. *Foreign Policy Into the 21st Century: The U.S. Leadership Challenge.* Washington, DC: Center for Strategic and International Studies.

Jones, Randall. 1992. *The Chinese Economic Area 3: Economic Integration Without a Free Trade Agreement.* Paris: OECD, Department of Economics and Statistics.

Jorgenson, Dale, and Ralph Landau, eds. 1993. *Tax Reform and the Cost of Capital: An International Comparison.* Washington, DC: Brookings Institution.

Judis, John B. 1997. "The Sun Also Rises: The Myth of Japan's Decline." *New Republic,* Nov. 3, 1997, 22–26.

Kaden, Lewis B., and Lee Smith. 1992. *America's Agenda: Rebuilding America's Strength.* Armonk, NY: M.E. Sharpe.

———. 1988. *The Cuomo Commission Report: A New American Formula for a Strong Economy.* New York: Touchstone.

Kagan, Donald. 1997. "Locarno's Lessons for NATO." *Wall Street Journal,* Oct. 28, 1997.

Kearns, Robert. 1992. *Zaibatu America: How Japanese Firms Are Colonizing Vital U.S. Industries.* New York: Free Press.

Kenen, Peter B. 2001. *International Financial Architecture.* Washington, DC: Institute for International Economics.

———, ed. 1995. *Understanding Interdependence: The Macroeconomics of the Open Economy.* Princeton, NJ: Princeton University Press.

————, ed. 1994. *Managing the World Economy: Fifty Years After Bretton Woods.* Washington, DC: Institute for International Economics.

————. 1992. *EMU After Maastricht.* Washington, DC: Group of Thirty.

Kennan, George. 1996. *At a Century's Ending: Reflections, 1982–1995.* New York: W.W. Norton.

Kennedy, Paul. 1987. *The Rise and Fall of the Great Empires.* New York: Random House.

————. 1993. *Preparing for the 21st Century.* New York: Random House.

Kidwell, David S., et al. 2003. *Financial Institutions, Markets, and Money.* 8th ed. Fort Worth, TX: Dryden Press.

Kindleberger, Charles P. 1997. "Mania and How to Prevent Them" (Interview). *Challenge* 40 (6): 21–31.

————. 1993. *A Financial History of Western Europe.* 2nd ed. New York: Oxford University Press.

Kissinger, Henry. 1994. *Diplomacy.* New York: Simon & Schuster.

Kitson, Michael, and Solomos Solomou. 1990. *Protectionism and Economic Revival: The British Interwar Economy.* Cambridge, MA: Cambridge University Press.

Kohout, John J., III, et al. 1995. "Alternative Grand Strategy Options for the United States." *Comparative Strategy.* 14:361–420.

Korten, David C. 1995. *When Corporations Rule the World.* San Francisco: Berret-Koehler Publishers; West Hartford, CT: Kumarian Press.

Kosai, Yutaka. 1986. *The Era of High-Speed Growth: Notes on the Post-War Japanese Economy.* trans. Jacqueline Kaminski. Tokyo: University of Tokyo Press.

Krugman, Paul. 1997. *The Age of Diminished Expectations.* 3rd ed. Cambridge, MA: MIT Press.

————. 1990. *The Age of Diminished Expectations: U.S. Economic Policy in the 1990s.* Cambridge, MA: MIT Press.

————. 1989. *Exchange Rate Instability.* Cambridge, MA: MIT Press.

————. 1986. *Strategic Trade Policy and the New International Economics.* Cambridge, MA: MIT Press.

Kuo, Chich-Heng. 1991. *International Capital Movements and the Developing World: The Case of Taiwan.* New York: Praeger.

Kuttner, Robert. 1997. "Workers on the Auction Block: Is Labor Just a Market?" *Working USA,* May/June 1997.

————. 1991. *The End of Laissez-Faire: National Purpose and the Global Economy After the Cold War.* New York: Alfred A. Knopf.

————. 1989. *Managed Trade and Economic Sovereignty.* Washington, DC: Economic Policy Institute.

————. 1982. "The Free Trade Fallacy." *New Republic,* Mar. 28, 1983, 16–21.

Lamont, Douglas F. 1986. *Forcing Our Hand: America's Trade Wars in the 1980's.* Lexington, MA: Lexington Books.

Lawrence, Robert Z., and Char Schultze, eds. 1990. *An American Trade Strategy: Options for the 1990's.* Washington, DC: Brookings Institution.

Layard, Richard, et al. 1994. *The Unemployment Crisis.* Oxford: Oxford University Press.

Lehman, John F. 1988. *Command of the Sea.* New York: Scribner's.

Leigh, Duane E. *Does Training Work for Displaced Workers: A Survey of Existing Experience.* Kalamazoo, MI: W.E. Upjohn Institute for Industrial Research.

Levinson, Jim, et al., eds. 1995. *New Directions in Trade Policy.* Ann Arbor: University of Michigan Press.

Lewis, John Wilson, and Litai Xue. 1994. *China's Strategic Seapower: The Politics of Force Modernization in the Nuclear Age.* Stanford, CA: Stanford University Press.

Lincoln, Edward J. 1990. *Japan's Unequal Trade.* Washington, DC: Brookings Institution.

———. 1988. *Japan: Facing Economic Maturity.* Washington, DC: Brookings Institution.

Lind, Michael. 1995. *The Next American Nation: The New Nationalism and the Fourth American Revolution.* New York: Free Press.

List, Friedrich. 1841. *The National System of Political Economy.* Trans. Sampson S. Lloyd. Fairfield, NJ: Reprinted by Augustus M. Kelley, 1991.

Livingston, Robert Gerald. 1997. "Life After Kohl?" *Foreign Affairs* 76 (6): 2–7.

Lockwood, William W., ed. 1965. *The State and Economic Enterprise in Japan: Essays in the Political Economy of Growth.* Princeton, NJ: Princeton University Press.

Lodge, George C. 1990. *Perestroika for America: Restructuring Business-Government Relations for World Competitiveness.* Boston: Harvard Business School Press.

Lodge, George C., and Ezra F. Vogel, eds. 1987. *Ideology and National Competitiveness: An Analysis of Nine Countries.* Boston: Harvard Business School Press.

Lovett, William A. 2002. "Bargaining Challenges and Conflicting Interests: Implementing the Doha Round," *American University International Law Review* 24:410–425.

———. 2001a. "The WTO: A Train Wreck in Progress." *Fordham International Law Review*, Spring 2001.

———. 2001b. *Banking and Financial Institutions Law.* 5th ed. St. Paul, MN: West Publishing.

———. 1996a. "World Trade Policies: Limits on Economic Integration." *International Market Change and the Law.* Ed Mähönen. 2 (1): 151–193. Turku, Finland: Turku Law School.

———. 1996b. ed. *United States Shipping Policies and the World Market.* Westport, CT: Greenwood Press.

———. 1996c. "Lessons from the Recent Peso Crisis in Mexico." *Tulane Journal of International and Comparative Law* 4 (2): 143–159.

———. 1994a. "Current World Trade Agenda: GATT, Regionalism, and Unresolved Asymmetry Problems." *Fordham Law Review* 52 (7): 2001–2045

———. 1994b. Testimony and Statement, "The World Trade Organization." Hearings, U.S. House of Representatives, Committee on Ways and Means, 103rd Cong., 2nd sess., June 10, 1994. Washington, DC: U.S. Government Printing Office, 1994.

———. 1993. "Rethinking U.S. Industrial-Trade Policy in the Post–Cold War Era." *Tulane Journal of International and Comparative Law* 1:135–189.

———. 1987. *World Trade Rivalry: Trade Equity and Competing Industrial Policies.* Lexington, MA: Lexington Books.

———. 1984. *Competitive Industrial Policies and the World Bazaar.* U.S. House of Representatives, Subcommittee on Economic Stabilization, Committee on Banking, Finance, and Urban Affairs, 98th Cong., 2nd sess. Washington, DC: U.S. Government Printing Office.

———. 1982. *Inflation and Politics: Fiscal, Monetary, and Wage-Price Discipline.* Lexington, MA: Lexington Books.

Lowenfeld, Andreas. 2002. *International Economic Law.* Oxford: Oxford University Press.

Macgregor, Douglas A. 1997. *Breaking the Phalanx: A New Design for Land Power in the 21st Century.* Center for Strategic and International Studies. Westport, CT: Greenwood Press.

MacMillan, Margaret. 2001. *Paris, 1919.* New York: Random House.

Madrick, Jeffrey. 1995. *The End of Affluence: The Causes and Consequences of America's Economic Dilemma.* New York: Random House.

Mahbubani, Kishore. 1994. "Asia and a United States in Decline." *Washington Quarterly* 17 (2): 5–23.

Mandelbaum, Michael. 1996. *The Dawn of Peace in Europe.* New York: Twentieth Century Fund Press.

Markusen, Ann, and Catherine Hill. 1992. *Converting the Cold War Economy: Investing in Industries, Workers, and Communities.* Washington, DC: Economic Policy Institute.

Marshall, Alfred. 1923. *Money, Credit, and Commerce.* London: Macmillan.

Marshall, Ray, and Marc Tucker. 1992. *Thinking for a Living: Education and the Wealth of Nations.* New York: Basic Books.

Mastel, Greg. 1997. *The Rise of the Chinese Economy: The Middle Kingdom Emerges.* Economic Strategy Institute; Armonk, NY: M.E. Sharpe.

———. 1996. *American Trade Laws After the Uruguay Round.* Armonk, NY: M.E. Sharpe.

Matlock, Jack F. 1995. *Autopsy of an Empire: The American Ambassador's Account of the Collapse of the Soviet Union.* New York: Random House.

McCraw, Thomas K., ed. 1989. *America Versus Japan: A Comparative Study.* Boston: Harvard Business School Press.

McKinnon, Ronald I. 1996. *The Rules of the Game: International Money and Exchange Rates.* Cambridge, MA: MIT Press.

McKinnon, Ronald, and Ohno Kenichi. 1997. *Dollar and Yen: Resolving Economic Conflict Between the United States and Japan.* Cambridge, MA: MIT Press.

Mead, Walter Russell. 2001. *Special Providence.* New York: Knopf.

Middlemas, Keith, and John Barnes. 1969. *Baldwin: A Biography.* London: Weidenfeld & Nicolson.

Mikesell, Raymond F. 1994. *The Bretton Woods Debates: A Memoir.* Princeton Economics Papers No. 192. Princeton, NJ: International Finance Section.

Mikitani, Ryoichi, and Adam Posen. 2000. *Japan's Financial Crisis.* Washington, DC: Institute for International Economics.

Mikuni, Akio, and R. Taggart Murphy. 2002. *Japan's Policy Trap.* Washington, DC: Brookings Institution.

Miller, Benjamin. 1995. "International Systems and Regional Security: From Competition to Cooperation, Dominance or Disengagement?" *Journal of Strategic Studies* 18 (2): 52–100.

Miller, James P. 1997. "Buffet Sounds Cautious Note About Stocks," Heard on the Street. *Wall Street Journal,* May 6, 1997.

Minsky, Hyman P. 1986. *Stabilizing an Unstable Economy.* New Haven: Yale University Press.

———. 1982. *Can "It" Happen Again? Essays on Instability and Finance.* Armonk, NY: M.E. Sharpe.

Mishel, Lawrence, Jared Bernstein, and John Schmitt. 1997. *The State of Working America, 1996–97.* Washington, DC: Economic Policy Institute; Armonk, NY: M.E. Sharpe.

Mishel, Lawrence, and Jared Bernstein. 1995. *The State of Working America, 1994–95.* Washington, DC: Economic Policy Institute; Armonk, NY: M.E. Sharpe.

————. 1993. *The State of Working America, 1992–93.* Washington, DC: Economic Policy Institute; Armonk, NY: M.E. Sharpe.

Mishel, Lawrence, and David M. Frankel. 1991. *The State of Working America, 1990–91.* Washington, DC: Economic Policy Institute; Armonk, NY: M.E. Sharpe.

Mishel, Lawrence, and Jacqueline Simon. 1988. *The State of Working America.* Washington, DC: Economic Policy Institute.

Morganthau, Hans J. 1954. *Politics Among Nations: The Struggle for Power and Peace.* New York: Alfred A. Knopf.

Morici, Peter. 1997. *The Trade Deficit: Where Does It Come From and What Does It Do?* Washington, DC: Economic Strategy Institute.

Murphy, R. Taggart. 1997. *The Weight of the Yen.* New York: W.W. Norton.

Murray, Charles. 1984. *Losing Ground: American Social Policy, 1950–1980.* New York: Basic Books.

Mussa, Michael. 2002. *Argentina and the Fund.* Washington, DC: Institute for International Economics.

Myers, Steven Lee. 1997. "U.S. and Russians Agree to Put Off Deadline on Arms: New Accords Give Moscow Until 2007 to Dismantle Its Launch Systems." *New York Times*, Sept. 27, 1997.

Nelson, Richard R. 1984. *High-Technology Policies: A Five-Nation Comparison.* Washington, DC: American Enterprise Institute.

Newman, Katherine S. 1993. *Declining Fortunes: The Withering of the American Dream.* New York: Basic Books.

Nye, Joseph S. 1992. "What New World Order?" *Foreign Affairs* 71 (2): 83–96.

Ohmae, Kenichi. 1990. *The Borderless World: Power and Strategy in the Interlinked Economy.* New York: Harper Business.

Organization for Economic Cooperation and Development. 1997. *Implementing the OECD Jobs Strategy: Member Countries Experience.* Paris: OECD.

————. 1994. *Industrial Policy in OECD Countries: Annual Review 1994.* Paris: OECD.

Perot, Ross, with Pat Choate. 1993. *Save Your Job, Save Our Country: Why NAFTA Must Be Stopped—Now!* New York: Hyperion.

Perry, Mark. 1989. *Four Stars: The Inside Story of the Forty-Year Battle Between the Joint Chiefs of Staff and America's Civilian Leaders.* Boston: Houghton Mifflin.

Peterson, Peter G. 1993. *Facing Up: How to Rescue the Economy from Crushing Debt and Restore the American Dream.* New York: Simon & Schuster.

Peterson, Wallace C. 1994. *Silent Depression: The Fate of the American Dream.* New York: W.W. Norton.

————. 1982. *Our Overloaded Economy: Inflation, Unemployment, and the Crisis in American Capitalism.* Armonk, NY: M.E. Sharpe.

Peterson, Wallace C., and Paul Estenson. 1992. *Income, Employment, and Economic Growth.* 7th ed. New York: W.W. Norton.

Phillips, Kevin. 1984. *Staying On Top.* New York: Randon House.

Podgursky, Michael. 1989. *Job Displacement and the Rural Worker.* Washington, DC: Economic Policy Institute.

Porter, Michael E. 1990. *The Competitive Advantage of Nations.* New York: Free Press.

————, ed. 1986. *Competition in Global Industries.* Boston: Harvard Business School.

Pozo, Susan, ed. 1996. *Exploring the Underground Economy: Studies of Unreported and Illegal Activity.* Kalamazoo, MI: Upjohn Institute for Employment Research.

President's Commission on Industrial Competitiveness. January 1985. *Global Com-*

petition: The New Reality, vols. 1 and 2. Washington, DC: U.S. Government Printing Office.

Prestowitz, Clyde V. 1988. *Trading Places: How We Allowed Japan to Take the Lead.* New York: Basic Books.

Priore, Michael J., and Charles F. Sabel. 1984. *The Second Industrial Divide: Possibilities for Prosperity.* New York: Basic Books.

Rabushka, Alvin. 1987. *The New China: Comparable Economic Development in Mainland China, Taiwan, and Hong Kong.* San Francisco: Pacific Research Institute for Public Policy; Boulder, CO: Westview Press.

Radelet, Steven, and Sachs, Jeffrey. 1997. "Asia's Re-emergence." *Foreign Affairs* 76 (6): 44–49.

Ragosta, John. 2000. "Unmasking the WTO." *Law and Policy in International Business* 31: 739–784.

Reich, Robert B. 1991a. "The Real Economy," *Atlantic Monthly,* February 1991.

———. 1991b. *The Work of Nations: Preparing Ourselves for 21st Century Capitalism.* New York: Alfred A. Knopf.

Reich, Robert B., and John D. Donahue. 1985. *New Ideas: The Chrysler Revival and the American System.* New York: Times Books.

Reich, Robert B., and Ira Magaziner. 1982. *Minding America's Business: The Decline and Rise of the American Economy.* New York: Harcourt Brace Jovanovich.

Richards, William Le Gro, Jr. 1996. *Offshore Financial Centers and Tax Havens.* Unpublished dissertation for S.J.D. program, Tulane Law School, New Orleans.

Root, Franklin R. 1994. *International Trade and Investment.* 7th ed. Cincinnati: South-Western Publishing.

Rubin, Seymour J., and Thomas R. Graham, eds. 1984. *Managing Trade Relations in the 1980s: Issues Involved in the GATT Ministerial Meeting—1982.* American Society of International Law. Totowa, NJ: Rowman & Allanheld.

Rubin, Seymour J., and Mark Jones. 1989. *Conflict and Resolution in U.S.–EC Trade Relations: At the Opening of the Uruguay Round.* New York: Oceana Publications.

Rubner, Alex. 1987. *The Export Cult: A Global Display of Economic Distortions.* Boulder, CO: Westview Press.

Ruggie, John Gerard. 1996. *Winning the Peace: America and World Order in the New Era.* New York: Twentieth Century Fund Press; New York: Columbia University Press.

Sampson, Gary. 2000. *Trade, Environment, and the Post-Seattle Agenda.* Washington, DC: Johns Hopkins University Press.

Scherer, F.M. 1992. *International High-Technology Competition.* Cambridge, MA: Harvard University Press.

Schott, Jeffrey J., ed. 1996. *The World Trading System: Challenges Ahead.* Washington, DC: Institute for International Economics.

———. 1994. *The Uruguay Round: An Assessment.* Washington, DC: Institute for International Economics.

———. 1990. *Completing the Uruguay Round: A Results-Oriented Approach to the GATT Trade Negotiations.* Washington, DC: Institute for International Economics.

Sheehan, Michael. 1995. *The Balance of Power: History and Theory.* London: Routledge.

Shelton, Judy. 1994. *Money Meltdown: Restoring Order to the Global Currency System*. New York: Free Press.

Shepherd, Geoffrey. 1983. *Europe's Industries: Public and Private Strategies for Change*. Ithaca, NY: Cornell University Press.

Shonfield, Andrew. 1958. *British Economic Policy Since the War*. London: Penguin Books.

Shutt, Harry. 1985. *The Myth of Free Trade: Patterns of Protectionism Since 1945*. Oxford: Basil Blackwell; London: Economist Publications.

Smith, Adam. 1776. *Wealth of Nations*. New York: Modern Library, 1937.

Smits, René. 1997. *The European Central Bank: Institutional Aspects*. Dordrecht, Netherlands: Kluwer Law International.

Solomon, Steven. 1995. *The Confidence Game: How Unelected Central Bankers Are Governing the Changed Global Economy*. New York: Simon & Schuster.

Stabile, Donald R., and Jeffrey A. Cantor. 1991. *The Public Debt of the United States: An Historical Perspective, 1775–1990*. New York: Praeger.

Starr, Martin K., ed. 1988. *Global Competitiveness: Getting the U.S. Back on Track*. New York: W.W. Norton.

Stein, Herbert. 1990. *The Fiscal Revolution in America*. Rev. ed. Washington, DC: American Enterprise Institute Press.

———. 1984. *Presidential Economics: The Making of Economic Policy From Roosevelt to Reagan and Beyond*. New York: Simon & Schuster.

Stiglitz, Joseph. 2002. *Globalization and Its Discontents*. New York: W.W. Norton.

Suro, Roberto. 1996. *Watching America's Door: The Immigration Backlash and the New Policy Debate*. New York: Twentieth Century Fund Press.

Tanzi, Vito. 1995. *Taxation in an Integrating World*. Washington, DC: Brookings Institution.

Templeton, Paul, ed. 1993. *The European Currency Crisis*. Cambridge, MA: Probus.

Thomas, Rich. 1997. "Why the United States Is Doomed to Deficits and U.S. Workers to Sweat," *Jobs and Capital* 6 (2): 14–21.

Thurow, Lester L. 1996. *The Future of Capitalism: How Today's Economic Forces Shape Tomorrow's World*. New York: William Morrow.

———. 1992. *Head to Head: The Coming Economic Battle Among Japan, Europe, and America*. New York: William Morrow.

Tolchin, Martin, et al. 1993. *Buying Into America: How Foreign Money Is Changing the Face of Our Nation*. Washington, DC: Farragut Publishing.

Tsao, James T.H. 1987. *China's Development Strategies and Foreign Trade*. Lexington, MA: Lexington Books.

Tsuru, Shigeto. 1995. *Japan's Capitalism: Creative Defeat and Beyond*. Cambridge: Cambridge University Press.

Tyson, Laura D'Andrea. 1993. *Who's Bashing Whom? Trade Conflict in High-Technology Industries*. Washington, DC: Institute for International Economics.

U.S. House of Representatives Hearings, Committee on Ways and Means. 1994. "The World Trade Organization." 103rd Cong., 2nd sess., June 10, 1994. Washington, DC: U.S. Government Printing Office, 1994.

Van Wolferen, Karel. 1989. *The Enigma of Japanese Power: People and Politics in a Stateless Nation*. New York: Alfred A. Knopf.

Vargish, George. 1992. *Where Have All the Jobs Gone?* Highland City, FL: Rainbow Press.

————. 1988. *What's Made in the USA?* New Brunswick, NJ: Transaction Books.

Viorst, Milton. 1997. "Algeria's Long Night." *Foreign Affairs* 76 (6): 86–99.

Volcker, Paul A., and Toyoo Gyohten. 1992. *Changing Fortunes: The World's Money and the Threat to American Leadership.* New York: Times Books.

Walker, Martin. 1996. *The President We Deserve: Bill Clinton, His Rise, Falls, and Comebacks.* New York: Crown Publishers.

Wallach, Lori. 1997a. Memorandum from Lori Wallach to Rep. David Bonior, Oct. 3, 1997.

————. 1997b. "Who Needs Fast Track?" Opinion. *Journal of Commerce*, Sept. 19, 1997.

Wei, Jia. 1994. *Chinese Foreign Investment Laws and Policies: Evolution and Transformation.* Westport, CT: Quorum (Greenwood) Press.

Winham, Gilbert R. 1986. *International Trade and the Tokyo Round Negotiation.* Princeton, NJ: Princeton University Press.

Witt, Matt, and Steve Trossman. 1997. "NAFTA, Round Two." *Working USA,* Sept./Oct.

Wolff, Alan William. 2001. *The Conduct of International Trade Relations.* Washington, DC: New America Foundation.

Wolman, William, and Anne Colamosca. 1997. *The Judas Economy: The Triumph of Capital, and the Betrayal of Work.* Reading, MA: Addison-Wesley.

Wood, Adrian. 1994. *North-South Trade, Employment and Inequality: Changing Fortunes in a Skill Driven World.* New York: Oxford University Press.

Wood, Christopher. 1992. *The Bubble Economy: Japan's Extraordinary Speculative Boom of the 80s and the Dramatic Bust of the 90s.* New York: Atlantic Monthly Press.

Woodward, Bob. 1994. *The Agenda: Inside the Clinton White House.* New York: Simon & Schuster.

Yamamura, Kozo. 1982. *Policy and Trade Issues of the Japanese Economy: American and Japanese Perspectives.* Seattle: University of Washington Press.

Zakaria, Fareed. 2003. *The Future of Freedom.* New York: W.W. Norton.

Zysman, John, and Laura Tyson, eds. 1983. *American Industry in International Competition: Government Policies and Corporate Strategies.* Ithaca, NY: Cornell University Press.

Index

About the Authors

William A. Lovett is a lawyer (JD New York University) and economist (MA Harvard, PhD Michigan State University). He worked in the Antitrust Division, U.S. Department of Justice (1962) and the Federal Trade Commission (1963–1969) as a lawyer and industrial organization economist. Since 1969 Lovett has taught at Tulane Law School, where he is presently Joseph Merrick Jones Professor of Law and Economics and the director, International Law, Trade, and Finance Program. His principal work has been economic regulation, antitrust, financial institutions, and international trade-finance. He has lectured or taught in Britain, Ireland, Norway, Sweden, Finland, France, Germany, Netherlands, Switzerland, Italy, Greece, Japan, China, Korea, Taiwan, Thailand, Singapore, the Philippines, Australia, Canada, Mexico, and Jamaica. Lovett's books on economic and trade policy include *Inflation and Politics: Fiscal, Monetary, and Wage-Price Discipline* (1982); *Banking and Financial Institutions Law* (five editions, 1984–2001); *Competitive Industrial Policies and the World Bazaar,* Staff Report, U.S. House of Representatives (1984); *World Trade Rivalry: Trade Equity and Competing Industrial Policies* (1987); *United States Shipping Policies and the World Market* (1996); and *U.S. Trade Policy* (1999 and 2004). In June 1994 Lovett was a lead witness on GATT 1994 and the World Trade Organization before the U.S. House Ways and Means Committee during one of the few Congressional hearings on this matter.

Alfred E. Eckes Jr. has an MA from the Fletcher School of Law and Diplomacy and a PhD in history from the University of Texas. He wrote his dissertation on the Bretton Woods international monetary system. His academic research has been mainly in contemporary economic and diplomatic history at Ohio State University (1969–1979) and as Ohio Eminent Research Professor in Contemporary History at Ohio University (1990–present). He also teaches international business in the Executive MBA program. From 1979 to 1981 he served as executive director of the U.S. House of Representatives Republican Conference and from 1981 to 1990 was a commissioner of the U.S. International Trade.Commission, serving as chair between 1982 and

1984. In 2002 he was Fulbright Sycip Distinguished Lecturer in the Philippines. Eckes has published six books relating to U.S. trade policy: *A Search for Solvency: Bretton Woods and the International Monetary System, 1941–1971* (1975); *The U.S. and the Global Struggle for Minerals* (1979); *Opening America's Market: U.S. Foreign Trade Policy Since 1776* (1995); *U.S. Trade Policy* (1999 and 2004); *Revisiting U.S. Trade Policy: Decisions in Perspective* (2000); and *Globalization and the American Century* (2003). These are leading works on the history of U.S. trade relations.

Richard L. Brinkman began his work in biology (BA Rutgers), but switched to economics (BA Rutgers; PhD Rutgers). His dissertation was on the European Common Market. Brinkman also earned an MA from the Fletcher School of Law and Diplomacy at Tufts University. An outstanding teacher at Portland State University since 1965, Brinkman has specialized in international economics, economic history, economic development, and cultural economics. He has taught and lectured extensively abroad, including Germany, Japan, China, South Africa, Canada, and Scandinavia. Brinkman's work emphasizes institutionalism and social economics, stressing the incompleteness of neoclassical economic models for international trade. He has been active in the Association for Evolutionary Economics (AFEE) and the Association for Social Economics (ASE) and has authored seventy-five articles and papers for professional journals and meetings, *Cultural Economics* (1981), and *U.S. Trade Policy* (1999 and 2004).

All three authors support expanding world trade, capital flows, and technology transfers. We believe that the "global economy" is well established and offers many blessings for humanity. But a naive dichotomy between *complete free trade* (not really practiced by many countries) and *general protectionism* clouds understanding. The world reality is an asymmetrical network of trading relations, with the United States being the most open major market, while most of the world (including Japan, China, Russia, and most developing countries) is more restricted. We insist that recent U.S. trade policy erred in neglecting reciprocity interests and in failing to maintain overall U.S. trade balance. Chronic U.S. current account and trade deficits were neither necessary nor desirable in promoting a healthy growth for world trade and broad economic development. Now the time has come for U.S. trade policies to support a more realistic, balanced, and sustainable pattern of world trade growth. This is urgent, not only for Americans, but for the whole world.